# MORAVIAN
# DAILY
# TEXTS

*Bible Texts with Hymn Verses
and Prayers for Every Day
in the Year*

# 2012

*Two Hundred Eighty-Second Year*

D1218668

**The Moravian Church in North America**
1021 Center St., Bethlehem, PA 18018
459 S. Church St., Winston-Salem, NC 27101
www.moravian.org

Moravian Daily Texts 2012

The text of this book is taken, with slight adaptation, from the
New Revised Standard Version of the Bible, copyright 1989 by
the Division of Christian Education of the National Council
of the Churches of Christ in the USA. Used by permission. All
rights reserved.

Cover photo: Mike Riess, Interprovincial Board of
Communication, Moravian Church in North America,
Bethlehem, Pa.

Book design: Sandy Fay, Laughing Horse Graphics, Inc.,
Doylestown, Pa.

Printed by McNaughton & Gunn, Inc., Saline, Mich.

Printed in the United States of America

ISBN: 978-1-933571-33-1 paperback edition

INTERPROVINCIAL BOARD
OF COMMUNICATION

MIX
Paper
FSC FSC® C011935

# NEW EVERY MORNING

*"The steadfast love of the Lord never ceases, his mercies never come to an end; they are new every morning."*

Lamentations 3:22,23

The first printed edition of the *Daily Texts* (Losungen) was published in Herrnhut, Saxony, in 1731. The title page of that edition quoted the passage from Lamentations and promised a daily message from God that would be new every morning. It was an outgrowth of a spiritual renewal of the Moravian Church (Unitas Fratrum) that dated from August 13, 1727.

In 1722 refugees from Bohemia and Moravia began arriving at the estate of Count Nicholas Ludwig von Zinzendorf (1700-1760), where he gave them a welcome and land on which to establish the settlement of Herrnhut ("Watch of the Lord").

Each day the settlers came together for morning and evening devotions, consciously placing their lives in the context of God's Word. On May 3, 1728, during the evening service, Count Zinzendorf gave the congregation a "watchword" for the next day. It was to be a "Losung" (watchword) to accompany them through the whole day.

Thereafter one or more persons of the congregation went daily to each of the 32 houses in Herrnhut to bring them the watchword for the day, and engage the families in pastoral conversations about the text.

From this oral tradition, the *Daily Texts* soon became fixed in printed form. Zinzendorf compiled 365 watchwords for the year and the first edition of the Losungen was published for 1731.

Even in the first editions there appeared the characteristic coupling of a Bible verse and hymn stanza. Zinzendorf called the hymns "collects" and considered them to be the answer of the congregation to the Word of God. The *Daily Texts* would be a great deal poorer without the mixture of God's Word and our human response.

The watchword soon became accompanied by a "doctrinal" text. The idea of an additional text grew out of a number of collections of texts from the Bible that were put together by Zinzendorf. Such additional lists (some of them for children) were used for special study within the groups in the community, and they came to be referred to as doctrinal texts.

For the *Daily Texts,* as for the whole Moravian Church, Count Zinzendorf's death (May 9, 1760), was a turning point.

His co-workers sensed the uniqueness of Zinzendorf's watchwords, textbooks, and lessons and had them published at Barby-on-the-Elbe in a four-volume collection 1762.

From then on the watchwords and doctrinal texts are distinguished by the way they are selected each year. The watchwords are chosen from various verse collections and, since 1788, they have been drawn by lot from a collection of around 2,000 suitable Old Testament texts. The doctrinal texts are not chosen by lot but are selected. The difference between the watchwords and doctrinal texts was explained in 1801 as follows: "The watchword is either a promise, an encouragement, an admonition or word of comfort; the doctrinal text contains a point of revealed doctrine."

By 1812 it was established that all watchwords would be drawn by lot from a selection of Old Testament texts, and the doctrinal texts would be selected from the New Testament. No doctrinal text is used more than once in a given year. By the end of the nineteenth century, the custom was established to relate the two texts in theme or thought.

### Into all the world

Another characteristic of the *Daily Texts* that was already apparent in the early years of its publication was its worldwide distribution. Missionaries who went as "messengers" from Herrnhut after 1732 had a *Daily Texts (Losungen)* in their luggage. They felt united with their home congregation through the daily contemplation of the same Scripture passages.

The *Daily Texts* of 1739 lists a multitude of places around the globe where messengers were witnessing for the Savior. The introduction read:

> "The Good Word of the Lord, 1739, From all
> the Prophets for His congregations, and servants at
> Herrnhut, Herrnhaag, Herrendijk [Holland], Pilgerruh
> [Denmark], Ebersdof, Jena, Amsterdam, Rotterdam,
> London, Oxford, Berlin, Greenland, St. Croix, St. John
> and St. Thomas [Virgin Islands], Berbice [Guyana],
> Palestine, Surinam, Savannah in Georgia, among
> the Moors in Carolina, with the wild Indians in Irene

[an island in the Savannah River in Georgia], in
Pennsylvania, among the Hottentots [South Africa], in
Guinea, in Latvia, Estonia and Lithuania, Russia, on the
White Sea, in Lappland, Norway, in Switzerland, [Isle of]
Man, Hittland [Scotland], in prison, on pilgrimage, to
Ceylon, Ethiopia, Persia, on visitation to the missionaries
among the heathen, and elsewhere on land and sea."

This distribution of the Moravians into every continent in
the known world seems all the more amazing when you consider that the settlement at Herrnhut was only 17 years old,
and the first missionaries had gone out only seven years earlier
in 1732.

Present membership of the worldwide Moravian Church is
over 700,000 in 19 provinces. The *Daily Texts* has a press run of
over 1,000,000 copies in the German language alone. This far
surpasses the 30,000 members of the Moravian Church in all of
Europe. Other language editions bring the total circulation of
this small devotional book to over 1.5 million copies. The Daily
Texts is now published in 51 languages and dialects, including
some of the following:

Afrikaans, Batak, Chichewa, Chinese (Hong Kong), Czech,
Danish, Dutch, English, Estonian, Finnish, French, German,
Hindi, Hmong, Hungarian, Indonesian, Inuktut (Labrador),
Japanese, Kiswahili (Tanzania), Latvian, Miskito (Nicaragua,
Honduras), Naga, Odiya, Ovambo (Nambia), Polish, Portu-
guese (Brazil), Rongmei, Russian, Swedish, Sepedi (South Af-
rica), Setswana (South Africa), Simalungan (Indonesia), Slovak,
Spanish (Argentina), Sranang (Surinam), Thai, Tibetan, Venda
(South Africa), Xhosa (South Africa), Zulu (South Africa).

The physical form of the *Daily Texts* varies considerably
from country to country. Some, like this North American edition, have a separate page for the verses, hymns, and prayers
of each day. Others have several days' texts printed on one
page, which makes a thin, pocket-size volume. Some are beautiful examples of the printing and bookbinding arts. Others are
simply mimeographed and stapled together.

These external nonessentials pale beside the fact that this
little book is probably the most widely read devotional guide in
the world, next to the Bible. It forms an invisible bond between
Christians on all continents, transcending barriers of confes-

sion, race, language, and politics. In its quiet way it performs a truly ecumenical service for the whole of Christendom.

## North American editions

The printing of the *Daily Texts* in North America dates back at least to 1767, when the Losungen was printed "at Bethlehem on the Forks of the Delaware by Johan Brandmuller." The printer's imprint bears the date of 1767 as well and may have been an extra printing for the German version done at Barby-on-the-Elbe in Germany, where most of the printing was done for the Moravian Church those days.

During the crucial days of the Revolution, the German-language edition was printed in Philadelphia by Heinrich Miller, who had worked for Benjamin Franklin when he first came to America. The daily text for July 4, 1776, was from Isaiah 55:5 —"Behold, you shall call nations that you know not, and nations that knew you not shall run to you" (RSV).

English versions were printed in London as early as 1746, and the title page bears the imprint of "James Hutton near the Golden Lion in Fetter Lane." Hutton was the well-known London printer associated with the Moravian Church who was a friend of John and Charles Wesley in the formative years of their ministry.

The 1850s were crucial years for the Moravian Church in North America as the congregations established in the United States broke away from direct control from the Moravian headquarters in Europe. Both German and English editions of the *Daily Texts* were regularly printed in Philadelphia or Bethlehem, Pennsylvania, and in a few years the custom was established to include the statistics of the provinces and districts of the Moravian Church in North America.

The biblical texts for each day are chosen in Herrnhut, Germany, and then sent around the world to those who prepare the different language editions. Since 1959 the edition published in the United States has included a prayer for each day. For this North American edition, the hymns are chosen or written, and the prayers are written by Moravian clergy and laypersons from the United States and Canada. Each month is prepared by a different individual or couple, of a variety of ages, so that the prayers reflect the great diversity of devotion in the Moravian Church.

# DAILY TOPICS FOR PRAYER

On August 27, 1727, certain members of the Moravian Church in Herrnhut, Saxony, formed a remarkable prayer union known as the "Hourly Intercession." This provided that, for every hour of the day and night, one of the volunteer intercessors would, for one hour in private, bear on his or her heart and mind the interests and hopes of the Kingdom of God in the world. This wonderful intercession continued for over 100 years.

On August 27, 1872, a Moravian Prayer union was formed in England as a form of resuscitation of the Hourly Intercession, and today its members are found in all areas of the Moravian world. You are invited to join in this prayer covenant. The following prayer suggestions may be helpful:

**Sunday: The Church At Worship.** For her purity and peace, unity and power. For the congregation to which we belong or with which we worship. For the ministry of the word of God. For the winning of people into fellowship with Christ. For all church schools, youth ministries, and other church groups at work.

**Monday: The Church At Work.** For the church in its mission next door and in other lands. For new congregations and specialized ministries. For the workers and leaders in these endeavors. For the worker volunteers to carry out the mission of the church.

**Tuesday: Home and School.** For households. For the Christian education of the young, and that our children may be led to give themselves to Christ. For all schools and teachers. For young people enrolled in colleges and universities. For the training of ministers in theological seminaries.

**Wednesday: For Those In Need.** For all in special need, whether as aged, sick, poor, or homeless. For those in prison. For all victims of famine, oppression, aggression, and war.

**Thursday: Our Nation and Our World.** For those who govern and for those who are governed. For the guidance of God to all who are in authority. For unity of nations and all agencies for peace. For the whole human family and equal rights for all. For the guidance and blessing of God as humanity has entered the space age.

**Friday: Our Own Church Fellowship.** For the purity, zeal, and practice of the church as a witnessing fellowship of the love of God. That the church may be a light to the world wherever its congregations are found, and that it may be active in redeeming mission in these communities.

**Saturday: The Witness of Christians.** That all who confess the name of Christ may grow in the grace and knowledge of Jesus Christ as Lord and Savior.

*"O thou King of kings and Lord of lords, who desirest that all people should dwell together in unity, let thy will be known and done among the nations; guide their feet into the way of peace. Remember us and all humanity in thy mercy. Deliver us from the sins which give rise to war and conflict, and strengthen within our hearts the will to establish righteousness and justice in the earth. Give unto us and to all who worship thee the sincere desire to live in peaceful and loving fellowship with all people. Fix our minds and hearts upon thine eternal purposes for your children on earth."*

— *A Prayer for Peace*

# THE DAILY TEXTS
## IN FAMILY WORSHIP

Almost from the very beginning the *Daily Texts* has been used as a guide for family worship as well as for private and personal devotions. The use of the *Daily Texts* in family worship will vary depending on the time available and the age of the children. One of the values of the *Daily Texts* is that it is adaptable to numerous patterns of use.

One pattern followed by many families is to begin the meal (usually breakfast or the evening meal) with the reading of the texts of the day and the accompanying hymn stanzas. After this, the family joins in the blessing or table grace. A suitable blessing may be chosen from among the following:

Come, Lord Jesus, our Guest to be,
and bless these gifts bestowed by thee.
Bless thy dear ones everywhere,
and keep them in thy loving care.

Be present at our table, Lord;
be here and everywhere adored;
from thine all-bounteous hand our food
may we receive with gratitude.

The worship of the family can then close with a prayer offered in the leader's own words or in those of the printed prayer offered in the *Daily Texts*. As a part of free prayer by the leader or in connection with the printed prayer, use can be made from day to day of the subjects of the Daily Topics for Prayer as given in the preceding pages.

# ACKNOWLEDGMENTS

Bible texts in this publication are quoted from the *New Revised Standard Version Bible*, copyright © 1989 by the Division of Christian Education of the National Council of the Churches of Christ in the United States of America, and are used by permission. Verses marked NIV are taken from *The Holy Bible New International Version*, copyright © 1973, 1978, 1984 by International Bible Society. Used by permission of Zondervan Publishing House. Verses marked KJV are taken from the King James Version, copyright © 1607. Verses marked NASB are taken from the New American Standard, copyright © 1997 by Thomas Nelson Publishers. Verses marked TANAKH are taken from the *Tanakh — The Holy Scriptures*, new JPS trans. © 1985 by the Jewish Publication Society, 3rd printing, all rights reserved.

Sunday readings are taken from the *Revised Common Lectionary*, copyright © 1992 by the Consultation on Common Texts (CCT).

Unless otherwise noted, hymn stanzas found in the *Daily Texts* are taken from the *Moravian Book of Worship*, 1995. The number found to the right of each stanza designates the source of the stanza in that hymnal. If the number is preceded by a p the hymn used is from one of the liturgies and the p designates the page number. The letter OW after a number denotes the *Liturgy and the Offices of Worship and Hymns*, 1908. The letters br after a number denotes the *British Moravian Hymn Book with Services*, 1960. The letter r after a number denotes the *Hymnal of the Moravian Church*, 1969. When hymns are copyrighted, information is given at the bottom of the page; we gratefully acknowledge permission to use copyrighted material.

Hymn stanzas are broken down by meter except when space would not allow.

The Scripture readings for Monday through Saturday are part of a plan to read through the Old and New Testaments in two years and the Psalms in one year.

## First Sunday after Christmas

**Sunday, January 1** — Isaiah 61:10-62:3; Psalm 148
Galatians 4:4-7; Luke 2:22-40

**Watchword for the Week** — But when the fullness of time had
come, God sent his Son, born of a woman, born under the law, in
order to redeem those who were under the law, so that we might
receive adoption as children. Galatians 4:4,5

# The fear of the Lord is Zion's treasure. Isaiah 33:6

Jesus' name, Jesus' name,                          324
source of life and happiness!
In this name true consolation
mourning sinners may possess;
here is found complete salvation.
Blessed Jesus, we your name will praise
all our days, all our days.

**There was a man in Jerusalem whose name was
Simeon; this man was righteous and devout,
looking forward to the consolation of Israel.
Simeon took Jesus in his arms and praised God,
saying, "Master, now you are dismissing your
servant in peace, according to your word; for my
eyes have seen your salvation." Luke 2:25,28-30**

In the arms of her who bore him,                   314
virgin pure, behold him lie
while his aged saints adore him
ere in perfect faith they die.
Alleluia, alleluia!
Lo, th'incarnate God Most High!

O Savior, those who saw you were once delighted
by your infant beauty. We see you now not as an
infant, but as one who calls our names. You call
us to live as you lived. Guide us by your presence.
Amen.

**Monday, January 2** — Psalm 1
Genesis 1:1-2:3; Matthew 1:1-17

### You have made the Lord your refuge. Psalm 91:9

> Peace, perfect peace, by thronging duties pressed?  710
> To do the will of Jesus, this is rest.
> Peace, perfect peace, with sorrows surging round?
> On Jesus' bosom naught but calm is found.

### Cast all your anxiety on him, because he cares for you. 1 Peter 5:7

> When peace, like a river, attendeth my way,        754
> when sorrows like sea billows roll;
> whatever my lot, you have taught me to say,
> it is well, it is well with my soul.

God of our future, things will happen this year which we can not foresee. Some may delight us, and others may cause us grief. At year's end, we will look back and know you were with us. "Great is thy faithfulness!" Amen.

**Tuesday, January 3** — Psalm 2
Genesis 2:4-25; Matthew 1:18-25

## You shall rise up before the grayheaded and honor the aged. Leviticus 19:32 (NASB)

> Praise to the Savior for his deep compassion,        383
> graciously caring for his chosen people;
> young men and women, aging folk and children,
> praise to the Savior!

## Do not rebuke an older man harshly, but exhort him as if he were your father. Treat younger men as brothers, older women as mothers, and younger women as sisters, with absolute purity. 1 Timothy 5:1-2 (NIV)

> O God, your constant care and love        804*
> are shed upon us from above,
> throughout our lives in ev'ry stage,
> from infancy to later age.

God of all ages, thank you for grandparents, parents, elders in the church and community and pastors with age and experience. They teach us so much and give us great strength. We feel your presence in their existence among us. Amen.

* © 1976 by The Hymn Society. Used by permission of Hope Publishing Company.

**Wednesday, January 4** — Psalm 3
Genesis 3,4; Matthew 2:1-12

## You shall not steal; you shall not deal falsely; and you shall not lie to one another. Leviticus 19:11

> Blessed are they who show their mercy                595
> to the guilty and the poor,
> for to them, set free from judgment,
> shall be opened heaven's door.
> Blessed, the sincere and truthful
> from the lie's deception free,
> for the God of truth and beauty
> they in joy will surely see.

## Love does not rejoice in wrongdoing, but rejoices in the truth. 1 Corinthians 13:6

> May ev'ry heart receive his loving spirit            671
> and know the truth that makes life truly free;
> then, in that spirit may we live united,
> and find in God our deep security.

Holy Spirit, you have created in us a desire for holiness and a hunger for the sacred. Nothing blesses us more than to follow your guidance. Let your will be done in us as it is in Heaven. Amen.

**Thursday, January 5** — Psalm 4
Genesis 5; Matthew 2:13-23

## With many dreams come vanities and a multitude of words; but fear God. Ecclesiastes 5:7

Lo! The hosts of evil round us                    751
scorn the Christ, assail his ways!
From the fears that long have bound us,
free our hearts to faith and praise.
Grant us wisdom, grant us courage,
for the living of these days,
for the living of these days.

## Lord, who will not fear and glorify your name? For you alone are holy. Revelation 15:4

At the name of Jesus                    480
ev'ry knee shall bow,
ev'ry tongue confess him
King of glory now;
'tis the Father's pleasure
we should call him Lord,
who from the beginning
was the mighty Word.

God, the world is so enticing to us — we want to taste everything. Our minds are cluttered with desire. You alone are worthy of our desire and worship. Today we devote ourselves wholly to you. Amen.

## Epiphany of the Lord

**Watchword for the Epiphany** — Arise, shine; for your light has come, and the glory of the Lord has risen upon you. Isaiah 60:1

**Friday, January 6** — Psalm 5
Genesis 6:1-7:10; Matthew 3

**Epiphany of the Lord** — Isaiah 60:1-6; Psalm 72:1-7,10-14
Ephesians 3:1-12; Matthew 2:1-12

# I delight to do your will, O my God; your law is within my heart. Psalm 40:8

> Consecrate me now to thy service, Lord,     607
> by the pow'r of grace divine;
> let my soul look up with a steadfast hope
> and my will be lost in thine.

# Christ says, "If you love me, you will keep my commandments." John 14:15

> Jesus, Master, I am yours;     614
> keep me faithful, keep me near;
> as your radiance through me pours
> all my homeward way to cheer.
> Jesus, at your feet I fall.
> O be now my all in all!

You are the light of the world. You are the light of our souls. Create in us a desire to do your will. Enable us to love you through our obedience. Let your light shine through us. Amen.

Saturday, January 7 — Psalm 6
Genesis 7:11-8:22; Matthew 4:1-11

**God, I think of you on my bed, and meditate on you in the watches of the night. Psalm 63:6**

> When morning gilds the skies,                    552
> my heart awaking cries:
> may Jesus Christ be praised!
> In all my work and prayer
> I ask his loving care:
> may Jesus Christ be praised!

**Will not God grant justice to his chosen ones who cry to him day and night? Will he delay long in helping them? Luke 18:7**

> Son of God, O hear my cry:                    744
> by the holy mystery
> of your dwelling here on earth,
> by your pure and holy birth,
> Lord, your presence let me see,
> manifest yourself to me!

God who answers prayers, hear the voices of billions crying out for deliverance. We join those abused, ravaged by war or steeped in poverty, in prayer. Hear our prayers for them and for ourselves. May your kingdom come to this world. Amen.

### First Sunday after the Epiphany

**Watchword for the Week** — Ascribe to the Lord the glory of his name; worship the Lord in holy splendor. Psalm 29:2

**Sunday, January 8** — Genesis 1:1-15; Psalm 29
Acts 19:1-7; Mark 1:4-11

## Woe to those who plan iniquity, because it is in their power to do it. Micah 2:1 (NIV)

"I'll bless you, and you shall be set for a blessing!"  616
Thus said God, the Lord, to his servant of old;
O may we, in grace and in number increasing,
through work show our faith and in service be bold;
upon your truth founded, we shall not move,
let us ever follow, and fearless prove;
so shall we in doctrine, in word and behavior,
to ev'ryone witness that Christ is our Savior.

## Jesus said, "The measure you give will be the measure you get." Mark 4:24

O God of unrelenting grace,                            738*
whose judgment yet we daily face,
forgive us now, good Lord.
You are so distant and so near;
for you we long, yet you we fear,
O known, and yet beyond record.

Holy God, we feel the conviction of our wrongs. Nothing justifies them. Even our sins of long ago rush back into our memories. We cry for mercy and for cleansing. Make us pure, we pray. Amen.

* © 1993 by Hermann I. Weinlick

**Monday, January 9** — Psalm 7:1-9
Genesis 9; Matthew 4:12-25

**Woe to those who rely on horses, who trust in the multitude of their chariots but do not seek help from the Lord. Isaiah 31:1 (NIV)**

> Lord, your body ne'er forsake,                    p86
> ne'er your congregation leave;
> we in you our refuge take,
> of your fullness we receive:
> ev'ry other help be gone,
> you are our support alone;
> for on your supreme commands
> all the universe depends.

**Your faith might rest not on human wisdom but on the power of God. 1 Corinthians 2:5**

> Then let us adore and give him his right,         p105
> all glory and pow'r and wisdom and might,
> all honor and blessing, with angels above,
> and thanks never ceasing for infinite love.

Lord, we know of the cruelties of war shown to us vividly in video clips. Yet, we are unable and sometimes unwilling to be peacemakers. O God, come and save us. Be our Prince of peace. Amen.

**Tuesday, January 10** — Psalm 7:10-17
Genesis 10:1-11:9; Matthew 5:1-16

**Rend your hearts and not your clothing. Return to the Lord, your God. Joel 2:13**

> Come, you sinners, poor and needy,    765
> weak and wounded, sick and sore,
> Jesus, Son of God, will save you,
> full of pity, love, and pow'r.
> I will arise and go to Jesus;
> he will embrace me in his arms;
> in the arms of my dear Savior,
> O there are ten thousand charms.

**Jesus said, "The time is fulfilled, and the kingdom of God has come near; repent, and believe in the good news." Mark 1:15**

> Lord Jesus, think on me    764
> and purge away my sin;
> from selfish passions set me free
> and make me pure within.

Forgive us, our Redeemer, when we take on a show of piety but not a heart of piety. Create in us a clean heart, and renew a right spirit within us. Restore to us the joy of salvation. Amen.

**Wednesday, January 11 — Psalm 8**
Genesis 11:10-12:9; Matthew 5:17-26

**See, the former things have come to pass, and new things I now declare; before they spring forth, I tell you of them. Isaiah 42:9**

Finish, then, your new creation;      474
pure and spotless let us be;
let us see your great salvation
perfectly restored and free.
Changed from glory into glory,
till in heav'n we take our place,
till we cast our crowns before you,
lost in wonder, love, and praise.

**The darkness is passing away and the true light is already shining. 1 John 2:8**

Morning Star, O cheering sight!      281
Ere thou cam'st, how dark earth's night!
Morning Star, O cheering sight!
Ere thou cam'st, how dark earth's night!
Jesus mine, in me shine;
in me shine, Jesus mine;
fill my heart with light divine.

God of creating light, you were in the beginning before anything existed. You continue to create. All that you touch becomes new and sacred. Thank you for the light in us and for making us new today. Amen.

**Thursday, January 12** — Psalm 9:1-10
Genesis 12:10-13:18; Matthew 5:27-42

**The Lord said to Gideon, "Peace be to you; do not
fear, you shall not die." Then Gideon built an
altar there to the Lord, and called it, The Lord is
peace. Judges 6:23-24**

O God, my faithful God,                              615
O fountain ever flowing,
without whom nothing is,
all perfect gifts bestowing,
grant me a faithful life,
and give me, Lord, within,
commitment free from strife,
a soul unhurt by sin.

**Christ says, "In this world you will have trouble.
But take heart! I have overcome the world."
John 16:33 (NIV)**

Fear not, I am with you; O be not dismayed,          709
for I am your God and will still give you aid;
I'll strengthen you, help you and cause you to stand
upheld by my righteous, omnipotent hand.

Faithful God, we depend on your promises. When
we open our eyes in the morning, we look for you
throughout the day. When we close our eyes in the
evening, we trust in you while we sleep. Amen.

Friday, January 13 — Psalm 9:11-20
Genesis 14,15; Matthew 5:43-6:4

## Comfort, O comfort my people, says your God. Isaiah 40:1

Bless, O Lord, we pray, your congregation;    445
bless each home and family;
bless the youth, the rising generation;
blessed may your dear children be;
bless your servants, grant them help and favor;
you to glorify be their endeavor.
Lord, on you we humbly call;
let your blessing rest on all.

## For God, who said, "Let light shine out of darkness," made his light shine in our hearts to give us the light of the knowledge of the glory of God in the face of Christ. 2 Corinthians 4:6 (NIV)

O come, O bright and morning star,    274
and bring us comfort from afar!
Dispel the shadows of the night,
and turn our darkness into light.

Our Creator, how amazing it is that you have
embedded in our hearts the same power you used
in creation! You make us children of light. Come
near us this day as we ponder the face of Christ.
Amen.

Saturday, January 14 — Psalm 10:1-11
Genesis 16,17; Matthew 6:5-18

## May his glory fill the whole earth. Psalm 72:19

> Praise the Lord! For he is glorious;                 454
> never shall his promise fail;
> God has made his saints victorious;
> sin and death shall not prevail.
> Praise the God of our salvation;
> hosts on high, his pow'r proclaim;
> heav'n and earth and all creation,
> praise and glorify his name.

## Christ says, "Go into all the world and proclaim the good news to the whole creation." Mark 16:15

> My gracious master and my God,                 548
> assist me to proclaim,
> to spread through all the earth abroad
> the honors of your name.

Thank you, Holy Spirit, for instilling in us passion
and joy for the tasks of going and proclaiming.
You've sent us because you love us and we go
because we love you. Guide us in this mission
today. Amen.

## Second Sunday after the Epiphany

**Watchword for the Week** — How weighty to me are your thoughts, O God! How vast is the sum of them! Psalm 139:17

**Sunday, January 15** — 1 Samuel 3:1-10,(11-20); Psalm 139:1-6,13-18 1 Corinthians 6:12-20; John 1:43-51

# Ah, you who join house to house, who add field to field, until there is room for no one but you. Isaiah 5:8

Come, O Christ, and reign among us,                648
King of love and Prince of peace;
hush the storm of strife and passion,
bid its cruel discords cease.
By your patient years of toiling,
by your silent hours of pain,
quench our fevered thirst of pleasure;
stem our selfish greed of gain.

# For what will it profit them to gain the whole world and forfeit their life? Mark 8:36

Take my wealth, all I possess,                     647
make me rich in faithfulness.
Take my mind that I may use
ev'ry pow'r as you should choose.

Giving God, you have created all that exists, but our greed compels us to covet things you have given to others. Have mercy on us for our sin of wanting more. Help us to find joy in our own gifts. Amen.

**Monday, January 16 — Psalm 10:12-18**
Genesis 18; Matthew 6:19-34

**Take care, or you will be seduced into turning away, serving other gods and worshipping them. Deuteronomy 11:16**

I need thee ev'ry hour;        740
stay thou near by;
temptations lose their pow'r
when thou art nigh.
I need thee, O I need thee,
ev'ry hour I need thee!
O bless me now, my Savior —
I come to thee!

**For us there is one God, the Father, from whom are all things and for whom we exist, and one Lord, Jesus Christ, through whom are all things and through whom we exist. 1 Corinthians 8:6**

Immortal, invisible, God only wise,      457
in light inaccessible hid from our eyes,
most blessed, most glorious, O Ancient of Days,
almighty, victorious, your great name we praise.

Our Father in heaven, the things we cherish more than we cherish you, things we make our life's priorities are precious to us. Forgive us when we invent our own gods to serve. Amen.

**Tuesday, January 17 — Psalm 11**
Genesis 19:1-29; Matthew 7:1-12

## Yours is the kingdom, O Lord, and you are exalted as head above all. 1 Chronicles 29:11

Fairest Lord Jesus!                                        470
King of creation!
Son of God and Son of man!
Truly I'd love thee,
truly I'd serve thee,
light of my soul, my joy, my crown.

## Speaking the truth in love, we must grow up in every way into him who is the head, into Christ. Ephesians 4:15

Heart with loving heart united,                            401*
met to know God's holy will.
Let his love in us ignited
more and more our spirits fill.
He the Head, we are his members;
we reflect the light he is.
He the Master, we disciples,
he is ours and we are his.

Lord, you are high and lifted up. Your glory fills
our lives. We pray the experiences of this day will
deepen our faith in you. Help us to keep our lives
centered on you. Amen.

* © 1983 by Walter Klaassen

**Wednesday, January 18** — Psalm 12
Genesis 19:30-20:18; Matthew 7:13-23

**The Lord is our judge, the Lord is our ruler, the
Lord is our king; he will save us. Isaiah 33:22**

On him we'll venture all we have,                    479
our lives, our all, to him we owe.
None else is able us to save,
naught but the Savior will we know;
this we subscribe with heart and hand,
resolved through grace thereby to stand.

**Immediately the father of the child cried out,
"I believe; help my unbelief!" Mark 9:24**

Help then, O Lord, our unbelief;                    713
and may our faith abound
to call on you when you are near
and seek where you are found.

O Savior, you are Lord over our doubts and our
confidence, our questions and our convictions. You
are with us when our faith trembles and when your
light fills our souls. Thank you for your faithfulness.
Amen.

**Thursday, January 19 — Psalm 13**
Genesis 21; Matthew 7:24-8:4

**O give thanks to the Lord, for he is good; for his
steadfast love endures forever. Psalm 106:1**

> We now with a joyful mind                    p19
> praise you, Lord, for you are kind;
> for your mercies shall endure,
> ever faithful, ever sure.

**Whatever you do, in word or deed, do everything
in the name of the Lord Jesus, giving thanks to
God the Father through him. Colossians 3:17**

> May the mind of Christ my Savior             585
> live in me from day to day,
> by his love and pow'r controlling
> all I do and say.

Merciful God, forgive us when we become distracted
today by our tasks and appointments. We desire to
keep you in the center of our lives, but the demands
on us make that hard. We pray for your help.
Amen.

**Friday, January 20 — Psalm 14**
Genesis 22; Matthew 8:5-22

## Abram said to Lot, "Let there be no strife between you and me, and between your herders and my herders; for we are kindred." Genesis 13:8

'Tis a pleasant thing to see                           670
brothers in the Lord agree,
sisters of a God of love
live as they shall live above,
acting each a Christian part,
one in word and one in heart.

## If you forgive others their trespasses, your heavenly Father will also forgive you. Matthew 6:14

How can your pardon reach and bless                    777
the unforgiving heart
that broods on wrongs and will not let
old bitterness depart,
old bitterness depart?

Christ, you taught us to pray and to forgive. Our
weak desire to forgive can sometimes undermine
our prayers. Teach us the ministry of mercy so our
prayers before you can give us life. Amen.

Saturday, January 21 — Psalm 15
Genesis 23:1-24:25; Matthew 8:23-34

**O Lord God, you have only begun to show
your servant your greatness and your might!
Deuteronomy 3:24**

> Jesus shall reign where'er the sun                    404
> does its successive journeys run;
> his Kingdom stretch from shore to shore,
> till moons shall wax and wane no more.

**Set all your hope on the grace that Jesus Christ
will bring you when he is revealed. 1 Peter 1:13**

> Let ev'ry creature rise and bring                     404
> the highest honors to our King;
> angels descend with songs again,
> and earth repeat the loud Amen.

Eternal God, your promises for our future fill us
with excitement. We spend this day, tomorrow and
the next day with you. You have promised to keep
us for all eternity. Your glory fills our hearts. Amen.

### Third Sunday after the Epiphany

**Watchword for the Week** — Trust in him at all times, pour out your
heart before him; God is a refuge for us. Psalm 62:8

**Sunday, January 22** — Jonah 3:1-5,10; Psalm 62:5-12
1 Corinthians 7:29-31; Mark 1:14-20

## God made human beings straightforward, but they have devised many schemes. Ecclesiastes 7:29

> O teach us all your perfect will                734
> to understand and to fulfill:
> when human insight fails, give light;
> this will direct our steps aright.

## Christ says, "If you continue in my word, you are truly my disciples; and you will know the truth, and the truth will make you free." John 8:31-32

> Thanks we give and adoration                559
> for your gospel's joyful sound.
> May the fruits of your salvation
> in our hearts and lives abound.
> Ever faithful, ever faithful
> to your truth may we be found.

You are the way, the truth and the life. We gather
today to share your truth with each other. Bless us
and enable us to discover insights about love and
faith while we are together. Amen.

**Monday, January 23** — Psalm 16:1-6
Genesis 24:26-66; Matthew 9:1-13

## You brought up my life from the Pit, O Lord my God. Jonah 2:6

Am I of my salvation                                    795
assured through thy great love?
May I on each occasion
to thee more faithful prove.
Hast thou my sins forgiven?
Then, leaving things behind,
may I press on to heaven
and bear the prize in mind.

## Christ Jesus came into the world to save sinners —of whom I am the foremost. 1 Timothy 1:15

My lasting joy and comfort here                         768
is Jesus' death and blood;
I with this passport can appear
before the throne of God.
Admitted to the realms above,
I then shall see the Christ I love,
where countless pardoned sinners meet
adoring at his feet.

The Gospel is your gift, O Savior—the good news of
your deliverance from despair. We are astonished
that you do this for us who often fail to be faithful
to you. We give you thanks throughout this day.
Amen.

**Tuesday, January 24** — Psalm 16:7-11
Genesis 25; Matthew 9:14-26

## In the congregations will I bless the Lord. Psalm 26:12 (NKJV)

All glory, honor, thanks, and praise          518*
to Christ our Lord and Savior,
that still his church in these our days
may know his boundless favor:
for brothers and sisters united by love
stand firm o'er the earth far extended,
as countless more legions in heaven above
extol how his grace them attended.

## Let us consider how to provoke one another to love and good deeds, not neglecting to meet together, as is the habit of some. Hebrews 10:24-25

What brought us together, what joined our hearts?   675
The pardon which Jesus, our High Priest, imparts;
'Tis this which cements the disciples of Christ,
who are into one by the Spirit baptized.

God of fellowship in Christ, bless us in our
congregations, in our sharing, in our unity in the
Spirit. Call us together as the body of Christ. Save us
from walking our journeys isolated from each other.
Amen.

*   © 1982 by C. Daniel Crews

**Wednesday, January 25** — Psalm 17:1-7
Genesis 26; Matthew 9:27-38

# The Lord will send his angel before you.
# Genesis 24:7

> Blessings abound where'er he reigns,                404
> the pris'ners leap to lose their chains,
> the weary find eternal rest,
> and all who suffer want are blessed.

## The angel said to Peter, "Fasten your belt and put on your sandals." He did so. Acts 12:8

> The angel spoke, and suddenly                      296
> appeared a shining throng
> of angels, praising God, who now
> begin their joyful song,
> begin their joyful song.

Faithful God, when we feel the weakest, you become our strength. You send your presence through those who come to us—sometimes angels, sometimes each other. Thank you for the nearness we feel this day through your servants. Amen.

Thursday, January 26 — Psalm 17:8-15
Genesis 27:1-29; Matthew 10:1-16

**Naaman said, "Your servant will no longer offer sacrifice to any god except the Lord." 2 Kings 5:17**

> O let me feel you near me;                           603
> the world is ever near:
> I see the sights that dazzle,
> the tempting sounds I hear.
> My foes are ever near me,
> around me and within;
> but, Jesus, draw still nearer
> and shield my soul from sin!

**Jesus Christ is the true God and eternal life. Little children, keep yourselves from idols. 1 John 5:20-21**

> Jesus calls us from the worship                      600
> of the vain world's golden store,
> from each idol that would keep us,
> saying, "Christian, love me more."

God of all riches, there are many things that distract us by their glitter—enticing things and treasures that promise much. We desire to serve only you. We give you our hearts, our lives, our wealth. Amen.

Friday, January 27 — Psalm 18:1-6
Genesis 27:30-28:9; Matthew 10:17-25

**God is our refuge and strength, a very present help in trouble. Therefore we will not fear. Psalm 46:1-2**

> God is my strong salvation,                    769
> no enemy I fear;
> he hears my supplication,
> dispelling all my care;
> if he, my head and master,
> defend me from above,
> what pain or what disaster
> can part me from his love?

**Paul wrote: Whenever I am weak, then I am strong. 2 Corinthians 12:10**

> Restrain me lest I harbor pride,               733
> lest I in my own strength confide;
> though I am weak, show me anew
> I have my pow'r, my strength from you.

Heavenly Protector, when we are threatened by the world around us, watch over us. When our fears weaken us, be our strength. When discouragement squelches the joy of life, shine your light into our lives and into your world. Amen.

Saturday, January 28 — Psalm 18:7-15
Genesis 28:10-29:14; Matthew 10:26-42

**Moses said, "If now I have found favor in your sight, O Lord, I pray, let the Lord go with us."**
**Exodus 34:9**

Guide me, O my great Redeemer,                    790
pilgrim through this barren land.
I am weak, but you are mighty;
hold me with your pow'rful hand.
Bread of heaven, bread of heaven,
feed me now and evermore,
feed me now and evermore.

**Those whom God predestined he also called;**
**and those whom he called he also glorified.**
**Romans 8:30**

Mighty God, we humbly pray,                         586
let your pow'r now lead the way
that in all things we may show
that we in your likeness grow.

Divine teacher, just as you are the truth and the
life, you are also the way. Teach us to walk in your
path. We desire to reflect your image. Guide us so
we will encounter you within our souls. Amen.

### Fourth Sunday after the Epiphany

**Watchword for the Week** — The fear of the Lord is the beginning of wisdom; all those who practice it have a good understanding. Psalm 111:10

**Sunday, January 29** — Deuteronomy 18:15-20; Psalm 111
1 Corinthians 8:1-13; Mark 1:21-28

**The Lord is your keeper; the Lord is your shade at your right hand. The sun shall not strike you by day, nor the moon by night. Psalm 121:5-6**

My Shepherd will supply my need;                    730
the Lord God is his name.
In pastures fresh he makes me feed,
beside the living stream.
He brings my wand'ring spirit back
when I forsake his ways,
and leads me for his mercy's sake
in paths of truth and grace.

**Now to him who is able to keep you from falling, and to make you stand without blemish in the presence of his glory with rejoicing, to the only God our Savior, through Jesus Christ our Lord, be glory, majesty, power, and authority. Jude 24-25**

O Joy, all joys excelling,                    484
the Bread of Life, the Way,
you came to make your dwelling
in sinful hearts to stay.
My spirit's hungry craving
you can forever still;
from deepest anguish saving,
with bliss my cup can fill.

God, you watch over us like a father and guide us like a mother. Your eye is always on us, ready to help us instantly. We rest in your strong hands. We worship you today, for you are faithful. Amen.

**Monday, January 30** — Psalm 18:16-24
Genesis 29:15-30:24; Matthew 11:1-10

**O Lord, restore me to health and make me live.
Isaiah 38:16**

> Stretch forth your hand, our health restore,          267
> and make us rise to fall no more;
> O let your face upon us shine
> and fill the world with love divine.

**She had heard about Jesus, and came up behind
him in the crowd and touched his cloak, for she
said, "If I but touch his clothes, I will be made
well." He said to her, "Daughter, your faith has
made you well." Mark 5:27-28,34**

> Just as I am, poor, wretched, blind;          762
> sight, riches, healing of the mind,
> yea, all I need, in thee to find,
> O Lamb of God, I come, I come!

God of wellness, we know fear when disease strikes
us hard. We seek cures from doctors and pray for
healing. Most of all, we lay our lives in your hands.
Make us whole in spirit and touch our bodies.
Amen.

**Tuesday, January 31** — Psalm 18:25-29
Genesis 30:25-31:21; Matthew 11:11-24

**A son honors his father. If then I am a father,
where is the honor due me? says the Lord.
Malachi 1:6**

> All praise and thanks to God          533
> the Father now be given,
> the Son and Spirit blessed,
> who reign in highest heaven —
> the one eternal God,
> whom heav'n and earth adore;
> for thus it was, is now,
> and shall be evermore.

**To the King of the ages, immortal, invisible, the
only God, be honor and glory forever and ever.
1 Timothy 1:17**

> To you, most holy Lord,          633
> we sing with hearts and voices;
> in you, with one accord,
> your church on earth rejoices!
> We bend before your throne
> and humbly chant your praise;
> we worship you alone,
> whose love has crowned our days.

Heavenly Father, it's hard for us to face the brutal
truth that we often ignore you. We separate
ourselves from you. We withhold our hearts from
the very one who created them. Forgive us and
receive us, we pray. Amen.

**Wednesday, February 1** — Psalm 18:30-36
Genesis 31:22-55; Matthew 11:25-12:8

**O Lord my Lord, act on my behalf for your
name's sake; because your steadfast love is good,
deliver me. Psalm 109:21**

Come, Almighty to deliver,                          474
let us all your life receive;
suddenly return, and never,
never more your temple leave.
You we would be always blessing,
serve you as your hosts above,
pray, and praise you without ceasing,
glory in your perfect love.

**Christ says, "I give my sheep eternal life, and
they will never perish. No one will snatch them
out of my hand." John 10:28**

O Christians, haste, your mission high fulfilling,  618
to tell to all the world that God is light,
that he who made all nations is not willing
one life should perish, lost in shades of night.

Almighty God, we are mindful of your steadfast
love and protection over our lives. Thank you for
acting on our behalf as we journey through life.
May we always feel secure in your haven of love.
Amen.

**Thursday, February 2** — Psalm 18:37-45
Genesis 32:1-21; Matthew 12:9-21

## I will save you from all your uncleannesses.
## Ezekiel 36:29

Save us from weak resignation     751
to the evils we deplore;
let the gift of your salvation
be our glory evermore.
Grant us wisdom, grant us courage
serving you whom we adore,
serving you whom we adore.

**You know that you were ransomed from the futile ways inherited from your ancestors, not with perishable things like silver or gold, but with the precious blood of Christ, like that of a lamb without defect or blemish.**
**1 Peter 1:18-19**

Alleluia! Sing to Jesus!     373
His the scepter, his the throne;
alleluia! His the triumph,
his the victory alone.
Hark! The songs of peaceful Zion
thunder like a mighty flood.
Jesus, out of ev'ry nation,
has redeemed us by his blood.

Heavenly Father, we thank you for your cleansing power. May we follow in the footsteps of our ancestors as we look to you for guidance! We praise you together with the Holy Spirit for anointing us with the precious blood of Jesus Christ. Amen.

**Friday, February 3** — Psalm 18:46-50
Genesis 32:22-33:20; Matthew 12:22-32

## When I thought, "My foot is slipping," your steadfast love, O Lord, held me up. Psalm 94:18

O God, in whom our trust we place,                     509
we thank you for your word of grace;
help us its precepts to obey
till we shall live in endless day.

## Let us therefore approach the throne of grace with boldness, so that we may receive mercy and find grace to help in time of need. Hebrews 4:16

Savior, now with contrite hearts                       741
we approach your throne of love,
asking pardon for our sins,
peace and comfort from above.
You once suffered on the cross
to atone for sinners' guilt;
may we never, Lord, forget
that for us your blood was spilled.

Creator God, your steadfast love endures forever.
We pray you will infuse us with the strength and
power of the Holy Spirit as we boldly approach your
throne of grace, asking forgiveness for our sins.
Amen.

Saturday, February 4 — Psalm 19:1-6
Genesis 34; Matthew 12:33-45

## Noah found favor in the sight of the Lord. Genesis 6:8

> O let my eyes be lightened                    484
> by sight of your dear face;
> my life below be brightened
> by tasting of your grace;
> without you, mighty Savior,
> to live is naught but pain;
> to have your love and favor
> is happiness and gain.

## The Son of Man will gather his elect from the four winds, from the ends of the earth to the ends of heaven. Mark 13:27

> Even so, Lord, quickly come                    450
> to your final harvest-home;
> gather all your people in,
> free from sorrow, free from sin,
> there forever purified
> in your presence to abide.
> Come, with all your angels, come,
> raise the glorious harvest-home.

Lord God, as you gather your children from the ends of the earth, may we remain faithful. We know our final place will be with you in your heavenly kingdom! Amen.

## Fifth Sunday after the Epiphany

**Watchword for the Week** — Great is our Lord, and abundant in power; his understanding is beyond measure. Psalm 147:5

**Sunday, February 5** — Isaiah 40:21-31; Psalm 147:1-11,20c
1 Corinthians 9:16-23; Mark 1:29-39

## On that day the root of Jesse shall stand as a signal to the peoples; the nations shall inquire of him. Isaiah 11:10

Bring near your great salvation,                         394
O Lamb for sinners slain;
fill up the roll of your elect,
then take your pow'r, and reign!
Appear, Desire of nations,
your exiles long for home;
show in the heav'n your promised sign;
then, Prince and Savior, come.

## Paul wrote: If you, a wild olive shoot, were grafted in to share the rich root of the olive tree, do not boast over the branches. If you do boast, remember that it is not you that support the root, but the root that supports you. Romans 11:17-18

We have received Christ Jesus,                          434
the Lord who sets us free
as sisters and as brothers
in one community,
a people deeply rooted
in Jesus' love and life.
We know who we are called to be:
Christ's body given melody
to sing God's praise resoundingly.
Alleluia!

God, today we gather to sing our alleluias to you. On this our day of worship, we acknowledge that it is not us but Jesus Christ who made it all possible through his love to each of us. Help us to stand together as a living branch extended from that love. Amen.

**Monday, February 6** — Psalm 19:7-14
Genesis 35:1-36:8; Matthew 12:46-13:9

**See, the Lord's hand is not too short to save, nor his ear too dull to hear. Rather, your iniquities have been barriers between you and your God. Isaiah 59:1-2**

In Christ there is no east or west —                      781
he breaks all barriers down:
by Christ redeemed, by Christ possessed,
in Christ we live as one.

**Do you not know that wrongdoers will not inherit the kingdom of God? Do not be deceived! 1 Corinthians 6:9**

O bless his holy name,                                     452
and joyful thanks proclaim
through all the earth;
be grateful and receive
God's blessing; and believe;
his love does not deceive.
Now share your mirth!

Father God, thank you for being attentive to the cry of your people! Guide us to the path which will help us to refrain from wrongdoings so we may glory with our brothers and sisters in your kingdom's light. Amen.

**Tuesday, February 7 — Psalm 20**
Genesis 36:9-43; Matthew 13:10-23

**More majestic than the thunders of mighty waters, more majestic than the waves of the sea, majestic on high is the Lord! Psalm 93:4**

> O Majestic Being,                                    554
> may our souls and bodies
> at all times be at your service!
> Like the holy angels
> who bow down before you,
> may we ceaselessly adore you,
> and through grace, Jesus' grace,
> in our whole demeanor,
> offer praise and honor.

**Jesus woke up and rebuked the wind, and said to the sea, "Peace! Be still!" Then the wind ceased, and there was a dead calm. Mark 4:39**

> Eternal Father, strong to save,                      725
> whose arm has bound the restless wave,
> who bade the mighty ocean deep
> its own appointed limits keep:
> O hear us when we cry to thee
> for those in peril on the sea.

Lord of heaven and earth, you are high above all creation. You continue to provide for us the sustenance needed to sustain our lives. May we live lives worthy of the peace that Jesus brings to all humankind! Amen.

**Wednesday, February 8** — Psalm 21
Genesis 37; Matthew 13:24-35

**For your own sake, Lord, let your face shine upon your desolated sanctuary. Daniel 9:17**

> Sun of righteousness, arise;                         521*
> dawn upon our clouded skies;
> shine within your church today
> that the world may see and say,
> "Have mercy, Lord."

**You are built upon the foundation of the apostles and prophets, with Christ Jesus himself as the cornerstone. In him the whole structure is joined together and grows into a holy temple in the Lord; in whom you also are built together spiritually into a dwelling place for God. Ephesians 2:20-22**

> Christ is our cornerstone,                            517
> on him alone we build;
> with his true saints alone
> the courts of heav'n are filled;
> on his great love our hopes we place
> of present grace and joys above.

Eternal and ever-loving God, shine your light within our hearts. We thank you for Jesus Christ, the cornerstone, and for the Holy Spirit with whom you have allowed us to dwell. May we grow within the realm of the triune God! Amen.

* Tr. by C. Daniel Crews (1994)

**Thursday, February 9** — Psalm 22:1-8
Genesis 38; Matthew 13:36-46

**If you extend your soul to the hungry and satisfy
the afflicted soul, then your light shall dawn in
the darkness. Isaiah 58:10 (NJKV)**

> By the Spirit we are gifted                          624*
> to fulfill Christ's ministry.
> With the poor we share our riches,
> giving captives liberty.
> Hungry, thirsty—we will feed them;
> greet the stranger; care and heal;
> clothe the naked, free the pris'ner;
> serve with gladness and with zeal.

**Show them the proof of your love.
2 Corinthians 8:24**

> Jesus makes my heart rejoice,                        662
> I'm his sheep and know his voice;
> he's a Shepherd, kind and gracious,
> and his pastures are delicious;
> constant love to me he shows,
> yea, my very name he knows.

God, help us to be always kindhearted to one
another so others will see your light shining within
us and glorify your holy name. Amen.

*  © 1988 by W. Thomas Stapleton

Friday, February 10 — Psalm 22:9-21
Genesis 39; Matthew 13:47-58

**A shoot shall come out from the stump of Jesse, and a branch shall grow out of his roots. Isaiah 11:1**

> Songs of thankfulness and praise,    313
> Jesus, Lord, to you we raise,
> manifested by the star
> to the sages from afar;
> branch of royal David's stem
> in your birth at Bethlehem;
> anthems be to you addressed,
> God in flesh made manifest.

**Christ says, "I am the vine, you are the branches. Those who abide in me and I in them bear much fruit, because apart from me you can do nothing." John 15:5**

> One our Master, one alone,    525
> none but Christ as Lord we own;
> "brethren of his law" are we —
> "As I loved you, so love ye."
> Branches we in Christ, the Vine,
> living by his life divine;
> as the Father with the Son,
> so, in Christ, we all are one.

Creator God, thank you for the earthly lineage of our Lord Jesus Christ! As we study his life's journey, may his words abide within us as we gather fruits worthy to be harvested in his kingdom! Amen.

Saturday, February 11 — Psalm 22:22-28
Genesis 40:1-41:16; Matthew 14:1-14

**Proclaim, give praise, and say, "Save, O Lord, your people." Jeremiah 31:7**

Sing hallelujah, praise the Lord!   543
Sing with a cheerful voice;
exalt our God with one accord,
and in his name rejoice.
Ne'er cease to sing, O ransomed host,
praise Father, Son, and Holy Ghost,
until in realms of endless light
your praises shall unite.

**Lord, grant to your servants to speak your word with all boldness. Acts 4:29**

Lord, have mercy, Lord, have mercy   636
on each land and place
where your servants, where your servants
preach the word of grace;
life and pow'r on them bestow,
them with needful strength endow,
that with boldness, that with boldness
they may you confess.

Gracious God, save your people from weak resignation and incline our hearts to speak your word of grace with boldness as we interact with others within our various communities. Amen.

## Sixth Sunday after the Epiphany

**Watchword for the Week** — Weeping may linger for the night, but joy comes with the morning. Psalm 30:5

**Sunday, February 12** — 2 Kings 5:1-14; Psalm 30
1 Corinthians 9:24-27; Mark 1:40-45

## O Lord, I love the house in which you dwell, and the place where your glory abides. Psalm 26:8

I love your kingdom, Lord,     513
the place of your abode,
the church our blessed Redeemer saved
with his own precious blood.

## After three days the parents found Jesus in the temple, sitting among the teachers, listening to them and asking them questions. Luke 2:46

Jesus taught both by example     665*
and with words of lasting worth;
Christ has given ways to sample
hints of heaven here on earth!
In the same way Christian teachers
model true humanity,
demonstrating in their witness
glimpses of eternity!

O Lord, we invite you into our midst as we assemble with our brothers and sisters in our places of worship. Bless our leaders whom you have inspired to bring us the message taken from your Holy Bible. Amen.

* © 1994 by John A. Dalles

**Monday, February 13** — Psalm 22:29-31
Genesis 41:17-57; Matthew 14:15-24

## We also will serve the Lord, for he is our God. Joshua 24:18

> Consecrate me now to thy service, Lord,                    607
> by the pow'r of grace divine;
> let my soul look up with a steadfast hope
> and my will be lost in thine.

## It is required of stewards that they be found trustworthy. 1 Corinthians 4:2

> O Jesus, I have promised                    603
> to serve you to the end;
> be now and ever near me,
> my master and my friend.
> I shall not fear the battle
> if you are by my side,
> nor wander from the pathway
> if you will be my guide.

Father God, we worship the beauty of your holiness. May our love and service to you be honorable as we spend time in your presence. Amen.

**Tuesday, February 14** — Psalm 23
Genesis 42; Matthew 14:25-15:9

**Assemble the people for me, and I will let them hear my words, so that they may learn to fear me as long as they live on the earth, and may teach their children to do so. Deuteronomy 4:10**

O God of unrelenting grace,                          738*
whose judgment yet we daily face,
forgive us now, good Lord.
You are so distant and so near;
for you we long, yet you we fear,
O known, and yet beyond record.

**Do your best to present yourself to God as one approved by him, a worker who has no need to be ashamed, rightly explaining the word of truth. 2 Timothy 2:15**

Hear us, O Lord, as we now pray,                     536**
dedicate us to your way;
lead us to work that bears your fruit,
giving knowledge of your truth.
Open our door and enter in,
rescue from darkness and from sin.
Strengthen according to your might,
share with us the promised life.

Lord God, we hear your call to discipleship. May we be worthy to serve you and help us to revere your presence as we learn your words of life. May we teach these words to those with whom we come in contact. Amen.

* © 1993 by Hermann I. Weinlick

** © 1991 by Beth E. Hanson

**Wednesday, February 15** — Psalm 24
Genesis 43; Matthew 15:10-20

## Noah was a righteous man, blameless in his generation; Noah walked with God. Genesis 6:9

Dear Lord and Father of mankind,                    739
forgive our foolish ways;
reclothe us in our rightful mind;
in purer lives thy service find,
in deeper rev'rence, praise.

## By faith Noah, warned by God about events as yet unseen, respected the warning and built an ark to save his household. Hebrews 11:7

All who have gone before us                    389*
have shown us how to live
a life of faith and service—
to pray, to praise, to give!
And so as we remember,
more so, we pray that we
may follow their example,
God's ministers to be!
All who've gone before us,
Christ's victory now share!
God, bless them all!
God, bless them all in your eternal care!

Lord God, help us to be as faithful as our ancestors
of old who loved you and trusted your guidance
within their lives and households. Amen.

* © 1992 by John A. Dalles

**Thursday, February 16** — Psalm 25:1-7
Genesis 44; Matthew 15:21-28

**You are my help and my deliverer; do not delay, O my God. Psalm 40:17**

> Open now the crystal fountain 790
> where the healing waters flow;
> let the fire and cloudy pillar
> lead me all my journey through.
> Strong deliv'rer, strong deliv'rer,
> ever be my strength and shield;
> ever be my strength and shield.

**A leper came to Jesus begging him, and kneeling he said to him, "If you choose, you can make me clean." Moved with pity, Jesus stretched out his hand and touched him, and said to him, "I do choose. Be made clean!" Mark 1:40-41**

> Now we bring ourselves to you; 741
> cleanse us, Lord, we humbly pray;
> undeserving though we be,
> draw us closer ev'ry day.
> Lord, our refuge, hope, and strength!
> Keep, O keep us safe from harm,
> shield us through our earthly life
> by your everlasting arm.

O God our help in ages past, may we take up our cross and emulate our Lord Jesus who was not afraid to be a servant by helping all in need. Amen.

Friday, February 17 — Psalm 25:8-22
Genesis 45; Matthew 15:29-16:4

**Happy are those who make the Lord their trust.
Psalm 40:4**

> Other refuge have I none;                    724
> hangs my helpless soul on thee;
> leave, ah, leave me not alone,
> still support and comfort me.
> All my trust on thee is stayed,
> all my help from thee I bring;
> cover my defenseless head
> with the shadow of thy wing.

**If for this life only we have hoped in Christ,
we are of all people most to be pitied.
1 Corinthians 15:19**

> My hope is built on nothing less                771
> than Jesus' blood and righteousness;
> no merit of my own I claim
> but wholly lean on Jesus' name.

Lord God, our hope is in you and we are thankful
your love for us remains unconditional. May we
as a people delight in that love as we walk in your
path of righteousness. Amen.

Saturday, February 18 — Psalm 26
Genesis 46:1-27; Matthew 16:5-20

**Here is my servant, whom I uphold, my chosen, in whom my soul delights. Isaiah 42:1**

> O seed of Israel's chosen race,                403
> now ransomed from the fall,
> hail him who saves you by his grace,
> and crown him Lord of all!
> Hail him who saves you by his grace,
> and crown him Lord of all!

**Jesus Christ received honor and glory from God the Father when that voice was conveyed to him by the Majestic Glory, saying, "This is my Son, my Beloved, with whom I am well pleased." 2 Peter 1:17**

> Worship, honor, pow'r and blessing              330
> you are worthy to receive;
> loudest praises without ceasing
> right it is for us to give.
> Help, O bright angelic spirits,
> all your noblest anthems raise,
> help us sing our Savior's merits,
> help to chant Immanuel's praise.

Heavenly Father in whom the world delights, we give you honor and praise. You sent your Son into the world to redeem us of our sins. Your voice still echoes, "This is my beloved Son." Thank you for the confirmation that Jesus Christ is Lord. Amen.

## Last Sunday after the Epiphany
## Transfiguration of our Lord

**Watchword for the Week** — For we do not proclaim ourselves; we proclaim Jesus Christ as Lord and ourselves as servants for Jesus' sake. 2 Corinthians 4:5

**Sunday, February 19** — 2 Kings 2:1-12; Psalm 50:1-6
2 Corinthians 4:3-6; Mark 9:2-9

### The Lord is in the right, for I have rebelled against his word. Lamentations 1:18

Pardon, Lord, and are there those                779
who my debtors are, or foes?
I, who by forgiveness live,
here their trespasses forgive.

### The son said to him, "Father, I have sinned against heaven and before you; I am no longer worthy to be called your son." Luke 15:21

Breathe, O breathe your loving Spirit            474
into ev'ry troubled breast;
let us all in you inherit,
let us find the promised rest.
Take away the love of sinning;
Alpha and Omega be;
end of faith, as its beginning,
set our hearts at liberty.

Lord God, although unworthy servants, we come before you confessing our sins and asking you to create within us clean hearts and renew a right spirit within us. We strive to follow the teachings of your holy word within our lives. Amen.

**Monday, February 20** — Psalm 27:1-6
Genesis 46:28-47:31; Matthew 16:21-28

## Do not fear or be dismayed! Joshua 8:1

In heav'nly love abiding,                    732
no change my heart shall fear;
and safe is such confiding,
for nothing changes here.
The storm may roar around me,
my heart may low be laid,
but God is round about me,
and can I be dismayed?

## Do not be afraid; I am the first and the last, and the living one. Revelation 1:17-18

Hail, Alpha and Omega, hail,                    703
O Author of our faith,
the Finisher of all our hopes,
the Truth, the Life, the Path.

Father God, when disappointment arises and fear
is all we can see ahead of us, let us hold on to our
Savior, the Alpha and the Omega, the one who
lives forever and ever. Amen.

**Tuesday, February 21** — Psalm 27:7-14
Genesis 48; Matthew 17:1-13

**Have you not known? Have you not heard?
The Lord is the everlasting God, the Creator of
the ends of the earth. He does not faint or grow
weary; his understanding is unsearchable.
Isaiah 40:28**

> Lifegiving Creator of both great and small;          457
> of all life the maker, the true life of all;
> we blossom, then wither like leaves on the tree,
> but you live forever who was and will be.

**God has not left himself without a witness in
doing good—giving you rains from heaven and
fruitful seasons, and filling you with food and
your hearts with joy. Acts 14:17**

> Come, you thirsty, come and welcome,          765
> God's free bounty glorify;
> true belief and true repentance,
> ev'ry grace that brings you nigh.

Creator God, you will not faint or grow weary
of your people. Your love is endless and your
provisions are bountiful. We joyfully give you
thanks and praise for your goodness towards your
whole creation. Amen.

## Ash Wednesday

**Wednesday, February 22** — Psalm 28
Genesis 49; Matthew 17:14-27

**Ash Wednesday** — Joel 2:1-2,12-17; Psalm 51:1-17
2 Corinthians 5:20b-6:10; Matthew 6:1-6,16-21

**You have delivered my soul from death, my eyes from tears, my feet from stumbling. Psalm 116:8**

> Christ, the life of all the living,    334
> Christ, the death of death, our foe,
> Christ, for us yourself once giving
> to the darkest depths of woe:
> through your suff'ring, death and merit,
> life eternal we inherit;
> thousand, thousand thanks are due,
> dearest Jesus, unto you.

**Peter got out of the boat, started walking on the water, and came toward Jesus. But when he noticed the strong wind, he became frightened, and beginning to sink, he cried out, "Lord, save me!" Jesus immediately reached out his hand and caught him. Matthew 14:29-31**

> Bring to our troubled minds,    681*
> uncertain and afraid,
> the quiet of a steadfast faith,
> calm of a call obeyed.

Creator of the universe, only you can deliver our souls from death. When we become overwhelmed with the activities of the world, let us keep our eyes fixed on Jesus, our Lord and Savior. Amen.

* © by Emmanuel College, Toronto. Used by permission.

Thursday, February 23 — Psalm 29
Genesis 50; Matthew 18:1-14

**Do not fear, for you will not be ashamed.
Isaiah 54:4**

> God sent his Son, they called him Jesus,                706
> he came to love, heal, and forgive;
> he lived and died to buy my pardon,
> an empty grave is there to prove my Savior lives.

**When they bring you to trial and hand you over,
do not worry beforehand about what you are to
say; but say whatever is given you at that time,
for it is not you who speak, but the Holy Spirit.
Mark 13:11**

> By your holy word instruct them;                        660
> fill their minds with heav'nly light;
> by your pow'rful grace constrain them
> always to approve what's right;
> let them know your yoke is easy,
> let them prove your burden's light.

Merciful Father, we thank you for always being with
us. We are thankful for the power to see clearly the
task set before us provided by the Holy Spirit who
dwells within our hearts. Amen.

**Friday, February 24** — Psalm 30:1-5
Exodus 1:1-2:10; Matthew 18:15-35

## I rejoice in your salvation. 1 Samuel 2:1 (NASB)

I bind this day to me forever                           p237
by power of faith Christ's incarnation;
his baptism in Jordan river;
his death on cross for my salvation;
his bursting from the spiced tomb;
his riding up the heavenly way;
his coming at the day of doom;
I bind unto myself today.

**When Jesus rose early on the first day of the week, he appeared first to Mary Magdalene. She went and told those who had been with him and who were mourning and weeping. Mark 16:9,10**

Rise up, O saints of God!                               628*
From vain ambitions turn;
Christ rose triumphant that your hearts
with nobler zeal might burn.

Precious Lord, we rejoice with the angels and the disciples in the salvation of our Lord and Savior Jesus Christ who died for our sins and was raised as King of kings. Amen.

* © 1978 by Norman O. Forness

**Saturday, February 25** — Psalm 30:6-12
Exodus 2:11-3:22; Matthew 19:1-12

**O God, you are my God, I seek you, my soul thirsts for you. Psalm 63:1**

> Did you not bid us love you, God and King,     490
> love you with all our heart and strength and mind?
> I see the cross—there teach my heart to cling.
> O let me seek you and O let me find!

**Christ says, "Strive first for the kingdom of God and his righteousness, and all these things will be given to you as well." Matthew 6:33**

> Seek ye first the kingdom of God     605
> and his righteousness,
> and all these things shall be added unto you —
> Allelu, alleluia!

Most holy Lord and God, to you we give all honor and praise. Help us always to seek first your kingdom and its righteousness as instructed by our Lord Jesus Christ. Amen.

## First Sunday in Lent

**Watchword for the Week** — Good and upright is the Lord; therefore he instructs sinners in the way. Psalm 25:8

**Sunday, February 26** — Genesis 9:8-17; Psalm 25:1-10
1 Peter 3:18-22; Mark 1:9-15

## I will set my eyes upon them for good. I will build them up, and not tear them down; I will plant them, and not pluck them up. Jeremiah 24:6

'Tis the most blessed and needful part                768
to have in Christ a share,
and to commit our way and heart
unto his faithful care;
this done, our steps are safe and sure,
our hearts' desires are rendered pure,
and naught can pluck us from his hand,
which leads us to the end.

## So neither the one who plants nor the one who waters is anything, but only God who gives the growth. 1 Corinthians 3:7

Grant, Lord, that with thy direction,                673
"Love each other," we comply,
aiming with unfeigned affection
thy love to exemplify;
let our mutual love be glowing;
thus the world will plainly see
that we, as on one stem growing,
living branches are in thee.

God of heaven and earth, as we gather for worship,
let us praise you as Lord who is able to shape us
as a people of one mind. You are the one who
also provides for us the life-giving water needed to
sustain our growth. Amen.

**Monday, February 27** — Psalm 31:1-5
Exodus 4:1-5:9; Matthew 19:13-22

**All the ends of the earth shall remember and turn to the Lord; and all the families of the nations shall worship before him. Psalm 22:27**

Worship, honor, glory, blessing,                    454
Lord, we offer as our gift;
young and old, your praise expressing,
our glad songs to you we lift.
All the saints in heav'n adore you;
we would join their glad acclaim;
as your angels serve before you,
so on earth we praise your name.

**God desires everyone to be saved and to come to the knowledge of the truth. 1 Timothy 2:4**

Amazing grace! How sweet the sound                    783
that saved a wretch like me!
I once was lost, but now am found,
was blind, but now I see.

Lord, help us to remain faithful while we take our journey as a people to worship you in the beauty of your holiness. Give us a better understanding, knowledge and saving grace as we walk in your devout light! Amen.

Tuesday, February 28 — Psalm 31:6-9
Exodus 5:10-6:12; Matthew 19:23-30

## Those who cling to worthless idols forfeit the grace that could be theirs. Jonah 2:8 (NIV)

We turn to Christ anew                           425*
who hear his call today,
his way to walk, his will pursue,
his word obey.
To serve him as our king
and of his kingdom learn,
from sin and ev'ry evil thing
to him we turn.

## The love of money is a root of all kinds of evil, and in their eagerness to be rich some have wandered away from the faith and pierced themselves with many pains. 1 Timothy 6:10

Just as I am, poor, wretched, blind;            762
sight, riches, healing of the mind,
yea, all I need, in thee to find,
O Lamb of God, I come, I come!

Lord God, we confess our weaknesses. We need your help to turn away from the idols we have created. May we always put our trust in you and worship you—the one true God. Amen.

**Wednesday, February 29** — Psalm 31:10-20
Exodus 6:13-7:24; Matthew 20:1-16

## Man born of woman is of few days and full of trouble. Job 14:1 (NIV)

You have cancelled my transgressions,                    p202
Jesus, by your precious blood;
may I find therein salvation,
happiness, and peace with God;
and since you, for sinners suff'ring
on the cross were made an off'ring,
from all sin deliver me,
that I wholly yours may be.

## It is sown in dishonor, it is raised in glory. It is sown in weakness, it is raised in power. 1 Corinthians 15:43

We know that Christ is raised and dies no more.    366
Embraced by death he broke its fearful hold;
and our despair he turned to blazing joy.
Alleluia!

Father God, help us follow in the footsteps of our Lord Jesus who was born, remained sinless and was raised in the power of your glory. Amen.

### March 1, 1457:
#### Beginning of the Unity of the Brethren in Bohemia

**Thursday, March 1** — Psalm 31:21-24
Exodus 8; Matthew 20:17-28

**This is God, our God forever and ever. He will be our guide forever. Psalm 48:14**

> Guide me, O my great Redeemer,  790
> pilgrim through this barren land.
> I am weak, but you are mighty;
> hold me with your pow'rful hand.
> Bread of heaven, bread of heaven,
> feed me now and evermore,
> feed me now and evermore.

**Let us hold fast to the confession of our hope without wavering, for he who has promised is faithful. Hebrews 10:23**

> On him we'll venture all we have,  479
> our lives, our all, to him we owe.
> None else is able us to save,
> naught but the Savior will we know;
> this we subscribe with heart and hand,
> resolved through grace thereby to stand.

Faithful God, on this special day marking the birth of our church, we are mindful of those who have gone before, especially those saints in 1457 who held fast to their hope. Like them, may we today walk forward unwavering, trusting in your guidance and faithfulness. Amen.

**Friday, March 2** — Psalm 32
Exodus 9; Matthew 20:29-21:11

## God knows what is in the darkness, and light dwells with him. Daniel 2:22

Immortal, invisible, God only wise,                    457
in light inaccessible hid from our eyes,
most blessed, most glorious, O Ancient of Days,
almighty, victorious, your great name we praise.

## Whatever is hidden is meant to be disclosed, and whatever is concealed is meant to be brought out into the open. Mark 4:22 (NIV)

Great Father of glory, pure Father of light,          457
your angels adore you, all veiling their sight;
all praise we would render, O lead us to see
the light of your splendor, your love's majesty.

Revealing God, we know your intent is always to open yourself to us in every way imaginable. Help us to have the ears to hear and the eyes to see the truths that you are constantly laying out before us. Guide us to live in accordance with those truths. Amen.

**Saturday, March 3 — Psalm 33:1-5**
Exodus 10; Matthew 21:12-22

**You, O God, are my king from of old; you bring salvation upon the earth. Psalm 74:12 (NIV)**

Crown him the Lord of years,                                405
the risen Lord sublime,
Creator of the rolling spheres,
the Master of all time.
All hail, Redeemer, hail!
For you have died for me;
your praise and glory shall not fail
throughout eternity.

**Wherever Jesus went, into villages or cities or farms, they laid the sick in the marketplaces, and begged him that they might touch even the fringe of his cloak; and all who touched it were healed. Mark 6:56**

Savior, you came to give                                    380
those who in darkness live
healing and sight,
health to the sick in mind,
sight to the inward blind:
now to all humankind
let there be light!

God of healing power, we intercede today for all in illness of body, mind or spirit. Give comfort in their discomfort, ease in their disease, rest in their restlessness and strength in their weakness. Above all, assure each one of your presence. Amen.

## Second Sunday in Lent

**Watchword for the Week** — God says, "I will establish my covenant between me and you, and your offspring after you throughout their generations." Genesis 17:7

**Sunday, March 4** — Genesis 7:1-7,15-16; Psalm 22:23-31
Romans 4:13-25; Mark 8:31-38

**You who live in the shelter of the Most High, who abide in the shadow of the Almighty, will say to the Lord, "My refuge and my fortress; my God, in whom I trust." Psalm 91:1-2**

We hail you as our Savior, Lord,                    267
our refuge and our great reward;
without your grace we waste away
like flow'rs that wither and decay.

**God did not give us a spirit of cowardice, but rather a spirit of power and of love and of self-discipline. 2 Timothy 1:7**

Add to your believing                               582
deeds that prove it true —
knowing Christ as Savior,
make him Master too:
follow in his footsteps,
go where he has trod,
in the world's great trouble
risk yourself for God.

God of justice, we confess our lack of compassion for a world in need. Continue to confront us with the needs that exist all over the world and, as a part of our own Lenten pilgrimage, guide us in our responses. We wish to be faithful representatives of Christ to the hurts and pains experienced by so many and fulfill our part of the covenant. Amen.

Monday, March 5 — Psalm 33:6-11
Exodus 11:1-12:20; Matthew 21:23-32

**But Moses said to God, "Who am I that I should go to Pharaoh, and bring the Israelites out of Egypt?" God said, "I will be with you." Exodus 3:11-12**

"Fear not, I am with you; O be not dismayed,       709
for I am your God and will still give you aid;
I'll strengthen you, help you and cause you to stand
upheld by my righteous, omnipotent hand.

**It is not those who commend themselves that are approved, but those whom the Lord commends. 2 Corinthians 10:18**

He to the lowly soul                              584
will still himself impart
and for his dwelling and his throne
will choose the pure in heart.

As we recall in a common Advent hymn: "Not in our own strength, Lord, we move; your kingdom falls not when we fall, but forward presses day by day until your truth is known to all." Dear Lord, remind us always that it is only by your grace that we have been justified. Amen.

**Tuesday, March 6 — Psalm 33:12-22**
Exodus 12:21-51; Matthew 21:33-46

**May God continue to bless us; let all the ends of
the earth revere him. Psalm 67:7**

> From all that dwell below the skies                551
> let the Creator's praise arise;
> let the Redeemer's name be sung
> through every land, by every tongue.

**Blessed be the God and Father of our Lord
Jesus Christ, who has blessed us in Christ with
every spiritual blessing in the heavenly places.
Ephesians 1:3**

> May the grace of Christ our Savior                441
> and the Father's boundless love,
> with the Holy Spirit's favor
> rest upon us from above.

Generous God, you have so generously blessed us
in manifold ways. How can we be but grateful?
Forgive us for taking that grace for granted and
lead us into deeper thankfulness. Amen.

**Wednesday, March 7** — Psalm 34:1-7
Exodus 13:1-14:18; Matthew 22:1-14

**For the Lord your God is God of gods and Lord
of lords, the great God, mighty and awesome,
who is not partial and takes no bribe.
Deuteronomy 10:17**

> Lord of all being, throned afar,                    p122
> your glory flames from sun and star;
> center and soul of ev'ry sphere,
> yet to each loving heart how near!

**From him and through him and to him are all
things. To him be the glory forever. Romans 11:36**

> He rules the world with truth and grace,            294
> and makes the nations prove
> the glories of his righteousness
> and wonders of his love,
> and wonders of his love,
> and wonders, wonders of his love.

Almighty, omnipotent God, we adore you
and we praise you. You inspire awe within us
as we contemplate the magnificence of your
creative ability joined with the splendor of your
unconditional love for us, your creatures. What a
glorious combination! Amen.

Thursday, March 8 — Psalm 34:8-18
Exodus 14:19-15:21; Matthew 22:15-22

**My people have committed two evils: they have forsaken me, the fountain of living water, and dug out cisterns for themselves, cracked cisterns that can hold no water. Jeremiah 2:13**

> Lord God, with shame I now confess                    p32
> I've turned away from you;
> forgive me all my sin today,
> my heart and soul renew.

**Christ says, "Come to me, all you that are weary and are carrying heavy burdens, and I will give you rest." Matthew 11:28**

> Are we weak and heavy laden,                          743
> cumbered with a load of care?
> Precious Savior, still our refuge,
> take it to the Lord in prayer!
> Do your friends despise, forsake you?
> Take it to the Lord in prayer!
> In his arms he'll take and shield you;
> you will find a solace there.

Forgiving God, we confess our failures to serve you and our decisions to openly sin against you, others, self, and your good creation. We claim your forgiveness as we seek rest from the burdens produced by our sinfulness. Amen.

Friday, March 9 — Psalm 34:19-22
Exodus 15:22-16:36; Matthew 22:23-40

**My words that I have put in your mouth shall not depart out of your mouth, or out of the mouths of your children, or out of the mouths of your children's children. Isaiah 59:21**

> We do not live by bread alone,
> but by ev'ry word
> that proceeds from the mouth of God.
> Allelu, alleluia!

605

**The word of the Lord endures forever. That word is the good news that was announced to you. 1 Peter 1:25**

> The word of God, which ne'er shall cease,
> proclaims free pardon, grace, and peace,
> salvation shows in Christ alone,
> the perfect will of God makes known.

509

We give thanks to you, gracious God, for the gift of Christ—your communication of who you are and what you want us to be. We have experienced your good news and we are determined to pass it on to future generations through our words and actions. Guide us in this endeavor. Amen.

Saturday, March 10 — Psalm 35:1-10
Exodus 17:1-18:6; Matthew 22:41-23:12

**For God alone my soul waits in silence; from him comes my salvation. Psalm 62:1**

Lord, we your presence seek;                    584
we ask this blessing true:
give us a pure and lowly heart,
a temple fit for you.

**Christ says, "Whatever things you ask when you pray, believe that you receive them, and you will have them." Mark 11:24 (NKJV)**

Ask and it shall be given unto you,             605
seek and you shall find,
knock and the door shall be opened unto you —
Allelu, alleluia!

Grant us, this day, dear Lord, the assurance that you are a constant companion. We live in the hope that you will grant us our every need instead of our every selfish want. Amen.

## Third Sunday in Lent

**Watchword for the Week** — For the message about the cross is foolishness to those who are perishing, but to us who are being saved it is the power of God. 1 Corinthians 1:18

**Sunday, March 11** — Exodus 20:1-17; Psalm 19
1 Corinthians 1:18-25; John 2:13-22

# The name of the Lord is a strong tower; the righteous run into it and are safe. Proverbs 18:10

Lord, I would clasp thy hand in mine,     787
nor ever murmur nor repine,
content, whatever lot I see,
since 'tis my God that leadeth me.

# Jesus said, "Who comes to me, hears my words, and acts on them is like a man building a house, who dug deeply and laid the foundation on rock." Luke 6:47-48

We are God's house of living stones,     512
built for his own habitation;
he fills our hearts, his humble thrones,
granting us life and salvation.
Yet to this place, an earthly frame,
we come with thanks to praise his name;
God grants his people true blessing.

Omnipotent God, we continue our Lenten journey knowing Christ Jesus has walked this path before us. Because we live on this side of his cruel death and resurrection, we know that sin and death do not have the final word. Our safety is found in your grace and love. Amen.

**Monday, March 12** — Psalm 35:11-18
Exodus 18:7-19:9; Matthew 23:13-22

**The Lord executes justice for the orphan and the widow, and loves the strangers, providing them food and clothing. You shall also love the stranger. Deuteronomy 10:18,19**

Christ be with me, Christ within me,                    p237
Christ behind me, Christ before me,
Christ beside me, Christ to win me,
Christ to comfort and restore me,
Christ beneath me, Christ above me,
Christ in quiet, Christ in danger,
Christ in hearts of all that love me,
Christ in mouth of friend and stranger.

**We ought to support such people, so that we may become co-workers with the truth. 3 John 8**

When I walk through the shades of death,         730
your presence is my stay;
one word of your supporting breath
drives all my fears away.
Your hand, in sight of all my foes,
shall still my table spread;
my cup with blessings overflows;
your oil anoints my head.

God of justice, you are never biased. However, you always favor the powerless, the marginalized, the downtrodden, the hungry, the homeless and the addicted. You call upon us to do the same so we might be co-workers with the truth. Give us courage to face the forces of power and work for justice in every arena of our lives. Amen.

Tuesday, March 13 — Psalm 35:19-28
Exodus 19:10-20:21; Matthew 23:23-32

**O Lord our God—we set our hope on you.
Jeremiah 14:22**

> Hope of the world,                                527r
>     you Christ of great compassion,
> speak to our fearful hearts by conflict rent;
> save us, your people, from consuming passion,
> who by our own false hopes and aims are spent.

**We wait for the blessed hope and the
manifestation of the glory of our great God and
Savior, Jesus Christ. Titus 2:13**

> My faith looks trustingly                          705
> to Christ of Calvary,
> my Savior true!
> Lord, hear me while I pray,
> take all my guilt away,
> strengthen in ev'ry way
> my love for you!

Almighty God, we lift our hearts to you; and our
eyes are fixed upon your unchanging glory. We
rejoice in the promises of the coming of our Lord
Jesus Christ in power and majesty. Amen. (from
Reign of Christ Liturgy, MBW p109)

**Wednesday, March 14 — Psalm 36**
Exodus 20:22-21:27; Matthew 23:33-39

**So Moses and Aaron went to Pharaoh, and said to him, "Thus says the Lord, 'Let my people go, so that they may worship me.'" Exodus 10:3**

> God of grace and God of glory,          751
> on your people pour your power;
> crown your ancient Church's story;
> bring its bud to glorious flower.
> Grant us wisdom, grant us courage
> for the facing of this hour,
> for the facing of this hour.

**God opposes the proud, but gives grace to the humble. 1 Peter 5:5**

> Lo! The hosts of evil round us          751
> scorn the Christ, assail his ways!
> From the fears that long have bound us,
> free our hearts to faith and praise.
> Grant us wisdom, grant us courage,
> for the living of these days,
> for the living of these days.

Gracious God, give us the courage and the strength today to stand up to the powers of evil in our lives. These can walk all over the powerless and sometimes close their ears and eyes to cries for help. Pour your power into us to act. Amen.

**Thursday, March 15** — Psalm 37:1-6
Exodus 21:28-22:24; Matthew 24:1-25

## The Lord will give strength to His people. Psalm 29:11 (NKJV)

> Faith finds in Christ our ev'ry need                700
> to save or strengthen us indeed;
> we now receive the grace sent down,
> which makes us share his cross and crown.

## In Christ Jesus you have been enriched in every way—in all your speaking and in all your knowledge. 1 Corinthians 1:5 (NIV)

> Lord, speak to me, that I may speak                646
> in living echoes of your tone.
> As you have sought, so let me seek
> your erring children lost and lone.

Gracious Redeemer, we thank you for empowering us today to speak for you. May we listen closely so the words we speak are truly the words you would have us speak. In addition, may our actions state an unmistakable message from you. Amen.

**Friday, March 16** — Psalm 37:7-15
Exodus 22:25-23:26; Matthew 24:26-35

**My child, give me your heart, and let your eyes observe my ways. Proverbs 23:26**

As a mother feels the heartbeat                    659
of her baby held so near,
and is moved to awe and laughter
at this infant life so dear,
so in Christ God feels our heartbeat,
enters in our joy and fear;
gives us bread and wine and mem'ry
that our vision may be clear.

**Jesus, looking at him, loved him and said, "You lack one thing; go, sell what you own, and give the money to the poor, and you will have treasure in heaven; then come, follow me." Mark 10:21**

We give you but your own                           657
in any gifts we bring;
all that we have is yours alone,
a trust from you, our King.

Generous and giving God, we confess today that we are not always good stewards of our hearts or our resources. Forgive us and help us realize all that we possess belongs to you. Create within us sharing and giving hearts. Amen.

Saturday, March 17 — Psalm 37:16-22
Exodus 23:27-25:9; Matthew 24:36-44

**Those of low estate are but a breath, those of
high estate are a delusion; in the balances they
go up; they are together lighter than a breath.
Psalm 62:9**

> The shadow of your cross, Lord,                    329
> be my abiding place;
> I ask no other sunshine than
> the sunshine of your face;
> content to let the world go by,
> to know no gain nor loss,
> my sinful self my only shame,
> my glory all your cross.

**Christ says, "Truly I tell you, whoever does not
receive the kingdom of God as a little child will
never enter it." Mark 10:15**

> Jesus loves me! This I know,                        726
> for the Bible tells me so.
> Little ones to him belong;
> they are weak but he is strong.
> Yes, Jesus loves me, yes, Jesus loves me,
> yes, Jesus loves me, the Bible tells me so.

Thank you, Jesus, for loving even us. In childlike
faith, we come to you. Take away our pride while
reminding us that you find even us worthy of your
love. Thank you, Jesus. Amen.

### Fourth Sunday in Lent

**Watchword for the Week** — By grace you have been saved through faith, and this is not your own doing; it is the gift of God. Ephesians 2:8

**Sunday, March 18** — Numbers 21:4-9; Psalm 107:1-3,17-22 Ephesians 2:1-10; John 3:14-21

## Consider too that this nation is your people. Exodus 33:13

> Jesus, great High Priest of our profession,          400
> we in confidence draw near;
> grant us, then, in mercy, the confession
> of our grateful hearts to hear;
> you we gladly own in ev'ry nation,
> Head and Master of your congregation,
> conscious that in ev'ry place
> you are giving life and grace.

## God's solid foundation stands firm, sealed with this inscription: "The Lord knows those who are his." 2 Timothy 2:19 (NIV)

> How firm a foundation, you saints of the Lord,          709
> is laid for your faith in his excellent world!
> What more can he say than to you he has said,
> to you who for refuge to Jesus have fled?

During these days of Lent, dear Lord, express to all nations that you have provided for us a firm foundation. As we continue our journey toward the observance of that terrible day when our sins were laid bare at the cross, remind us that we are yours and therefore, we too may taste the resurrection victory. Amen.

**Monday, March 19** — Psalm 37:23-26
Exodus 25:10-40; Matthew 24:45-51

**Jeremiah said, "For the hurt of my poor people I am hurt. Is there no balm in Gilead? Is there no physician there?" Jeremiah 8:21-22**

> There is a balm in Gilead 500
> to make the wounded whole,
> there is a balm in Gilead
> to heal the sin-sick soul.

**She felt in her body that she was freed from her suffering. At once Jesus realized that power had gone out from him. Mark 5:29-30 (NIV)**

> Thanks to his love's wide outpouring 316
> and to the Spirit's imploring,
> joy in our hearts is abiding,
> suff'ring and pain are subsiding.

Healing God, you can bring wholeness to your people. Our sin is known by you and, as we confess it, you bring forgiveness and healing. We pray in the name of Jesus who loves us and who gave himself for us. Amen.

**Tuesday, March 20** — Psalm 37:27-33
Exodus 26; Matthew 25:1-13

**Both we and our ancestors have sinned;
we have committed iniquity, have done wickedly.
Psalm 106:6**

> Here we kneel to seek your presence,                    557*
> share our sin, confess our shame,
> touch the joy whose very essence
> cleanses, strengthens, cancels blame.
> Grace invited, faith united,
> fellowship of love set free.

**To one who without works trusts him who
justifies the ungodly, such faith is reckoned as
righteousness. Romans 4:5**

> His grace subdues the pow'r of sin;                    548
> he sets the pris'ner free;
> his blood can make the foulest clean,
> his blood availed for me.

Most holy and almighty God, our Savior, we confess
our disobedience. We, like sheep, have gone astray,
all of us turning to our own way. We have sinned
and have done wrong. The good that we knew to
do we have not done. We know that we have been
unworthy servants and have fallen short of your
glory. Help us, deliver us, and forgive our sins,
O God of our salvation, for the sake of your Son,
Jesus Christ, who loved us and gave himself for us.
Amen. (from General Liturgy I, MBW p2)

**Wednesday, March 21** — Psalm 37:34-40
Exodus 27:1-28:14; Matthew 25:14-30

**Do not be wise in your own eyes; fear the Lord,
and turn away from evil. Proverbs 3:7**

> Now we bring ourselves to you;                    741
> cleanse us, Lord, we humbly pray;
> undeserving though we be,
> draw us closer ev'ry day.
> Lord, our refuge, hope, and strength!
> Keep, O keep us safe from harm,
> shield us through our earthly life
> by your everlasting arm.

**Christ Jesus became for us wisdom from God,
and righteousness and sanctification and
redemption. 1 Corinthians 1:30**

> Great God of all wisdom, of science and art,      p128*
> O grant us the wisdom that comes from the heart.
> Technology, learning, philosophy, youth—
> all leave us still yearning for your word of truth.

Forgive us for our pride, dear Lord, and for thinking
so highly of ourselves that we miss the essence
of your grace. Restore us and lead us into deeper
faithfulness and righteousness so others will get a
glimpse of you in us. Amen.

**Thursday, March 22 — Psalm 38:1-8**
Exodus 28:15-43; Matthew 25:31-46

May your eyes be open toward this temple night
and day, this place of which you said, "My name
shall be there." 1 Kings 8:29

> To your temple, Lord, I come,                                    553
> for it is my worship home.
> This earth has no better place,
> here I see my Savior's face.

Jesus said, "Do not make my Father's house a
house of merchandise!" John 2:16 (NKJV)

> We build with mortar, brick and wood,                      440*
> this monument to praise our God,
> to share our fellowship in kind,
> and educate the searching mind,
> within the comfort of these halls,
> within the safety of these walls,
> we pray our faith be not confined
> by that which human hand designed.

We give thanks, O God, for the church that has
nurtured us, helped us to grow in faith, supported
us with its love and accepted us when we are
rejected by others. The church has been your hands
and your heart to us and has accepted us with all
our hypocrisies. Amen.

\*   © 1994 by Ralph E. Freeman

**Friday, March 23** — Psalm 38:9-16
Exodus 29:1-30; Matthew 26:1-13

## Lord, there is no one like you to help the powerless against the mighty. 2 Chronicles 14:11 (NIV)

Though hordes of devils fill the land                    788*
all threat'ning to devour us,
we tremble not, unmoved we stand;
they cannot overpow'r us.
Let this world's tyrant rage;
in battle we'll engage!
His might is doomed to fail;
God's judgment must prevail!
One little word subdues him.

## Paul wrote: My God will fully satisfy every need of yours according to his riches in glory in Christ Jesus. Philippians 4:19

Who are these in bright array,                           p88
thousand times ten thousand strong,
round the altar night and day,
singing one triumphant song:
"Worth is the Lamb once slain,
blessing, honor, glory, pow'r,
wisdom, riches, to obtain,
new dominion ev'ry hour!"

Christ Jesus, you are our mighty fortress and in you
we find our sin and evil is conquered. Thank you
for breaking the rod of the oppressor and winning
our salvation. We dedicate ourselves anew to you
this day. Amen.

**Saturday, March 24** — Psalm 38:17-22
Exodus 29:31-30:16; Matthew 26:14-30

**I know, my God, that you search the heart, and
take pleasure in uprightness. 1 Chronicles 29:17**

Highly favored congregation,                    515
loved by Jesus and esteemed,
ne'er forget your destination,
why from this vain world redeemed.

**Christ says, "Whenever you stand praying,
forgive, if you have anything against anyone; so
that your Father in heaven may also forgive you
your trespasses." Mark 11:25**

"Forgive our sins as we forgive,"              777
you taught us, Lord, to pray;
but you alone can grant us grace
to live the words we say,
to live the words we say.

It is so easy, forgiving God, to accept your
forgiveness. It is even fairly easy to confess our sins
to you. What is much more difficult is for us to
reach out and forgive those who we feel have done
us some kind of harm. Today, we are determined
to remember any person who we feel has done
us wrong and to bring that person to you in
intercession. We ask you to give us the strength
to forgive that person. Amen.

## Fifth Sunday in Lent

**Watchword for the Week** — Create in me a clean heart, O God, and put a new and right spirit within me. Psalm 51:10

**Sunday, March 25** — Jeremiah 31:31-34; Psalm 51:1-12
Hebrews 5:5-10; John 12:20-33

**They will neither hunger nor thirst, nor will the desert heat or the sun beat down upon them. He who has compassion on them will guide them and lead them beside springs of water. Isaiah 49:10 (NIV)**

Apostles, prophets, martyrs,                         p107
and all the sacred throng
who wear the spotless raiment,
who raise the ceaseless song;
for those passed on before us,
our Savior, we adore,
and walking in their footsteps,
would serve you more and more.

**This Spirit he poured out on us richly through Jesus Christ our Savior, so that, having been justified by his grace, we might become heirs according to the hope of eternal life. Titus 3:6-7**

It is in God that we shall hope,                       761*
and not in our own merit.
We rest our fears in his good word
and trust his Holy Spirit.
His promise keeps us strong and sure;
we trust the holy signature
inscribed upon our temples.

As we begin this final time before Holy Week, dear Lord, help us to use it to reflect more fully on the sacrifice you made for us as you made your way to the cross. Forgive our undisciplined life, our indifferent witness and our yielding to fear. Transform us this day by your grace and your love. Amen.

Monday, March 26 — Psalm 39:1-6
Exodus 30:17-31:11; Matthew 26:31-35

**The Lord said to Jeremiah, "Now I have put my words in your mouth." Jeremiah 1:9**

> While your ministers proclaim          553
> peace and pardon in your name,
> through their voice, by faith, may I
> hear you speaking from the sky.

**Do not be afraid, but speak and do not be silent! Acts 18:9**

> Keep me from saying words              615
> that later need recalling;
> guard me, lest idle speech
> may from my lips be falling;
> but when, within my place,
> I must and ought to speak,
> then to my words give grace,
> lest I offend the weak.

We stand before you, dear Lord, and ask, "When did I see you hungry and feed you, thirsty and give you drink? When did I see you a stranger and welcome you, naked and clothe you, sick or in prison and visit you?" It is our sincere desire that your answer will be, "When you did it to one of the least of these, you did it to me." Help us today to stand with the powerless and the marginalized. Amen.

**Tuesday, March 27** — Psalm 39:7-13
Exodus 31:12-32:29; Matthew 26:36-46

**Praise him, sun and moon; praise him, all you
shining stars! For he commanded, and they were
created. Psalm 148:3,5**

Praise the Lord! You heav'ns, adore him,          454
praise him, angels in the height;
sun and moon, rejoice before him;
praise him, all you stars and light.
Praise the Lord! For he has spoken;
worlds his mighty voice obeyed;
laws which never shall be broken
for their guidance he has made.

**You are worthy, our Lord and God, to receive
glory and honor and power, for you created all
things, and by your will they existed and were
created. Revelation 4:11**

He only is the Maker                              453
of all things near and far;
he paints the wayside flower,
he lights the evening star;
the winds and waves obey him,
by him the birds are fed;
much more to us, his children,
he gives our daily bread.

We offer thanks to you, Creator God, for all good
gifts—the seasons of the year and of the spirit,
and the experiences of joy, pleasure and gladness.
We offer thanks also for the sorrow and grief and
solitudes of life and for the strength through which
we are able to meet them. We pray for those who
work hard to preserve our planet and we commit
ourselves to work with them this day. Amen.
(paraphrased from General Liturgy 4, MBW p29)

**Wednesday, March 28** — Psalm 40:1-8
Exodus 32:30-33:23; Matthew 26:47-58

**And when you turn to the right or when you turn to the left, your ears shall hear a word behind you, saying, "This is the way; walk in it." Isaiah 30:21**

> You are the way; to you alone                    661
> from sin and death we flee;
> and those who would the Father seek
> your followers must be.

**Jesus said, "I am the way, and the truth, and the life. No one comes to the Father except through me." John 14:6**

> To God be the glory—great things he has done!   550
> So loved he the world that he gave us his Son,
> who yielded his life an atonement for sin,
> and opened the lifegate that all may go in.

Lord Jesus, you are not our interpretation of your way, but YOU are simply the way. Knowing this, we commit ourselves to you anew this day confident in knowing that it is you who opens the gate. We seek your guidance in being open about the interpretations others use regarding the details of that way. Amen.

**Thursday, March 29** — Psalm 40:9-17
Exodus 34; Matthew 26:59-75

## Inquire first for the word of the Lord.
## 2 Chronicles 18:4

O word of God incarnate,                                505
O wisdom from on high,
O truth unchanged, unchanging,
O light of our dark sky:
we praise you for the radiance
that from the scripture's page,
a lantern to our footsteps,
shines on from age to age.

## Continue in what you have learned and firmly
## believed. 2 Timothy 3:14

Because the Lord our God is good,                       539
his mercy is forever sure.
His truth at all times firmly stood,
and shall from age to age endure.

Guide us, dear Lord, in our efforts to discern your
will for our lives. As we turn to the scriptures,
your guide for our faith and life, may we use
all the resources at our disposal to understand
and interpret their meaning for us. Keep us from
shallow faith and unquestioning obedience and
instead, help us to use our questions and doubts to
be able to grow in our commitment to you. Amen.

**Friday, March 30** — Psalm 41
Exodus 35; Matthew 27:1-10

## That which had not been told them they shall see. Isaiah 52:15

Be thou my vision, O Lord of my heart;                    719
Nought be all else to me save that thou art—
thou my best thought, by day or by night,
waking or sleeping, thy presence my light.

## And the disciples went out and proclaimed the good news everywhere, while the Lord worked with them and confirmed the message by the signs that accompanied it. Mark 16:20

Your lofty themes, all mortals, bring;                    551
in songs of praise divinely sing;
the great salvation loud proclaim,
and shout for joy the Savior's name.

Like those early disciples, may we be so committed to serving you that the world will surely see you in the deeds we perform. Empower us to be your agents of justice in an unjust world, agents of unity in a divided world, agents of healing in a sin-sick world, agents of welcome in a bigoted world and agents of peace in a war-torn world. Amen.

Saturday, March 31 — Psalm 42:1-5
Exodus 36; Matthew 27:11-31

## I call upon God, and the Lord will save me. Psalm 55:16

O my God, be ever near me;                    568
for your rest, for your feast,
more and more prepare me.
Still assure me of my calling;
keep me near, in your care,
saved from final falling.

## On God we have set our hope that he will rescue us again. 2 Corinthians 1:10

My hope is built on nothing less                    771
than Jesus' blood and righteousness;
no merit of my own I claim
but wholly lean on Jesus' name.
On Christ the solid rock, I stand;
all other ground is sinking sand,
all other ground is sinking sand.

God of the ages, you have been faithful. We confess our faithlessness. As we call upon you today, we know that you have rescued us. You are our hope. Thank you for your grace and love today and every day. Amen.

### Palm Sunday

**Watchword for the Week** — Jesus said, "You will see the Son of Man seated at the right hand of Power, and coming with the clouds of heaven." Mark 14:62

**Sunday, April 1** — Isaiah 50:4-9a; Psalm 31:9-16
Philippians 2:5-11; Mark 11:1-11

**See, I am setting before you today a blessing and a curse: the blessing, if you obey the commandments of the Lord your God; and the curse, if you do not obey the commandments of the Lord your God. Deuteronomy 11:26-28**

> Jesus calls us; by your mercies,                         600
> Savior, may we hear your call,
> give our hearts to your obedience,
> serve and love you best of all.

**The kingdom of heaven is like a merchant in search of fine pearls; on finding one pearl of great value, he went and sold all that he had and bought it. Matthew 13:45-46**

> Take my wealth, all I possess,                           647
> make me rich in faithfulness.
> Take my mind that I may use
> ev'ry pow'r as you should choose.

Holy Redeemer, we thank you for the blessing of grace and for showing us the eternal promise through the life, death and resurrection of your son, our pearl of great value. In the name of Jesus. Amen.

**Monday, April 2** — Psalm 42:6-11
Exodus 37; Matthew 27:32-44

## Let the hearts of those who seek the Lord rejoice.
## Psalm 105:3

Faithful heart, rejoice today!                    275*
Praise the King of glory.
Tell of God's wondrous story.
Now he comes as an evening's soft rain,
comes to wash away all of sin's stain,
comes to you that you might through him gain.

## Why do you look for the living among the dead?
## Luke 24:5

Christians, dismiss your fear;                     p91
let hope and joy succeed;
the joyful news with gladness hear,
"The Lord is ris'n indeed!"
The promise is fulfilled
in Christ our only Head;
justice with mercy's reconciled,
he lives who once was dead.

Blessed Savior, hear our prayer of rejoicing for your
gift of the promise of new life. Let us learn to trust
in your path and lighten our hearts with joy. In
Christ's name we pray. Amen.

* © 1994 by Brian Henkelmann

**Tuesday, April 3 — Psalm 43**
Exodus 38; Matthew 27:45-56

**Speak tenderly to Jerusalem, and proclaim to her that her hard service has been completed, that her sin has been paid for. Isaiah 40:2 (NIV)**

> At last the march shall end;                    786
> the wearied ones shall rest;
> the pilgrims find their home at last,
> Jerusalem the blessed.

**Christ himself bore our sins in his body on the cross, so that, free from sins, we might live for righteousness. 1 Peter 2:24**

> Once he came in blessing                        273
> all our sins redressing,
> came in likeness lowly,
> Son of God most holy;
> bore the cross to save us,
> hope and freedom gave us.

Dear God, we are so grateful that our debts have been released through the grace of your son, Jesus Christ. May we strive to pay forward the grace and love you have given us. In his name. Amen.

**Wednesday, April 4** — Psalm 44:1-8
Exodus 39:1-31; Matthew 27:57-66

## The Lord lift up his countenance upon you, and give you peace. Numbers 6:26

Lord, dismiss us with your blessing;                    559
fill our hearts with joy and peace.
Let us each, your love possessing,
triumph in redeeming grace.
O, refresh us, O, refresh us;
trav'ling through this wilderness.

## And the peace of God, which surpasses all understanding, will guard your hearts and your minds in Christ Jesus. Philippians 4:7

When peace, like a river, attendeth my way,         754
when sorrows like sea billows roll;
whatever my lot, you have taught me to say,
it is well, it is well with my soul.

May the Lord bless us and keep us, lift up his
countenance upon us and give us the peace that
surrounds us and emanates from our hearts. In the
name of Jesus. Amen.

## Maundy Thursday

**Watchword for Maundy Thursday** — He has gained renown by his wonderful deeds; the Lord is gracious and merciful. Psalm 111:4

**Thursday, April 5** — Psalm 44:9-16
Exodus 39:32-40:23; Matthew 28:1-20

## In your great mercies you did not make an end of your people or forsake them. Nehemiah 9:31

Sing, pray, and keep his ways unswerving,                712
offer your service faithfully,
and trust his word; though undeserving,
you'll find his promise true to be.
God never will forsake in need
the soul that trusts in him indeed.

## The Lord Jesus on the night when he was betrayed took a loaf of bread, and when he had given thanks, he broke it and said, "This is my body that is for you. Do this in remembrance of me." In the same way he took the cup also, after supper, saying, "This cup is the new covenant in my blood. Do this, as often as you drink it, in remembrance of me." 1 Corinthians 11:23-25

One the name in which we pray,                525
one our Savior day by day;
with one cup and with one bread
thus one cov'nant way we tread.
One in spirit, one in life,
one amid earth's frequent strife,
one in faith and one in love,
one in hope of heav'n above.

Father, forgive us for our sins of ignorance and restore our hope as we remember the suffering, death and resurrection of our Lord Jesus Christ. In his name we pray. Amen.

### Good Friday

**Watchword for Good Friday** — For God so loved the world that he gave his only Son, so that everyone who believes in him may not perish but may have eternal life. John 3:16

**Friday, April 6** — Psalm 44:17-26
Exodus 40:24-Leviticus 1:17; Mark 1:1-8

## Upon your walls, O Jerusalem, I have posted sentinels; all day and all night they shall never be silent. Isaiah 62:6

Here does the Lord of life proclaim                    p198
to all the world his saving name;
repenting souls, in him believe;
you wounded, look on him and live.

## I handed on to you what I in turn had received: that Christ died for our sins in accordance with the scriptures, and that he was buried, and that he was raised on the third day in accordance with the scriptures. 1 Corinthians 15:3-4

O word of God incarnate,                               505
O wisdom from on high,
O truth unchanged, unchanging,
O light of our dark sky:
we praise you for the radiance
that from the scripture's page,
a lantern to our footsteps,
shines on from age to age.

All-knowing and all-understanding Father, nourish us with your grace and allow us the understanding of joy after mourning, peace after tragedy and love beyond our comprehension. In Christ's holy name. Amen.

## Great Sabbath

**Saturday, April 7** — Psalm 45:1-9
Leviticus 2,3; Mark 1:9-20

**The mountains may depart and the hills be removed, but my steadfast love shall not depart from you, and my covenant of peace shall not be removed, says the Lord, who has compassion on you. Isaiah 54:10**

> He shall come down like showers          263
> upon the fruitful earth,
> and love, joy, hope, like flowers,
> spring in his path to birth;
> before him on the mountains
> shall Peace, the herald, go;
> and righteousness, in fountains,
> from hill to valley flow.

**Christ says, "Peace I leave with you; my peace I give to you. I do not give to you as the world gives. Do not let your hearts be troubled, and do not let them be afraid." John 14:27**

> Savior, when your love shall call us          559
> from our struggling pilgrim way,
> let no fear of death appall us,
> glad your summons to obey.
> May we ever, may we ever
> reign with you in endless day.

Lord, as St. Francis prayed, make us instruments of your peace. Guide us to console more than seeking consolation, to pardon more than asking for pardon and to know that in death we are born to eternal life. In Jesus' name. Amen.

## Easter Sunday

**Watchword for the Week** — But in fact Christ has been raised from the dead, the first fruits of those who have died. 1 Corinthians 15:20

**Sunday, April 8** — Acts 10:34-43; Psalm 118:1-2,14-24
1 Corinthians 15:1-11; Mark 16:1-8

## He was oppressed, and he was afflicted, yet he did not open his mouth; like a lamb that is led to the slaughter. Isaiah 53:7

Paschal Lamb, by God appointed,         330
all our sins on you were laid;
by almighty love anointed,
you have full atonement made.
All your people are forgiven
through the virtue of your blood;
opened is the gate of heaven;
we are reconciled to God.

## Christ has indeed been raised from the dead, the first fruits of those who have fallen asleep. 1 Corinthians 15:20 (NIV)

Now be God the Father praised, alleluia!     358
With the Son, from death upraised, alleluia!
And the Spirit, ever blessed; alleluia!
One true God, by all confessed. Alleluia!

Dear Jesus, you have burst the bonds of death, offering us a hope and promise of new life far beyond this small world of time and space. We seek language to thank you, to praise you, to love you. In your name we pray. Amen.

## Easter Monday

**Monday, April 9** — Psalm 45:10-17
Leviticus 4; Mark 1:21-34

## Must I not take care to say what the Lord puts into my mouth? Numbers 23:12

> Be present with your servants, Lord;    734
> we look to you with one accord;
> refresh and strengthen us anew,
> and bless what in your name we do.

## Whoever speaks must do so as one speaking the very words of God; whoever serves must do so with the strength that God supplies, so that God may be glorified in all things through Jesus Christ. 1 Peter 4:11

> Be thou my wisdom, and thou my true word;    719
> I ever with thee and thou with me, Lord;
> thou my great Father, I thy true son;
> thou in me dwelling, and I with thee one.

God, we pray that the words of our mouths and the thoughts of our hearts will be for your glory. We wish to serve you with strength and wisdom. In the name of Jesus, we pray. Amen.

**Tuesday, April 10** — Psalm 46
Leviticus 5:1-6:13; Mark 1:35-45

### Can mortals be righteous before God? Can human beings be pure before their Maker? Job 4:17

> This holy Word exposes sin,                          509
> convinces us that we're unclean,
> points out the wretched, ruined state
> of humankind, both small and great.

### Jesus Christ gave himself for us that he might redeem us from all iniquity and purify for himself a people of his own who are zealous for good deeds. Titus 2:14

> Jesus came, adored by angels,                        p55
> came with peace from realms on high;
> Jesus came for our redemption,
> lowly came on earth to die:
> alleluia, alleluia!
> Came in deep humility.

Gracious Savior, refresh and purify our hearts and minds to lead us to service in your name. Remind us gently that humility, not hubris is the path to serving you. In Jesus' name, Amen.

**Wednesday, April 11 — Psalm 47**
Leviticus 6:14-7:21; Mark 2:1-12

## God saw my affliction and the labor of my hands. Genesis 31:42

Take my hands and let them move                610
at the impulse of your love.
Take my feet and lead their way;
never let them go astray,
never let them go astray.

## Paul wrote, Be steadfast, immovable, always excelling in the work of the Lord, because you know that in the Lord your labor is not in vain. 1 Corinthians 15:58

Take my life that it may be                     610
all your purpose, Lord, for me.
Take my moments and my days;
let them sing your ceaseless praise,
let them sing your ceaseless praise.

Steadfast Lord, show us of small vision that our
work for you is never in vain. Show us you are
our rock and we know we can trust in you forever.
Amen.

**Thursday, April 12 — Psalm 48**
Leviticus 7:22-8:17; Mark 2:13-28

**Indeed, you are my lamp, O Lord, the Lord
lightens my darkness. 2 Samuel 22:29**

> We've a story to tell to the nations,                  621
> that shall turn their hearts to the right,
> a story of truth and mercy,
> a story of peace and light,
> a story of peace and light.
> For the darkness shall turn to dawning,
> and the dawning to noonday bright;
> and Christ's great kingdom shall come on earth,
> the kingdom of love and light.

**Christ says, "I have come as light into the world,
so that everyone who believes in me should not
remain in the darkness." John 12:46**

> May the God of hope go with us ev'ry day,             708
> filling all our lives with love and joy and peace.
> May the God of justice speed us on our way,
> bringing light and hope to ev'ry land and race.
> Praying, let us work for peace, singing,
>      share our joy with all.
> Working for a world that's new,
>      faithful when we hear Christ's call.

Christ Jesus, let your light continue to be a beacon
to us as we move from darkness to the hope and joy
and peace of your light. Illuminate our way with
your grace. In your name we pray. Amen.

**Friday, April 13 — Psalm 49:1-12**
Leviticus 8:18-9:11; Mark 3:1-12

**Let your steadfast love, O Lord, be upon us, even as we hope in you. Psalm 33:22**

> Consecrate me now to thy service, Lord,            607
> by the pow'r of grace divine;
> let my soul look up with a steadfast hope
> and my will be lost in thine.

**By grace you have been saved through faith, and this is not your own doing; it is the gift of God. Ephesians 2:8**

> O for a thousand tongues to sing                    548
> my great Redeemer's praise,
> the glories of my God and King,
> the triumphs of his grace!

Faithful and steadfast God, our gratitude is too great for words. You have offered us the gift of grace and you have shown us by your son's birth, death and resurrection how to accept this gift through faith. Amen.

**Saturday, April 14** — Psalm 49:13-20
Leviticus 9:12-10:20; Mark 3:13-19

**Great is our Lord, and abundant in power; his understanding is beyond measure. Psalm 147:5**

> Then let us adore and give him his right,                565
> all glory and pow'r and wisdom and might,
> all honor and blessing, with angels above,
> and thanks never ceasing for infinite love.

**Jesus said, "For mortals it is impossible, but not for God; for God all things are possible." Mark 10:27**

> Our heav'nly Father, source of love,                    p38
> to you our hearts we raise.
> Your all-sustaining power we prove,
> and gladly sing your praise.

All-knowing and all-sustaining God, we open our hearts today that we may reflect your wisdom by our actions in our communities. Help us to reach out to those in need of safety, shelter and sustenance in Jesus' name. Amen.

## Second Sunday of Easter

**Watchword for the Week** — If we walk in the light as God is in the light, we have fellowship with one another, and the blood of Jesus his Son cleanses us from all sin. 1 John 1:7

**Sunday, April 15** — Acts 4:32-35; Psalm 133
1 John 1:1-2:2; John 20:19-31

## I will make peace your governor and righteousness your ruler. Isaiah 60:17 (NIV)

> That night the apostles met in fear;                    369
> among them came their Master dear
> and said, "My peace be with you here."
> Alleluia!

## Everything is for your sake, so that grace, as it extends to more and more people, may increase thanksgiving, to the glory of God. 2 Corinthians 4:15

> 'Twas grace that taught my heart to fear              783
> and grace my fears relieved;
> how precious did that grace appear
> the hour I first believed.

Amazing God, lead us to share the news of your grace to all those around us through our words and actions. May we thus glorify your name. In Jesus' name, we pray. Amen.

**Monday, April 16 — Psalm 50:1-6**
Leviticus 11:1-28; Mark 3:20-35

## The Lord grants peace within your borders. Psalm 147:14

> We've a song to be sung to the nations,                  621
> that shall lift their hearts to the Lord,
> a song that shall conquer evil
> and shatter the spear and sword,
> and shatter the spear and sword.

## Blessed are the peacemakers, for they will be called children of God. Matthew 5:9

> Blessed are the brave and peaceful,                       595
> bringing peace where'er they live,
> God shall own them as his children
> and through them his peace will give.
> All for love and truth who suffer,
> in your God rejoice and sing;
> he, the end of all your striving,
> he, your Father, Lord, and King.

Dear God, lover of peace, thank you for showing us paths to peace in our daily lives. Help us to show others by our words and our lives that living peaceably is sharing your love. In Jesus' name we pray. Amen.

**Tuesday, April 17** — Psalm 50:7-15
Leviticus 11:29-13:8; Mark 4:1-20

**I will give them one heart, and put a new spirit within them. Ezekiel 11:19**

> Create in me a clean heart, O God,                        p79
> and renew a right Spirit within me.
> Cast me not away from your presence,
> and take not your Holy Spirit from me.
> Restore unto me the joy of salvation;
> anoint me with your Spirit free.
> Create in me a clean heart, O God,
> and renew a right Spirit within me.

**So if anyone is in Christ, there is a new creation: everything old has passed away; see, everything has become new! 2 Corinthians 5:17**

> A new creation comes to life and grows                    366
> as Christ's new body takes on flesh and blood.
> The universe restored and whole will sing:
> Alleluia!

Creator God, give us clear vision to see that you make all things new. Give us courage to understand your new creation even when it seems so much more comfortable to keep the old. In Christ's name we pray. Amen.

**Wednesday, April 18** — Psalm 50:16-23
Leviticus 13:9-46; Mark 4:21-29

**I will bless you as long as I live; I will lift up my hands and call on your name. Psalm 63:4**

> O my soul, bless God, the Father;     458
> all within me bless his name;
> bless the Father, and forget not
> all his mercies to proclaim.

**I will pray with the spirit, but I will pray with the mind also; I will sing praise with the spirit, but I will sing praise with the mind also. 1 Corinthians 14:15**

> Come now, O Lord, and teach us how to pray.     742
> Teach us to ask ourselves from day to day
> if we are yours and yours alone will be
> through earthly days and through eternity.

Father, we pray to you with our hearts, minds and spirits. Hear our prayers and lead us as we share your story with those around us. In Jesus' name we pray. Amen.

**Thursday, April 19** — Psalm 51:1-6
Leviticus 13:47-14:18; Mark 4:30-41

**You shall be called priests of the Lord; you shall be named ministers of our God. Isaiah 61:6**

> Lord, you give the great commission:                617*
> "Heal the sick and preach the word."
> Lest the church neglect its mission,
> and the gospel go unheard,
> help us witness to your purpose
> with renewed integrity;
> with the Spirit's gifts empow'r us
> for the work of ministry.

**You are a chosen race, a royal priesthood, a holy nation, God's own people, in order that you may proclaim the mighty acts of him who called you out of darkness into his marvelous light. 1 Peter 2:9**

> Praise the Lord, praise the Lord!                   528
> He with you deals bounteously.
> Highly favored church of Jesus,
> he chose you through mercy free
> to show forth his matchless praises
> and rich fruit, blessed for the Master's use,
> to produce, to produce.

Dear Father, we pray that we may serve as your ministers, showing love and peace to those around us, sharing faith and hope to all in this world. Empower us with your gifts. In Jesus' name we pray. Amen.

**Friday, April 20** — Psalm 51:7-12
Leviticus 14:19-57; Mark 5:1-20

## One generation shall laud your works to another, and shall declare your mighty acts. Psalm 145:4

Magnify the Lord with me,                          300*
ev'ry generation,
for the year of jubilee
dawns for ev'ry nation.
Christ the Prince of Peace is here,
no one dare ignore him;
welcome this, God's gift most dear,
eager to adore him.

**The blind and the lame came to him in the temple, and he cured them. But when the chief priests and the scribes saw the amazing things that he did, and heard the children crying out in the temple, "Hosanna to the Son of David," they became angry. Matthew 21:14-15**

All glory, laud, and honor                          342
to you, Redeemer, King,
to whom the lips of children
made sweet hosannas ring.
You are the King of Israel
and David's royal Son,
now in the Lord's name coming,
the king and Blessed One.

Gentle Physician who cures the blind and lame, we give praise and honor to you. We magnify your name by telling the world of your works. In Jesus' name we pray. Amen.

* © 1989 by Jaroslav J. Vajda

**Saturday, April 21 — Psalm 51:13-19**
Leviticus 15:1-24; Mark 5:21-43

**The fear of the Lord is instruction in wisdom.
Proverbs 15:33**

> Save us from weak resignation                 751
> to the evils we deplore;
> let the gift of your salvation
> be our glory evermore.
> Grant us wisdom, grant us courage
> serving you whom we adore,
> serving you whom we adore.

**Anyone who claims to know something does
not yet have the necessary knowledge; but
anyone who loves God is known by him.
1 Corinthians 8:2-3**

> O Spirit of the Lord, all life is yours;          516
> now on your church your pow'r and strength outpour,
> that many children may be born to you
> and through your knowledge may be brought anew
> to sing Christ's praise.

Father, you know us and love us still. Grant us the
courage to serve you and the wisdom to choose
your path. Help us to serve you by serving others in
your name. Amen.

### Third Sunday of Easter

**Watchword for the Week** — See what love the Father has given us, that we should be called children of God; and that is what we are. 1 John 3:1

**Sunday, April 22** — Acts 3:12-19; Psalm 4
1 John 3:1-7; Luke 24:36b-48

# I will add to their numbers, and they will not be decreased; I will bring them honor, and they will not be disdained. Jeremiah 30:19 (NIV)

"I'll bless you, and you shall be set for a blessing!"   616
Thus said God, the Lord, to his servant of old;
O may we, in grace and in number increasing,
through work show our faith and in service be bold;
upon your truth founded, we shall not move,
let us ever follow, and fearless prove;
so shall we in doctrine, in word and behavior,
to ev'ryone witness that Christ is our Savior.

# When the mustard seed is sown it grows up and becomes the greatest of all shrubs, and puts forth large branches, so that the birds of the air can make nests in its shade. Mark 4:32

We plow the fields, and scatter                        453
the good seed on the land,
but it is fed and watered
by God's almighty hand;
he sends the snow in winter,
the warmth to swell the grain,
the breezes and the sunshine
and soft refreshing rain.

Bountiful God, as we see small sprouts return to earth in springtime, evidence of new life's return after the winter, remind us of the good gifts sent from you, the promise of eternal life with you. Amen.

**Monday, April 23 — Psalm 52**
Leviticus 15:25-16:25; Mark 6:1-6

**All that the Lord has spoken we will do, and we will be obedient. Exodus 24:7**

Life-giving Creator of both great and small;          457
of all life the maker, the true life of all;
we blossom, then wither like leaves on the tree,
but you live forever who was and will be.

**Christ says, "By this everyone will know that you are my disciples, if you have love for one another." John 13:35**

May the mind of Christ my Savior          585
live in me from day to day,
by his love and pow'r controlling
all I do and say.

Jesus, the world will know we are your disciples by the love shown in our words and by our example to others. Let the words of our mouths, the thoughts of our hearts and our actions be to your glory. Amen.

Tuesday, April 24 — Psalm 53
Leviticus 16:26-18:5; Mark 6:7-13

## Do not cast me off in the time of old age; do not forsake me when my strength is spent. Psalm 71:9

If you but trust in God to guide you                    712
and place your confidence in him,
you'll find him always there beside you
to give you hope and strength within;
for those who trust God's changeless love
build on the rock that will not move.

## Even though our outer nature is wasting away, our inner nature is being renewed day by day. 2 Corinthians 4:16

May your rich grace impart                              705
strength to my fainting heart,
my zeal inspire;
as you have died for me,
my love, adoringly,
pure, warm and changeless be,
a living fire!

Dear God, you renew our strength in ways we
cannot imagine: teaching us hope and giving us
new ways to spend our energies for you. Direct our
paths, sustain our hearts; we serve you with awe.
Amen.

**Wednesday, April 25** — Psalm 54
Leviticus 18:6-19:11; Mark 6:14-29

**The righteous are like trees planted by streams of water, which yield their fruit in its season, and their leaves do not wither. Psalm 1:3**

> This is my Father's world,                            456
> and to my list'ning ears
> all nature sings and round me rings
> the music of the spheres.
> This is my Father's world;
> I rest me in the thought
> of rocks and trees, of skies and seas—
> his hand the wonders wrought.

**You will know them by their fruits. Matthew 7:16**

> May we your bounties thus                            657
> as stewards true receive,
> and gladly, Lord, as you bless us,
> to you our firstfruits give.

Dear God, in this time of spring when the earth shows new growth, help us to grow in love and witness to you in the world around us. In Jesus' name we pray. Amen.

**Thursday, April 26** — Psalm 55:1-8
Leviticus 19:12-20:8; Mark 6:30-44

## Be strong, and let your heart take courage, all you who wait for the Lord. Psalm 31:24

Through many dangers, toils, and snares,          783
I have already come;
'tis grace has brought me safe thus far,
and grace will lead me home.

## Pursue righteousness, godliness, faith, love, endurance, gentleness. 1 Timothy 6:11

Blessed are the strong but gentle,          595
trained to served a higher will,
wise to know th'eternal purpose
which their Father shall fulfill.
Blessed are they who with true passion
strive to make the right prevail,
for the earth is God's possession
and his purpose will not fail.

Father, teach us to live with courage, faith, love and gentleness in a world that does not always value these traits. Help us to be patient as we serve others and as we serve you. In Jesus' name we pray. Amen.

**Friday, April 27** — Psalm 55:9-15
Leviticus 20:9-21:12; Mark 6:45-56

**Why are you cast down, O my soul? And why are
you disquieted within me? Hope in God; For I
shall yet praise him, The help of my countenance
and my God. Psalm 42:11 (NKJV)**

Sometimes I feel discouraged,                          500
and think my work's in vain,
but then the Holy Spirit
revives my soul again.
There is a balm in Gilead
to make the wounded whole,
there is a balm in Gilead
to heal the sin-sick soul.

**After you have suffered for a little while, the God
of all grace, who has called you to his eternal
glory in Christ, will himself restore, support,
strengthen and establish you. 1 Peter 5:10**

Have we trials and temptations?                        743
Is there trouble anywhere?
We should never be discouraged;
take it to the Lord in prayer!
Can we find a friend so faithful
who will all our sorrows share?
Jesus knows our ev'ry weakness;
take it to the Lord in prayer!

Jesus, you know our sorrows and our struggles.
We pray for renewal and strength, not only for
ourselves but for all those who are weak and
discouraged today. Wrap us in your comfort;
restore us to your service. Amen.

APRILAPRIL

APRIL119APRIL

TAPRIL

APRIL

**Saturday, April 28 — Psalm 55:16-19**
Leviticus 21:13-22:16; Mark 7:1-8

## Say to those who are of a fearful heart, "Be strong, do not fear! Here is your God." Isaiah 35:4

The Savior's blood and righteousness          p201
my beauty is, my glorious dress;
thus well arrayed, I need not fear,
when in his presence I appear.

## These are the words of him who is the First and the Last, who died and came to life again, "I know your afflictions and your poverty—yet you are rich!" Revelation 2:8-9 (NIV)

Here is a pasture, rich and never failing,          593
here living waters in abundance flow;
none can conceive the grace with them prevailing,
who Jesus' shepherd-voice obey and know.
He banishes all fear and strife,
and leads them gently on to everlasting life.

Shepherd Jesus who knows our afflictions and our poverty, we praise you for the richness beyond compare that your life, death and resurrection gives us: a hope and a promise far greater than anything our small minds can imagine. Amen.

### Fourth Sunday of Easter

**Watchword for the Week** — Jesus says, "I am the good shepherd. The good shepherd lays down his life for the sheep." John 10:11

**Sunday, April 29** — Acts 4:5-12; Psalm 23
1 John 3:16-24; John 10:11-18

## The Lord executes justice for the oppressed; he gives food to the hungry. Psalm 146:7

He comes with rescue speedy 263
to those who suffer wrong,
to help the poor and needy,
and bid the weak be strong,
to give them songs for sighing,
their darkness turn to light,
whose souls, condemned and dying,
were precious in his sight.

## Jesus took the seven loaves, and after giving thanks he broke them and gave them to his disciples to distribute; and they distributed them to the crowd. Mark 8:6

Break now the bread of life, 502
dear Lord, to me,
as when you broke the loaves
beside the sea.
Beyond the sacred page
I seek you, Lord;
my spirit waits for you,
O living Word.

Dear Lord, with your love, our sighs turn to song, and through darkness we can walk toward light. Our spirits wait for you, our living Word. In Jesus' name we pray. Amen.

**Monday, April 30** — Psalm 55:20-23
Leviticus 22:17-23:22; Mark 7:9-23

## In distress you called, and I rescued you.
## Psalm 81:7

> For God, in grace and tenderness,    519
> regarded us in our distress;
> yea, to our aid himself he came;
> let all adore God's holy name.

## Jesus said to the disciples, "Why are you afraid? Have you still no faith?" Mark 4:40

> Blessed assurance, Jesus is mine!    714
> O what a foretaste of glory divine!
> Heir of salvation, purchase of God,
> born of his Spirit, washed in his blood.
> This is my story, this is my song,
> praising my Savior all the day long.
> This is my story, this is my song,
> praising my Savior all the day long.

Savior, thank you for the blessed assurance that we may wipe out fears with faith. Thank you for giving us your story to tell and sing all the day long. We are blessed beyond measure by your grace. Amen.

**Tuesday, May 1 — Psalm 56:1-8**
Leviticus 23:23-24:9; Mark 7:24-37

## My people will abide in a peaceful habitation, in secure dwellings. Isaiah 32:18

Peace be to this congregation,                              556
peace to ev'ry soul therein;
peace, which flows from Christ's salvation,
peace, the seal of cancelled sin,
peace that speaks its heav'nly Giver,
peace, to earthly minds unknown,
peace divine that lasts forever
here erect its glorious throne.

## We wait for new heavens and a new earth, where righteousness is at home. 2 Peter 3:13

Jesus, Prince of Peace, be near us;                              556
fix in all our hearts your home;
with your gracious presence cheer us;
let your sacred kingdom come;
raise to heav'n our expectation,
give our favored souls to prove
glorious and complete salvation
in the realms of bliss above.

Our true Home, in a violent world, make of our churches peaceful communities that show you at work among us, that show how life is to be lived, and that are indeed foretastes of our eternal home. Amen.

**Wednesday, May 2** — Psalm 56:9-13
Leviticus 24:10-25:17; Mark 8:1-13

## The Lord says, "I will be with them in trouble, I will rescue them and honor them." Psalm 91:15

We have one Savior and one Lord,                    *
the Christ, God's only Son.
He is the living Shepherd true,
who leads a scattered flock.
As members of Christ's church on earth
we share the guilt and shame
of severed ties and judging eyes
that rend the solid Rock.

## I commend you to God and to the message of his grace, a message that is able to build you up and to give you the inheritance among all who are sanctified. Acts 20:32

Rejoice in rich and varied gifts                    *
bestowed on us through grace
and valued on the promised path
the saints before have trod.
So, welcome all whose pilgrim feet
move toward the single goal
of meeting Christ in unity
around the throne of God.

Ever-present Help in trouble—trouble of our own
making and trouble beyond our control—we give
thanks for the witness through the years of those
who have found in you what they needed in order
to be built up and to move forward. Amen.

* by Gilbert Frank, 2003. Used by permission.

**Thursday, May 3** — Psalm 57:1-6
Leviticus 25:18-55; Mark 8:14-21

# I keep the Lord always before me. Psalm 16:8

Visions of glory, visions triumphant,                    *
bright wonders dance, Lord, charming our eyes;
yet, Lord, you call us to humble service,
doing your will, Lord, in the real world.

## So whether we are at home or away, we make it our aim to please him. 2 Corinthians 5:9

Help us to balance all of our choices;                   *
help us to look both forward and back;
help us to hear you in all our choices,
which sing the wisdom our voices lack.

Lord Jesus, so many things call us and tempt us. So many things want to be lord and center of our lives. Wherever we are today, at home or away, whatever choices we face, give us the wisdom and courage to be faithful to you. Amen.

* by C. Daniel Crews, 1999. Used by permission.

**Friday, May 4** — Psalm 57:7-11
Leviticus 26:1-35; Mark 8:22-38

**When I gather the people of Israel from the nations where they have been scattered, I will show myself holy among them in the sight of the nations. Ezekiel 28:25 (NIV)**

> The God of Abraham praise,     468
> who reigns enthroned above,
> the Ancient of eternal days,
> the God of love!
> The Lord, the great I Am,
> by earth and heav'n confessed—
> we bow before his holy name
> forever blessed.

**The gifts and the calling of God are irrevocable. Romans 11:29**

> He by his name has sworn,     468
> on this we shall depend,
> and as on eagles' wings upborne
> to heav'n ascend.
> There we shall see his face,
> his pow'r we shall adore
> and sing the wonders of his grace
> forevermore.

God of Sarah and Abraham, Isaac and Rebekah, today we are reminded of your special tie with the Jewish people and are reminded that our Lord Jesus was of the Jewish faith. May we both learn from and share with these brothers and sisters in faith. Amen.

**Saturday, May 5** — Psalm 58
Leviticus 26:36-27:15; Mark 9:1-10

## Call on me in the day of trouble; I will deliver you, and you shall glorify me. Psalm 50:15

What a friend we have in Jesus,                    743
all our sins and griefs to bear!
What a privilege to carry
ev'rything to God in prayer!
O what peace we often forfeit,
O what needless pain we bear,
all because we do not carry
ev'rything to God in prayer.

## The prayer of the righteous is powerful and effective. James 5:16

Are we weak and heavy laden,                    743
cumbered with a load of care?
Precious Savior, still our refuge,
take it to the Lord in prayer!
Do your friends despise, forsake you?
Take it to the Lord in prayer!
In his arms he'll take and shield you;
you will find a solace there.

Jesus, our Friend, you are so much more willing to help than we are to ask. As any friend affects those he or she touches, through our prayers, cause us more fully to resemble you and to care about the people you care about. Amen.

### Fifth Sunday of Easter

**Watchword for the Week** — Jesus says, "Abide in me as I abide in you. Just as the branch cannot bear fruit by itself unless it abides in the vine, neither can you unless you abide in me." John 15:4

**Sunday, May 6** — Acts 8:26-40; Psalm 22:25-31
1 John 4:7-21; John 15:1-8

## Why do you say, O Jacob, and speak, O Israel, "My way is hidden from the Lord, and my right is disregarded by my God"? Isaiah 40:27

> If the way be drear,                                      799
> if the foe be near,
> let no faithless fears o'ertake us,
> let not faith and hope forsake us;
> safely past the foe
> to our home we go.

## In this you greatly rejoice, though now for a little while you may have had to suffer grief in all kinds of trials. 1 Peter 1:6 (NIV)

> Jesus, still lead on                                      799
> till our rest be won;
> and although the way be cheerless,
> we will follow calm and fearless;
> guide us by your hand
> to the promised land.

Jesus, Pioneer and Perfecter of our faith, wherever we have been, you have been there, too. In whatever trials, darkness, confusion or grief we find ourselves, lead us. Amen.

**Monday, May 7** — Psalm 59:1-9
Leviticus 27:16-Numbers 1:16; Mark 9:11-29

**We give thanks to you, O God; we give thanks;
your name is near. People tell of your wondrous
deeds. Psalm 75:1**

> O would, my God, that I could praise you                    3r
> with thousand tongues by day and night!
> How many a song my lips should raise you,
> who orderest all things here aright.
> My thankful heart would ever be
> telling what God has done for me.

**The people in Jerusalem were shouting, "Blessed
is the coming kingdom of our ancestor David!
Hosanna in the highest heaven!" Mark 11:10**

> But I will tell, while I am living,                          3r
> God's goodness forth with every breath
> and greet each morning with thanksgiving,
> until my heart is still in death.
> Nay, when at last my lips grow cold,
> God's praise shall in my sighs be told.

Lord, how do we tell the world of your wondrous
deeds, of the blessedness of being part of your rule?
By showing, in this day and tomorrow, that you
are continuing to shape us, to make of us what you
want. Lord, let it be so. Amen.

**Tuesday, May 8** — Psalm 59:10-17
Numbers 1:17-54; Mark 9:30-37

**Hear the word of the Lord, because the Lord
has a charge to bring against you who live
in the land: "There is no faithfulness, no love,
no acknowledgment of God in the land."
Hosea 4:1 (NIV)**

> Lord Jesus, think on me                    764
> and purge away my sin;
> from selfish passions set me free
> and make me pure within.

**But the tax collector, standing far off, would
not even look up to heaven, but was beating his
breast and saying, "God, be merciful to me, a
sinner!" Luke 18:13**

> Lord Jesus, think on me,                    764
> nor let me go astray;
> through darkness and perplexity
> point out your chosen way.

Holy One, sometimes we are sinners because it is
simply the easiest way to live, doing what those
around us do. Empower us to see and to live
another way, the way we see in Jesus. Amen.

**Wednesday, May 9** — Psalm 60
Numbers 2; Mark 9:38-50

**The Lord our God is merciful and forgiving.
Daniel 9:9 (NIV)**

> My song is love unknown,                          482
> my Savior's love for me,
> love to the loveless shown
> that they might lovely be.
> O who am I that for my sake
> my Lord should take frail flesh, and die?

**But when the goodness and loving kindness
of God our Savior appeared, he saved us, not
because of any works of righteousness that we
had done, but according to his mercy. Titus 3:4-5**

> Christ came from heaven's throne               482
> salvation to bestow,
> but people scorned and none
> the longed-for Christ would know.
> But O my friend, my friend indeed,
> who at my need his life did spend.

Who are we? We are often loveless even to our
friends, to say nothing of our foes. But you, O
Friend, see in us—and in our friends and our
foes—strength and beauty and possibility we do
not see. Open our eyes. Amen.

**Thursday, May 10 — Psalm 61**
Numbers 3:1-32; Mark 10:1-12

## Hear, O Israel: The Lord is our God, the Lord alone. Deuteronomy 6:4

> Gracious Lord, gracious Lord,                    528
> blessed is our lot indeed
> in your ransomed congregation;
> here we on your merits feed,
> and the wellsprings of salvation,
> all the needy to revive and cheer,
> stream forth here, stream forth here.

## There are varieties of activities, but it is the same God who activates all of them in everyone. 1 Corinthians 12:6

> Praise the Lord, praise the Lord!                 528
> He with you deals bounteously.
> Highly favored church of Jesus,
> he chose you through mercy free
> to show forth his matchless praises
> and rich fruit, blessed for the Master's use,
> to produce, to produce.

You, Lord God, are one who blesses. You give us life. You give us your love. You give us the work of sharing your love, and the power to do it. For this we give you thanks and praise. Amen.

**Friday, May 11** — Psalm 62
Numbers 3:33-4:14; Mark 10:13-31

**Do not say, 'I am a youth,' because everywhere I send you, you shall go, and all that I command you, you shall speak. Jeremiah 1:7 (NASB)**

> All we are called to walk with Christ                    *
> throughout each earthly day.
> He bids us to take up our cross
> and follow in his way.

**Be strong in the grace that is in Christ Jesus.
2 Timothy 2:1**

> He gives us strength for every task                    *
> and makes our hearts grow wise
> as forth we go to help the world
> attain his kingdom's prize.

God, you call us, young and old, influential and unknown, to be part of your dream for your creation. Help us see how we can labor with you, how you equip us to be about your tasks and how your grace surrounds us in both our strength and our weakness. Amen.

* by Dirk French © 2006. Used by permission.

**Saturday, May 12** — Psalm 63
Numbers 4:15-49; Mark 10:32-45

## See, the Lord God comes with might, and his arm rules for him. Isaiah 40:10

Let the earth now praise the Lord,                    261
who has truly kept his word
and at last to us did send
Christ, the sinner's help and friend.

## Beware, keep alert; for you do not know when the time will come. Mark 13:33

Then when you will come again                         261
as the glorious king to reign,
I with joy will see your face,
freely ransomed by your grace.

O God of promises, you promised a messiah and surprised us with Jesus, who showed us in the flesh who you are. You promise that in the end all things will conform to your will. We wonder, how and when will that come to be? Strengthen our trust in that promise. Amen.

### Sixth Sunday of Easter

**Watchword for the Week** — Make a joyful noise to the Lord, all the earth; break forth into joyous song and sing praises. Psalm 98:4

**Sunday, May 13** — Acts 10:44-48; Psalm 98
1 John 5:1-6; John 15:9-17

**I am merciful, says the Lord; I will not be angry forever. Only acknowledge your guilt, that you have rebelled against the Lord your God. Jeremiah 3:12-13**

> There's a wideness in God's mercy          185r
> like the wideness of the sea;
> there's a kindness in his justice
> which is more than liberty.

**I will get up and go to my father, and I will say to him, "Father, I have sinned against heaven and before you." Luke 15:18**

> There is no place where earth's sorrows          185r
> are more felt than up in heaven;
> there is no place where earth's failings
> have such kindly judgment given.

Giver of second chances, sometimes we remember that you expect much of us and hold us to account, and we forget you never give up on us and are always ready to give us another chance. Open our hearts to give the same to our sisters and brothers. Amen.

**Monday, May 14** — Psalm 64
Numbers 5; Mark 10:46-52

## By this you shall know that among you is the living God. Joshua 3:10

> On the earth on Christmas night                    *
> you were born in meekness
> leaving all your heavenly might
> to embrace our weakness.

## With great power the apostles gave their testimony to the resurrection of the Lord Jesus, and great grace was upon them all. Acts 4:33

> Easter morning saw you rise,                       *
> hope and joy restoring,
> as disciples' wondering eyes
> glowed with love, adoring.

God of the ages, in many ways you have shown yourself to humanity, but supremely, with grace and power, in Jesus. You are a great mystery, but we know enough. Today we again give ourselves to your service. May your power be evident in us. Amen.

*   by C. Daniel Crews, 2001. Used by permission.

**Tuesday, May 15 — Psalm 65:1-8**
Numbers 6; Mark 11:1-11

**I will put my Spirit in you and you will live, and
I will settle you in your own land. Then you will
know that I the Lord have spoken, and I have
done it, declares the Lord. Ezekiel 37:14 (NIV)**

> Our Savior, many years ago                    *
> you brought us to this place,
> and still we seek to learn and grow
> to manifest your grace.
> With wider vision may we give
> ourselves to others while we live;
> O may we all with one accord
> still follow you, dear Lord.

**The last enemy to be destroyed is death.
1 Corinthians 15:26**

> O Lord, in love you came to earth              *
> to rise, but first to die;
> yet in your death we find our birth,
> all lives to sanctify.
> When all your saving work we view,
> our hearts are filled with love for you,
> and love for one another grows
> as your love overflows.

Giver of life and Victor over death, wherever we find
ourselves, help us find you and make ourselves at
home, knowing that the whole earth is yours. When
we find patterns of death, enable us also to find
new life. Amen.

*  by C. Daniel Crews, 1999. Written for 250th anniversary of the Moravian Church,
   Southern Province. Used by permission.

**Wednesday, May 16 — Psalm 65:9-13**
Numbers 7:1-35; Mark 11:12-26

**Restore us to yourself, O Lord, that we may
be restored; renew our days as of old.
Lamentations 5:21**

> Jesus, Lord of Life and Light,                    *
> every soul's salvation,
> glowing hope in sin's dark night,
> love's bright affirmation.

**Jesus said, "What do you think? If a shepherd
has a hundred sheep, and one of them has gone
astray, does he not leave the ninety-nine on the
mountains and go in search of the one that went
astray?" Matthew 18:12**

> Willingly you bore the cross,                      *
> shared our pain distressing,
> died to mend our tragic loss,
> turning curse to blessing.

Good Shepherd, you restore, you renew, you
retrieve. If we wander today, or just feel lost, help us
to find in you what we need: to know we are yours
and cannot ever really be lost. Amen.

*    by C. Daniel Crews, 2001. Used by permission.

### Ascension Day

**Watchword for the Ascension** — Christ says, "I, when I am lifted up from the earth, will draw all people to myself." John 12:32

**Thursday, May 17** — Psalm 66:1-7
Numbers 7:36-71; Mark 11:27-12:12

**Ascension of the Lord** — Acts 1:1-11; Psalm 47
Ephesians 1:15-23; Luke 24:44-53

## Maintain the right of the lowly and the destitute. Psalm 82:3

> In our churches, in our churches                    *
> open wide the door;
> love is never, love is never
> cast against the poor;
> social status has no say
> in the pattern of our way.
> All are welcome, all are welcome;
> riches we ignore.

## May our Lord Jesus Christ strengthen you in every good deed and word. 2 Thessalonians 2:16-17 (NIV)

> Show God's mercy, show God's mercy                    *
> unto one and all;
> do no judging, do no judging
> as we heed our call.
> This is how the church should be:
> filled with love and liberty
> in the Spirit, in the Spirit
> of our Savior's law.

Ascended Lord, on this day we remember your last appearance before the coming of the promised Spirit at Pentecost. As you are no longer limited to one time and place, may we not be limited in our welcome. Fill us with love and liberty. Amen.

* by Bill Gramley, 1993. Used by permission.

**Friday, May 18** — Psalm 66:8-15
Numbers 7:72-8:4; Mark 12:13-17

**Who then will offer willingly, consecrating themselves today to the Lord? 1 Chronicles 29:5**

Jesus, Master, whom I serve,                    p42
though so feebly and so ill,
strengthen hand and heart and nerve,
all your bidding to fulfill;
open now my eyes to see
all the work you have for me.

**Each of you must give as you have made up your mind, not reluctantly or under compulsion, for God loves a cheerful giver. 2 Corinthians 9:7**

Jesus, Master, will you use                    p42
one who owes you more than all?
As you will, I would not choose;
only let me hear your call.
Jesus, let me always be
in your service glad and free.

River of blessing, life would be so much more full and rich if we could accept your generosity and be more generous ourselves. But we are afraid. So often we care only for ourselves. Help us to look more like you. Amen.

**Saturday, May 19** — Psalm 66:16-20
Numbers 8:5-9:14; Mark 12:18-34

**Know therefore that the Lord your God is God; he is the faithful God, keeping his covenant of love to a thousand generations of those who love him and keep his commands. Deuteronomy 7:9 (NIV)**

Lord, you have been our dwelling place          p147
in ev'ry generation.
Your people still have known your grace
and your blessed consolation.
Through ev'ry age you heard our cry,
through ev'ry age we found you nigh,
our strength and our salvation.

**What if some were unfaithful? Will their faithlessness nullify the faithfulness of God? By no means! Romans 3:3-4**

Lord, nothing from your arms of love            p147
shall your own people sever.
Our helper never will remove;
our God will fail us never.
Your people, Lord, have dwelt secure;
our dwelling place you will endure
forever and forever.

Faithful One, so many people we depend on have let us down. And we have let others down. We are made to be faithful, because we are made in your image. Make of us faithful men and women. Amen.

### Ascension Sunday
### Seventh Sunday of Easter

**Watchword for the Week** — Jesus says, "Sanctify them in the truth; your word is truth." John 17:17

**Sunday, May 20** — Acts 1:15-17,21-26; Psalm 1
1 John 5:9-13; John 17:6-19

## Those who bring thanksgiving as their sacrifice honor me; to those who go the right way I will show the salvation of God. Psalm 50:23

> Now thank we all our God                    533
> with heart and hands and voices,
> who wondrous things has done,
> in whom his world rejoices;
> who, from our mother's arms,
> has blessed us on our way
> with countless gifts of love,
> and still is ours today.

## Thanks be to God, who gives us the victory through our Lord Jesus Christ. 1 Corinthians 15:57

> All praise and thanks to God                533
> the Father now be given,
> the Son, and Spirit blessed,
> who reign in highest heaven—
> the one eternal God,
> whom heav'n and earth adore;
> for thus it was, is now,
> and shall be evermore.

Lord, thank you. This is where the good life starts. We give you but your own, whatever our gift may be. Life is so much easier when we know that it doesn't all depend on us. Lord, thank you. Amen.

**Monday, May 21 — Psalm 67**
Numbers 9:15-10:36; Mark 12:35-44

**May the Lord, who is good, pardon everyone who sets their heart on seeking God. 2 Chronicles 30:18,19 (NIV)**

We pray thee, touch our hearts,                          *
dear God, O Lord of all creation,
that we may know thy blessed work
and scene of our salvation!
we pray thee, touch our soul,
O Christ, our brother in every venture,
that we thy great compassion find
and mercy without censure.

**Draw near to God, and he will draw near to you. James 4:8**

We pray thee, open now our minds,                        *
O Spirit of truth and wonder,
that we reach thy sacred peace
and bonds not made to sunder.
We pray thee, God, the Three-in-One,
to draw us to thy nearness
that we may confidently hope
to see thee once with clearness.

What a wonder! Creator of all things seen and unseen, you have come to us in our brother Jesus, and even now are near, leading us by your Spirit. Amen.

* by James Jackman, 1986. Used by permission.

**Tuesday, May 22** — Psalm 68:1-6
Numbers 11; Mark 13:1-13

# He heals the brokenhearted, and binds up their wounds. Psalm 147:3

> When gloomy desolation chills                    *
> the splendors of the flowered hills,
> when commerce ends her golden dreams,
> and nature falls to man's dark schemes,
> Lord, your celestial anthems swell
> to soar o'er lands where mortals dwell.

# They brought to Jesus all who were sick or possessed with demons. And he cured many who were sick with various diseases. Mark 1:32,34

> Though all the world in sorrow mourns             *
> and in death's shadow hides its face,
> still caught in hatred's poisonous thorns,
> resisting still the call of grace,
> in love our souls with Christ will fly,
> and songs of joy will sound on high.

Healer of our every ill, when we are afraid to admit
we need you, or afraid of new life, or afraid you
may need us to be a part of someone else's healing,
heal and comfort us. Amen.

* by Willie Israel, 1997. Used by permission.

**Wednesday, May 23** — Psalm 68:7-18
Numbers 12:1-13:16; Mark 13:14-27

**The Lord of hosts is with us; the God of Jacob is our refuge. Psalm 46:7**

A mighty fortress is our God,                    428r
a bulwark never failing,
our helper he amid the flood
of mortal ills prevailing:
for still our ancient foe
doth seek to work us woe;
his craft and power are great,
and, armed with cruel hate,
on earth is not his equal.

**Since all have sinned and fall short of the glory of God; they are now justified by his grace as a gift, through the redemption that is in Christ Jesus. Romans 3:23-24**

Did we in our own strength confide,              428r
our striving would be losing,
were not the right man on our side,
the man of God's own choosing.
Dost ask who that may be?
Christ Jesus, it is he,
Lord Sabaoth his name,
from age to age the same,
and he must win the battle.

Crucified One, you are with us, you are our refuge.
But what a different understanding of power you
give us! Your power is shown not in overwhelming
others but in giving yourself. May we live that kind
of power. Amen.

**Thursday, May 24** — Psalm 68:19-27
Numbers 13:17-33; Mark 13:28-37

## Is my hand shortened, that it cannot redeem? Isaiah 50:2

> We cannot see his face;                                                          *
> Christ lives beyond our vision,
> that we may, by his grace, fulfill his word and mission.
> For sightless faith alone becomes for us true bliss,
> until he draws us home and greets us with a kiss.

## The Lord is not slow about his promise, as some think of slowness, but is patient with you, not wanting any to perish, but all to come to repentance. 2 Peter 3:9

> The church on earth may stay                                                     *
> a thousand years or longer,
> sustained in every day
> as faith in Christ grows stronger.
> And yet if he appear
> before tomorrow's noon,
> for us who hold him dear
> it would not be too soon.

Holy One, you are hidden and mysterious, beyond our knowledge. But we see Jesus, and it is enough. We wait for those special moments in our lives— glimpses of eternity—when we know you more clearly. Amen.

* Nicholas Ludwig von Zinzendorf, trans. C. Daniel Crews and Nola Reed Knouse 1996.
  © Moravian Archives (Southern Province) and Moravian Music Foundation.
  Used by permission.

---

**Friday, May 25** — Psalm 68:28-35
Numbers 14; Mark 14:1-11

**You shall worship before the Lord your God; and you shall rejoice in every good thing which the Lord your God has given you and your house. Deuteronomy 26:10-11 (NKJV)**

> How lovely are the flowers wild, *
> the dogwood and blue violets,
> the dandelions and buttercups,
> found growing in God's fields.

**Give thanks to God the Father at all times and for everything in the name of our Lord Jesus Christ. Ephesians 5:20**

> How perfectly is formed each flower, *
> the hollyhock and hibiscus,
> the candytuft and Queen Anne's lace,
> made perfect by God's power.

Awesome God, we thank you for little things, for things we touch and smell and see and taste. In appreciating little things, help us to appreciate big things. May this one day, as it comes, be part of a life lived for you. Amen.

* by E. Artis Weber, 1990. Used by permission.

**Saturday, May 26 — Psalm 69:1-12**
Numbers 15:1-31; Mark 14:12-31

## Lord, you are righteous, but this day we are covered with shame. Daniel 9:7 (NIV)

> Christ's sure agony was Gethsemane.                         *
> His disciples seemed to care less
> for his sorrow and his sadness;
> no attention paid while our Savior prayed.

## At that moment the cock crowed for the second time. Then Peter remembered that Jesus had said to him, "Before the cock crows twice, you will deny me three times." And he broke down and wept. Mark 14:72

> Christ's pure litany in Gethsemane                          *
> to the Father, God almighty,
> from his soul pressed blood most holy;
> painful drop on drop filled the promised cup.

Lord Jesus, the story of Holy Week, of disciples who fell asleep and denied you, is too often the story of our lives. May your later words to those same disciples—"I send you" and "Feed my sheep"—direct us. Amen.

* by E. Artis Weber, 1988. Used by permission.

## Day of Pentecost

**Watchword for the Week** — O Lord, how manifold are your works! In wisdom you have made them all. Psalm 104:24

**Sunday, May 27** — Acts 2:1-21; Psalm 104:24-34,35b Romans 8:22-27; John 15:26-27,16:4b-15

## You remain the same, and your years will never end. Psalm 102:27 (NIV)

Spirit of God, burst forth in flame 491*
searing our conscience, staking your claim.
Burn up the clutter, brand us apart;
warm ev'ry recess of my cold heart.

## God is faithful; by him you were called into the fellowship of his Son, Jesus Christ our Lord. 1 Corinthians 1:9

Spirit of love, transform our ways, 491*
fill with new feeling all of our days;
replace our hatred, our anger, our fear
with new compassion, new struggle to care.

O faithful and powerful Spirit, you came on Pentecost and you come to us, your church, today. Stretch us to seek you, follow your leading, and be your powerful instruments. Amen.

* ©1980 by David Henkelmann

**Monday, May 28** — Psalm 69:13-21
Numbers 15:32-16:27; Mark 14:32-42

**Only fear the Lord, and serve him faithfully with all your heart; for consider what great things he has done for you. 1 Samuel 12:24**

> In faith we follow Christ                    *
> with song and celebration.
> He leads us to the cross,
> the price of our salvation.
> We cannot find the path
> through reason and strength alone.
> Belief provides the light
> that guides us to the throne.

**Those who welcomed his message devoted themselves to the apostles' teaching and fellowship, to the breaking of bread and the prayers. Acts 2:41,42**

> By faith we learn to trust                   *
> the deeds of one another.
> We bind ourselves with love
> for sister and for brother.
> Our family of God works
> hand in hand to grow
> a congregation strong
> and Christ's great truth to know.

Jesus Christ, Chief Elder of your church, so fill our life together that we may be the diverse but peaceful family that shows your plan for creation. Amen.

* by Chancy and Katie Kapp © 2008. Used by permission.

**Tuesday, May 29** — Psalm 69:22-29
Numbers 16:28-17:13; Mark 14:43-52

**Let us go with you, for we have heard that God is with you. Zechariah 8:23**

Lord, through changing days, unchanging,       435r
you the light our fathers knew,
through our widening ways, far ranging,
let your splendor claim us too;
go beside us,
lead and guide us
to whatever things are true.

**Conduct yourselves honorably among the Gentiles, so that, though they malign you as evildoers, they may see your honorable deeds and glorify God when he comes to judge. 1 Peter 2:12**

Past all sham of small succeeding       435r
sordid gains that call and woo,
lift us by the mighty leading
fit for your aspiring few;
hold us serving,
all unswerving,
whatsoever things are true.

Jesus, Prince of peace, go with us, that we may be the caring and justice-seeking people that the world so badly needs. Amen.

**Wednesday, May 30** — Psalm 69:30-36
Numbers 18:1-24; Mark 14:53-65

## How awesome is this place! This is none other than the house of God, and this is the gate of heaven. Genesis 28:17

Lord, awe and wonder fill the heart                    *
when we can feel your holy presence.
Unrivaled blessing you impart
when you reveal to us your essence.
Power and majesty you are,
wisdom and righteousness unbending,
love, grace, and mercy without ending.

## The house of God is the church of the living God, the pillar and ground of the truth. 1 Timothy 3:15 (NKJV)

Dwell in your temples on the earth—                    *
hearts where your Spirit is abiding,
but when the new world comes to birth,
unveil what now remains in hiding.
Come, Triune Godhead, as you are,
and with your love that ceases never
reign over all that is, forever.

Holy One, we bow in silence before you. May we find in that quiet center the heart of our lives. Amen.

* by Dirk French, 2006. Used by permission.

**Thursday, May 31** — Psalm 70
Numbers 18:25-19:22; Mark 14:66-72

## Great peace have those who love your law; nothing can make them stumble. Psalm 119:165

Breathe through the pulses of desire          739
thy coolness and thy balm;
let sense be dumb, its heats expire;
speak through the earthquake, wind, and fire,
O still, small voice of calm!

## Peace to all of you who are in Christ. 1 Peter 5:14

Drop thy still dews of quietness,          739
till all our strivings cease.
Take from our souls the strain and stress;
and let our ordered lives confess
the beauty of thy peace.

You call us, God, to peace—not the peace of sleep,
but the peace of people working together, helping
one another and listening to one another. Make us
instruments of your peace. Amen.

**Friday, June 1** — Psalm 71:1-8
Numbers 20:1-21:9; Mark 15:1-20

## Whoever fears the Lord has a secure fortress. Proverbs 14:26 (NIV)

You were their rock, their fortress, and their might;   390
you, Lord, their captain in the well-fought fight;
you in the darkness drear, their one true light.
Alleluia! Alleluia!

## Christ says, "Everyone then who hears these words of mine and acts on them will be like a wise man who built his house on rock." Matthew 7:24

Blessed name! the rock on which we build,          487
our shield and resting place,
our never-failing comfort, filled
with blessings of his grace.
O Jesus, Shepherd, Guardian, Friend,
our Prophet, Priest, and King,
our Lord, our Life, our Way, our End,
accept the praise we bring.

Strengthen us, almighty God, as we seek to bear
witness to your Son, to our church family and to the
world. Help us to persevere in the face of doubt and
hold ever true to our Savior, Jesus Christ. Amen.

**Saturday, June 2** — Psalm 71:9-18a
Numbers 21:10-22:6; Mark 15:21-32

**Truly, the fear of the Lord, that is wisdom; and to depart from evil is understanding. Job 28:28**

Saints before the altar bending,                293
watching long in hope and fear,
suddenly the Lord descending
in his temple shall appear.
Come and worship, come and worship,
worship Christ, the newborn king.

**If you invoke as Father the one who judges all people impartially according to their deeds, live in reverent fear during the time of your exile. 1 Peter 1:17**

Lord, teach us how to pray aright,                750
with rev'rence and with fear;
though dust and ashes in your sight,
we may, we must draw near.

O divine Wisdom, shine forth your light upon us, guiding us from evil into the arms of our Redeemer so we may come to know peace. In the name of Jesus. Amen.

### Trinity Sunday

**Watchword for the Week** — Holy, holy, holy is the Lord of hosts;
the whole earth is full of his glory. Isaiah 6:3

**Sunday, June 3** — Isaiah 6:1-8; Psalm 29
Romans 8:12-17; John 3:1-17

## Our God turned the curse into a blessing. Nehemiah 13:2

Come, thou Fount of ev'ry blessing,      782
tune my heart to sing thy grace;
streams of mercy, never ceasing,
call for songs of loudest praise.
Teach me some melodious sonnet,
sung by flaming tongues above.
Praise the mount—I'm fixed upon it—
mount of God's redeeming love.

## Do not repay evil for evil or abuse for abuse; but, on the contrary, repay with a blessing. It is for this that you were called—that you might inherit a blessing. 1 Peter 3:9

Where divine affection lives,      670
there the Lord his blessing gives;
there his will on earth is done;
there his heav'n is half begun.
Great example from above,
teach us all like you to love.

Holy Lord of hosts, we are eternally blessed by the
triune presence of our loving Creator; our Savior,
Jesus Christ; and our Advocate, the Holy Spirit.
Where once there was iniquity, help us now to bring
bountiful blessing. Amen.

**Monday, June 4** — Psalm 71:18b-24
Numbers 22:7-41; Mark 15:33-47

## When you have eaten your fill, take care that you do not forget the Lord. Deuteronomy 6:11-12

You are the bread of life,                    502
O Lord, to me.
Your holy Word the truth
that rescues me.
Give me to eat and live
with you above;
teach me to love your truth,
for you are love.

## Pray then in this way: Give us this day our daily bread. Matthew 6:9,11

Guide me, O my great Redeemer,               790
pilgrim through this barren land.
I am weak, but you are mighty;
hold me with your pow'rful hand.
Bread of heaven, bread of heaven,
feed me now and evermore,
feed me now and evermore.

Lord, you perpetually provide for us, filling our
body and soul with sustenance greater than any we
might forage for ourselves. As we partake of your
bounty, help us to remember all you have done for
us. Amen.

**Tuesday, June 5** — Psalm 72:1-11
Numbers 23; Mark 16:1-13

**Their children, who do not know this law, must hear it and learn to fear the Lord your God as long as you live. Deuteronomy 31:13 (NIV)**

> To you our vows with sweet accord, 677
> head of your church, we pay;
> we and our house will serve you, Lord;
> your word we will obey.
> Grant us and all our children grace
> in word and deed your name to praise,
> and in each family, your will
> and purpose to fulfill.

**Paul wrote to the congregation in Corinth: Here I am, ready to come to you this third time. And I will not be a burden, because I do not want what is yours but you; for children ought not to lay up for their parents, but parents for their children. 2 Corinthians 12:14**

> As it was without beginning, 458
> so it lasts without an end;
> to their children's children ever
> shall God's righteousness extend.

Great Teacher, grant us wisdom and guidance as we share our love and service for you with others, especially our youth. Help us to recognize your voice in their voices and to learn from them in return. Amen.

**Wednesday, June 6** — Psalm 72:12-20
Numbers 24,25; Mark 16:14- Luke 1:4

**And now, Lord God, keep forever the promise
you have made and do as you promised.
2 Samuel 7:25 (NIV)**

> Sing, pray, and keep his ways unswerving,                    712
> offer your service faithfully,
> and trust his word; though undeserving,
> you'll find his promise true to be.
> God never will forsake in need
> the soul that trusts in him indeed.

**From the descendants of David, according to
promise, God has brought to Israel a Savior,
Jesus. Acts 13:23 (NASB)**

> Christians, dismiss your fear;                                356
> let hope and joy succeed;
> the joyful news with gladness hear:
> "The Lord is ris'n indeed!"
> The promise is fulfilled
> in Christ our only Head;
> now justice, mercy, reconciled,
> he lives who once was dead.

Steadfast Savior, in a world where our commitment
to you is tested, help us remember that you keep
your promise, even when we fall short. May we
humbly accept your grace as we strive to do better
by you. Amen.

Thursday, June 7 — Psalm 73:1-12
Numbers 26:1-24; Luke 1:5-25

## I am a stranger on earth. Psalm 119:19 (NIV)

Join we all with one accord;                              525
praise we all our common Lord;
for we all have heard his voice,
all have made his will our choice.
Join we with the saints of old,
no more strangers in the fold,
one the Shepherd who us sought,
one the flock his blood has bought.

## Do you not know that in a race the runners all compete, but only one receives the prize? Run in such a way that you may win it. 1 Corinthians 9:24

Am I of my salvation                                      795
assured through thy great love?
May I on each occasion
to thee more faithful prove.
Hast thou my sins forgiven?
Then, leaving things behind,
may I press on to heaven
and bear the prize in mind.

Lord, let us not get so caught up in the blur of
worldly races that we are blinded to the ultimate
prize you place before us. Train us to engage in
those efforts that lead to you. Amen.

Friday, June 8 — Psalm 73:13-20
Numbers 26:25-56; Luke 1:26-38

**Just as I have watched over them to pluck up
and break down, so I will watch over them to
build and to plant, says the Lord. Jeremiah 31:28**

Kindle our hearts to burn with your flame.          489
Raise up your banners high in this hour.
Stir us to build new worlds in your name.
Spirit of God, O send us your pow'r!

**Jesus began to speak in parables. "A man
planted a vineyard, put a fence around it, dug
a pit for the wine press, and built a watchtower;
then he leased it to tenants and went to another
country." Mark 12:1**

In loving service may our lives be spent,          587
in other's gladness finding sweet content,
striving to show God's fellowship to all.
To show God's loving work—the servants' call.
In loving service may our lives be spent.

Guide and Guardian, we hear your call to tend the
vineyard, bearing fruit for the entire world as you
have taught by your example. Keep watch over us
as we serve in your name. Amen.

Saturday, June 9 — Psalm 73:21-28
Numbers 26:57-27:23; Luke 1:39-45

**There is forgiveness with you, so that you may be revered. Psalm 130:4**

Always giving and forgiving,                                    544
ever blessing, ever blessed,
wellspring of the joy of living,
ocean depth of happy rest!
Loving Father, Christ our brother,
let your light upon us shine;
teach us how to love each other,
lift us to the joy divine.

**As God's fellow workers we urge you not to receive God's grace in vain. 2 Corinthians 6:1 (NIV)**

So to our God we sing praises,                                  316
who all our spirits upraises,
and we rejoice in the telling
of his dear grace in us dwelling.

Gracious God, we come to you with humble hearts,
seeking reconciliation with you, with each other,
and with ourselves. Help us to receive your grace.
As you have forgiven us, may we also forgive others
and ourselves. Amen.

### Second Sunday after Pentecost

**Watchword for the Week** — Lord, hear my voice! Let your ears be attentive to the voice of my supplications! Psalm 130:2

**Sunday, June 10** — Genesis 3:8-15; Psalm 130
2 Corinthians 4:13-5:1; Mark 3:20-35

## By the sweat of your face you shall eat bread until you return to the ground, for out of it you were taken; you are dust, and to dust you shall return. Genesis 3:19

Frail children of dust, and feeble as frail,                566
in you do we trust, nor find you to fail;
your mercies how tender, how firm to the end,
our maker, defender, redeemer, and friend.

## Our Savior, Christ Jesus, has destroyed death and has brought life and immortality to light through the gospel. 2 Timothy 1:10 (NIV)

His sov'reign pow'r without our aid                          455
formed us of clay and gave us breath;
and when like wand'ring sheep we strayed,
he saved us from the pow'r of death.

Blessed Savior, we rejoice in your victory over death!
Let this knowledge guide and sustain us as we move
through the darkness of our lives toward the eternal
light of salvation you have shone into the world.
Amen.

**Monday, June 11** — Psalm 74:1-9
Numbers 28:1-29:6; Luke 1:46-56

**Speak, Lord, for your servant is listening.
1 Samuel 3:9**

> O let me hear you speaking 603
> in accents clear and still,
> above the storms of passion,
> the murmurs of self-will.
> O speak to reassure me,
> to hasten or control;
> and speak to make me listen,
> O guardian of my soul.

**Christ says, "Anyone who hears my word and
believes him who sent me has eternal life, and
does not come under judgment, but has passed
from death to life." John 5:24**

> Christ, the life of all the living, 334
> Christ, the death of death, our foe,
> Christ, for us yourself once giving
> to the darkest depths of woe:
> through your suff'ring, death and merit,
> life eternal we inherit;
> thousand, thousand thanks are due,
> dearest Jesus, unto you.

Dearest Jesus, thousand, thousand thanks to you
for teaching us that even in suffering and death,
there is hope in the promise of new life—eternal
life. May we, your servants, continue to listen and
share this good news. Amen.

**Tuesday, June 12 — Psalm 74:10-17**
Numbers 29:7-40; Luke 1:57-66

**The Lord God called to the man, and said to him, "Where are you?" He said, "I heard the sound of you in the garden, and I was afraid." Genesis 3:9,10**

> "Fear not, I am with you; O be not dismayed,       709
> for I am your God and will still give you aid;
> I'll strengthen you, help you and cause you to stand
> upheld by my righteous, omnipotent hand."

**Jesus said, "I have come to call not the righteous but sinners." Mark 2:17**

> Trusting only in thy merit,                            772
> would I seek thy face;
> heal my wounded, broken spirit,
> save me by thy grace.

So often fear and doubt lead us away from you, yet still you seek us, calling our name. O steadfast One, rather than shamefully hide, may we come forth and meet you, who loves us just as we are! Amen.

**Wednesday, June 13 — Psalm 74:18-23**
Numbers 30:1-31:12; Luke 1:67-80

## I made the earth, and created humankind upon it. Isaiah 45:12

Life-giving Creator of both great and small;          457
of all life the maker, the true life of all;
we blossom, then wither like leaves on the tree,
but you live forever who was and will be.

## Worship him who made heaven and earth, the sea and the springs of water. Revelation 14:7

We thank you, our Creator,                            453
for all things bright and good,
the seedtime and the harvest,
our life, our health, our food;
accept the gifts we offer
for all your love imparts,
and what you most would treasure—
our humble, thankful hearts.

We delight in the wonder of the world that you, our
divine Designer, have made. May we worship you
by tenderly cultivating all of your creation. Amen.

**Thursday, June 14** — Psalm 75
Numbers 31:13-47; Luke 2:1-20

## There is hope for your future, says the Lord. Jeremiah 31:17

> Be still, my soul: your God will undertake    757
> to guide the future, as in ages past.
> Your hope, your confidence, let nothing shake;
> all now mysterious shall be bright at last.
> Be still, my soul: the waves and winds still know
> the Christ who ruled them while he dwelt below.

## God did not withhold his own Son, but gave him up for all of us, will he not with him also give us everything else? Romans 8:32

> My hope is built on nothing less    771
> than Jesus' blood and righteousness;
> no merit of my own I claim
> but wholly lean on Jesus' name.
> On Christ the solid rock, I stand;
> all other ground is sinking sand,
> all other ground is sinking sand.

Why do we continue to question you, Lord? You have faithfully cared for us in joy and sorrow, yet we doubt and seek to control—to usurp—your power. In Christ, help us to know hope, even in suffering. Amen.

Friday, June 15 — Psalm 76
Numbers 31:48-32:27; Luke 2:21-32

**A bruised reed he will not break, and a dimly burning wick he will not quench. Isaiah 42:3**

Show'rs of blessing, show'rs of blessing          636
from the Lord proceed,
strength supplying, strength supplying
in the time of need;
for no servant of our King
ever lacked for anything.
He will never, he will never
break the bruised reed.

**Jesus said, "Those who are well have no need of a physician, but those who are sick." Mark 2:17**

Come, you sinners, poor and needy,          765
weak and wounded, sick and sore,
Jesus, Son of God, will save you,
full of pity, love, and pow'r.
I will arise and go to Jesus;
he will embrace me in his arms;
in the arms of my dear Savior,
O there are ten thousand charms.

Suffering Servant, you came into this world of sickness and sin offering healing and hope. Help us to tend to our bruised and broken bodies and spirits with the balm of your good news. Amen.

**Saturday, June 16 — Psalm 77:1-9**
Numbers 32:28-33:9; Luke 2:33-40

### You have put gladness in my heart more than when their grain and wine abound. Psalm 4:7

Joyful, joyful, we adore you,                                   544
God of glory, Lord of love;
hearts unfold like flow'rs before you,
op'ning to the sun above.
Melt the clouds of sin and sadness;
drive the dark of doubt away;
giver of immortal gladness,
fill us with the light of day!

### We brought nothing into the world, so that we can take nothing out of it. 1 Timothy 6:7

Sing praise to God who reigns above,                           537
the God of all creation,
the God of pow'r, the God of love,
the God of our salvation.
My soul with comfort rich he fills,
and ev'ry grief he gently stills:
to God all praise and glory!

How do we measure abundance—in our worldly
possessions or in the richness of our souls? O great
Provider, help us to lay aside the blanket of
belongings for the blanket of blessing that
envelops us in your love. Amen.

### Third Sunday after Pentecost

**Watchword for the Week** — It is good to give thanks to the Lord, to sing praises to your name, O Most High. Psalm 92:1

**Sunday, June 17** — Ezekiel 17:22-24; Psalm 92:1-4,12-15
2 Corinthians 5:6-10,14-17; Mark 4:26-34

## Woe to those who acquit the guilty for a bribe, but deny justice to the innocent. Isaiah 5:22,23 (NIV)

> May the God of hope go with us ev'ry day,            708
> filling all our lives with love and joy and peace.
> May the God of justice speed us on our way,
> bringing light and hope to ev'ry land and race.
> Praying, let us work for peace,
>     singing, share our joy with all.
> Working for a world that's new,
>     faithful when we hear Christ's call.

## The kingdom of God is righteousness and peace and joy in the Holy Spirit. The one who thus serves Christ is acceptable to God and has human approval. Romans 14:17-18

> While your glorious praise is sung,            553
> touch my lips, unloose my tongue
> that my joyful soul may bless
> Christ the Lord, my righteousness.

Where do we hide our eyes from injustice? Where do we fail to raise our voices in righteousness? Lord, grant us the courage to do your will in the world. In the name of Jesus. Amen.

**Monday, June 18** — Psalm 77:10-15
Numbers 33:10-56; Luke 2:41-52

**There is a river whose streams make glad the city of God, the holy habitation of the Most High. God is in the midst of the city; it shall not be moved. Psalm 46:4-5**

> Glorious things of you are spoken,                    522
> Zion, city of our God;
> he whose word cannot be broken
> formed you for his own abode;
> on the rock of ages founded,
> what can shake your sure repose?
> With salvation's walls surrounded
> you may smile at all your foes.

**The city has no need of sun or moon to shine on it, for the glory of God is its light, and its lamp is the Lamb. Revelation 21:23**

> Lift your eyes and see the light;                     789
> Zion's city is in sight!
> There our endless home shall be;
> there our Lord we soon shall see.

God of hospitality and hope, may we walk in your ways, seeking to bring the light of Zion to this world so that all may know the comforts of your holy habitation. Amen.

**Tuesday, June 19** — Psalm 77:16-20
Numbers 34; Luke 3:1-20

**You will be for me a kingdom of priests and a
holy nation. Exodus 19:6 (NIV)**

> Since we, though unworthy,                746
> through electing grace,
> 'mid your ransomed people
> have obtained a place,
> Lord, may we be faithful
> to our cov'nant found,
> to you, as our shepherd,
> and your flock fast bound.

**Like living stones, let yourselves be built into a
spiritual house, to be a holy priesthood, to offer
spiritual sacrifices acceptable to God through
Jesus Christ. 1 Peter 2:5**

> Church of God, elect and holy,              526*
> be the people Christ intends,
> strong in faith and swift to answer
> each command your master sends:
> royal priests, fulfill your calling
> through your sacrifice and prayer,
> give your lives in joyful service,
> sing his praise, his love declare.

O High Priest above, we celebrate our consecration
as your people and offer our lives to your calling.
Together we raise a spiritual sanctuary, tending to
the temples of our hearts, minds and bodies, which
we dedicate to you. Amen.

Wednesday, June 20 — Psalm 78:1-8
Numbers 35:1-30; Luke 3:21-38

**His anger is but for a moment; his favor is for a lifetime. Weeping may linger for the night, but joy comes with the morning. Psalm 30:5**

> O let my eyes be lightened                    484
> by sight of your dear face;
> my life below be brightened
> by tasting of your grace;
> without you, mighty Savior,
> to live is naught but pain;
> to have your love and favor
> is happiness and gain.

**God has destined us not for wrath but for obtaining salvation through our Lord Jesus Christ. 1 Thessalonians 5:9**

> Come now and sing in praise of Christ         481*
> who came to live on earth,
> who cried our tears and shared our joys,
> who roundly laughed with mirth.
> We praise the Christ who preached good news,
> who said, "Repent, believe,"
> who fed the crowds that pressed him round
> and made the blind to see.

Gracious God, we stand in awe before you. Your amazing grace is showered upon us, offering us salvation even when we've strayed. Help us to know your everlasting love through Jesus Christ, our Lord. Amen.

* © 1987 by M. Lynnette Delbridge

**Thursday, June 21** — Psalm 78:9-16
Numbers 35:31-Deuteronomy 1:18; Luke 4:1-13

**Why should the nations say, "Where is their God?" Our God is in the heavens; he does whatever he pleases. Psalm 115:2-3**

> Alleluia! Not as orphans      373
> are we left in sorrow now;
> alleluia! He is near us;
> faith believes, nor questions how.
> Though the cloud from sight received him
> when the forty days were o'er,
> shall our hearts forget his promise,
> "I am with you evermore"?

**The message about the cross is foolishness to those who are perishing, but to us who are being saved it is the power of God. 1 Corinthians 1:18**

> Once he came in blessing      273
> all our sins redressing,
> came in likeness lowly,
> Son of God most holy;
> bore the cross to save us,
> hope and freedom gave us.

Scribe of salvation, we confess that we doubt you, forgetting your promises fulfilled in Christ Jesus. As we reflect on the suffering of the cross, let us also remember that which is beyond—the promise of life anew! Amen.

**Friday, June 22** — Psalm 78:17-31
Deuteronomy 1:19-46; Luke 4:14-21

**Behold, here I am, let him do to me as seems
good to him. 2 Samuel 15:26 (NASB)**

> Breathe on me, breath of God,                    494
> my will to yours incline,
> until this selfish part of me
> glows with your fire divine.

**Your will be done, on earth as it is in heaven.
Matthew 6:10**

> Worship, honor, glory, blessing,                  p66
> Lord, we offer unto you;
> young and old, your praise expressing,
> sing your mercies ever new.
> All the saints in heav'n adore you;
> we would bow before your throne.
> As your angels serve before you,
> so on earth your will be done.

We covenant with you, O purposeful Providence.
Your will is written in our lives and works and
is lived out in the world you created and saved
through Jesus Christ, our Lord. Amen.

**Saturday, June 23 — Psalm 78:32-39**
Deuteronomy 2; Luke 4:22-30

## Let not my heart be drawn to what is evil. Psalm 141:4 (NIV)

'Tis the most blessed and needful part                    768
to have in Christ a share,
and to commit our way and heart
unto his faithful care;
this done, our steps are safe and sure,
our hearts' desires are rendered pure,
and naught can pluck us from his hand,
which leads us to the end.

## And do not bring us to the time of trial, but rescue us from the evil one. Matthew 6:13

Lead on, O King eternal,                                  753
till sin's fierce war shall cease,
and holiness shall whisper
the sweet amen of peace;
for not with sword's loud clashing,
nor roll of stirring drums,
but deeds of love and mercy,
the heav'nly kingdom comes.

We live in a woeful world that calls us to ponder painful paths away from our ardent aim. May we find safe harbor from sin's storms with you, our heart's true desire. In the name of Jesus. Amen.

## Fourth Sunday after Pentecost

**Watchword for the Week** — O give thanks to the Lord, for he is good; for his steadfast love endures forever. Psalm 107:1

**Sunday, June 24** — Job 38:1-11; Psalm 107:1-3,23-32
2 Corinthians 6:1-13; Mark 4:35-41

### Even now, in fact, my witness is in heaven, and he that vouches for me is on high. Job 16:19

From all that dwell below the skies                    551
let the Creator's praise arise;
let the Redeemer's name be sung
through every land, by every tongue.

### There is one God; there is also one mediator between God and humankind, Christ Jesus, himself human. 1 Timothy 2:5

No prayer is made by us alone,                         749
the Holy Spirit pleads,
and Jesus, on the eternal throne,
for sinners intercedes.

O loving One, words alone can barely express our gratitude for the wonderful witness of your love given to us in Jesus Christ, our merciful Mediator. As you vouch for us, may we be a worldly witness to you. Amen.

Monday, June 25 — Psalm 78:40-55
Deuteronomy 3; Luke 4:31-44

## God said to Moses, "I AM WHO I AM."
## Exodus 3:14

Hail, First and Last, the great I Am,                    703
in whom we live and move;
increase our little spark of faith,
and fill our hearts with love.

## I am the Alpha and the Omega, the beginning
## and the end. To the thirsty I will give water
## as a gift from the spring of the water of life.
## Revelation 21:6

Of the Father's love begotten                           483
ere the worlds began to be,
he is Alpha and Omega—
he the source, the ending he
of the things that are, that have been,
and that future years shall see
evermore and evermore.

Lord, may we never question the infinite presence
that is you, the great I Am. As we value you, may
we also value all of your creation, remembering
that all are worthy because all are from you. Amen.

**Tuesday, June 26** — Psalm 78:56-64
Deuteronomy 4:1-31; Luke 5:1-11

**Thus says the Lord, "I will rejoice in doing good
to them." Jeremiah 32:41**

All glory to our Lord and God                    485
for love so deep, so high, so broad—
the Trinity, whom we adore
forever and forevermore.

**For God so loved the world that he gave his only
Son, so that everyone who believes in him may
not perish but may have eternal life. John 3:16**

We've a message to give to the nations,          621
that the Lord who's reigning above
has sent us his Son to save us,
and show us that God is love,
and show us that God is love.

Just as the Lord rejoices in doing good for us, so
may we rejoice in our great-hearted Redeemer
through all we do. Let us testify to the entire
world—"God is love!" In the name of Jesus. Amen.

**Wednesday, June 27** — Psalm 78:65-72
Deuteronomy 4:32-5:21; Luke 5:12-26

## The Lord is my shepherd, I shall not want.
## Psalm 23:1

He leadeth me: O blessed thought!                 787
O words with heav'nly comfort fraught!
Whate'er I do, where'er I be,
still 'tis God's hand that leadeth me.
He leadeth me, he leadeth me;
by his own hand he leadeth me,
his faithful foll'wer I would be,
for by his hand he leadeth me.

## Christ says, "I came that they may have life, and have it abundantly. I am the good shepherd. The good shepherd lays down his life for the sheep." John 10:10-11

Chosen flock, your faithful Shepherd follow,    444
who laid down his life for you;
all your days unto his service hallow,
each to be disciples true;
evermore rejoice to do his pleasure,
be the fullness of his grace your treasure;
should success your labor crown,
give the praise to him alone.

God of abundance, we hear your familiar voice and
draw near to you, the one who leads us through
verdant vales of vitality. May the still waters of your
presence comfort our anxious spirits. In the name
of Jesus. Amen.

**Thursday, June 28** — Psalm 79:1-8
Deuteronomy 5:22-6:25; Luke 5:27-39

**Praise him for his acts of power; praise him for his surpassing greatness. Psalm 150:2 (NIV)**

> All praise and thanks to God                    533
> the Father now be given,
> the Son and Spirit blessed,
> who reign in highest heaven—
> the one eternal God,
> whom heav'n and earth adore;
> for thus it was, is now,
> and shall be evermore.

**In Jesus Christ every one of God's promises is a "Yes." For this reason it is through him that we say the "Amen," to the glory of God. 2 Corinthians 1:20**

> The Lord has promised good to me,               783
> his word my hope secures;
> he will my shield and portion be
> as long as life endures.

We praise you, great Promise-Keeper, and give thanks for gifts aplenty! As your resounding "Yes" answered all of our prayers in Christ, let us respond, "Amen" again and again, to your glory! In the name of Jesus. Amen.

**Friday, June 29** — Psalm 79:9-13
Deuteronomy 7; Luke 6:1-11

## In your hand are power and might, so that no one is able to withstand you. 2 Chronicles 20:6

His righteous government and power     320
shall over all extend;
on judgment and on justice based,
his reign shall have no end.

## God raised the Lord and will also raise us by his power. 1 Corinthians 6:14

Mighty God, we humbly pray,     586
let your pow'r now lead the way
that in all things we may show
that we in your likeness grow.

As the powers of this world fall victim to greed and injustice, let us not forget the power of the mighty One who raises us, victims made victorious by the hand of hope that holds us close. Amen.

**For your name's sake, O Lord, pardon my guilt,
for it is great. Psalm 25:11**

> Forgive me, Lord, for this I pray,                    569
> the wrong that I have done this day.
> May peace with God and neighbor be,
> before I sleep, restored to me.

**Jesus said, "Father, forgive them; for they do not
know what they are doing." Luke 23:34**

> Lord Jesus, think on me                               764
> and purge away my sin;
> from selfish passions set me free
> and make me pure within.

Merciful One, we humbly kneel before you and
offer our confession. May we live out our contrition
as witnesses to your gospel, drawing closer to you in
all that we do. Amen.

### Fifth Sunday after Pentecost

**Watchword for the Week** — The steadfast love of the Lord never ceases, his mercies never come to an end. Lamentations 3:22

**Sunday, July 1** — Lamentations 3:22-33; Psalm 30
2 Corinthians 8:7-15; Mark 5:21-43

## You are wearied with your many consultations. Isaiah 47:13

> At last the march shall end;                          786
> the wearied ones shall rest;
> the pilgrims find their home at last,
> Jerusalem the blessed.

## Let each of you lead the life that the Lord has assigned, to which God called you. 1 Corinthians 7:17

> Jesus, Master, will you use                           p42
> one who loves you more than all?
> As you will, I would not choose;
> only let me hear your call.
> Jesus, let me always be
> in your service glad and free. Amen.

Dear Lord, we are slaves to our busy date books. Sometimes we forget we work for the Lord. We must do your work, on your time, and then we will find time to do the rest. Amen.

**Monday, July 2 — Psalm 80:8-11**
Deuteronomy 9:7-10:22; Luke 6:27-38

### Keep far from a false charge. Exodus 23:7

Thou, O Christ, art all I want;                    724
more than all in thee I find;
raise the fallen, cheer the faint,
heal the sick and lead the blind.
Just and holy is thy name,
I am all unrighteousness,
false and full of sin I am,
thou art full of truth and grace.

**Rid yourselves, therefore, of all malice, and all
guile, insincerity, envy, and all slander. Like
newborn infants, long for the pure, spiritual
milk, so that by it you may grow into salvation.
1 Peter 2:1-2**

Jesus, by your presentation,                        314
when they blessed you, weak and poor,
make us see your great salvation,
seal us with your promise sure;
and present us in your glory
to your Father, cleansed and pure.

Dear Father, we need to take inventory of spiritual
things. We must be aware of things we say and
do so we do not become too involved in life's
complications. Be with us. Amen.

Tuesday, July 3 — Psalm 80:12-19
Deuteronomy 11; Luke 6:39-49

**Many are saying, "Who will show us any good?"
Lift up the light of Your countenance upon us, O
Lord! Psalm 4:6 (NASB)**

> They live to him who bought them with his blood,   516
> baptized them with his Spirit, pure and good;
> and in true faith and ever-burning love,
> their hearts and hopes ascend to seek above
> th'eternal good.

**Christ says, "I am the light of the world.
Whoever follows me will never walk in darkness
but will have the light of life." John 8:12**

> I heard the voice of Jesus say,                            606
> "I am this dark world's Light;
> look unto me, your morn shall rise,
> and all your day be bright."
> I looked to Jesus, and I found
> in him my Star, my Sun;
> and in that Light of life I'll walk,
> till trav'ling days are done.

Lord Jesus, keep us from stumbling in darkness
when you are anxious to enlighten our paths every
day. Thank you for this light! In your name we
pray. Amen.

**Wednesday, July 4** — Psalm 81:1-5
Deuteronomy 12; Luke 7:1-17

**The Lord God helps me; therefore I have not been disgraced. Isaiah 50:7**

> Good news! Our Christ has come!                    630*
> Oppression now may cease.
> Christ claims the side of those
> who've lost their rights and peace.
> God's Spirit moves to free the slave
> and fill the empty with good things.

**Now in Christ Jesus you who once were far off have been brought near by the blood of Christ. Ephesians 2:13**

> The church on earth, in humble strain,              471
> exalts the Christ, our Savior,
> and sings, "The Lamb for us was slain,
> our foe is lost forever;
> for Christ has redeemed us with his precious blood
> out of ev'ry nation and kindred,
> and made us thereby kings and priests unto God.
> To him thanksgiving be rendered."

Lord, by your saving grace we know we do not need to earn our salvation. Keep us close to you so we do not forget your grace. Remind us whenever we pray the prayers you have taught us. Amen.

---

* © Sharon M. Benson (1988). Used by permission.

**Thursday, July 5** — Psalm 81:6-10
Deuteronomy 13:1-14:21; Luke 7:18-30

**The spirit of the Lord shall rest on him, the spirit of wisdom and understanding, the spirit of counsel and might, the spirit of knowledge and the fear of the Lord. Isaiah 11:2**

> Rise, my soul, adore your Maker;        568
> angels sing, praises bring,
> with them be partaker.
> Father, Lord of ev'ry spirit,
> in your might, lead me right
> through my Savior's merit.

**In Christ God was reconciling the world to himself, not counting their trespasses against them, and entrusting the message of reconciliation to us. 2 Corinthians 5:19**

> Proclaim the gracious word:       p138*
> God loves the whole wide earth,
> to lift, to save, to reconcile,
> to grant essential worth!

When we become aware of drifting into sin, keep us close to your reconciliation. Lord, actively claim all your grace and spirit to cover our careless sin. Thank you. Amen.

\* © 1980 by Jane Parker Huber

**Friday, July 6** — Psalm 81:11-16
Deuteronomy 14:22-15:18; Luke 7:31-38

**John Hus Festival†** — Isaiah 49:1-7; Psalm 135:1-13
1 Corinthians 1:18-24; Mark 8:34-38

## The Holy One of Israel is your Redeemer, the God of the whole earth he is called. Isaiah 54:5

My Redeemer, overwhelmed with anguish,          346
went to Olivet for me;
there he kneels, his heart does heave and languish
in a bitter agony;
fear and horror seize his soul and senses,
for the hour of darkness now commences;
ah, how he does weep and groan
our rebellion to atone.

## No one can say "Jesus is Lord" except by the Holy Spirit. 1 Corinthians 12:3

For Hus the fearless martyr                      391*
we give you thanks and praise,
whose bright and pure example
still shines in these our days.
May we with dedication
so preach and live your love
that all may hear your witness
and strive for heav'n above.

Lord Jesus, we are aware of the difficult life you accepted in God's will. We are grateful for the saints and martyrs who followed in your path and give us light. Amen.

† On July 6, 1415, John Hus was martyred at the Council of Constance.

Saturday, July 7— Psalm 82:1-4
Deuteronomy 15:19-17:7; Luke 7:39-50

## And you forget the Lord your Maker, who stretched out the heavens and laid the foundations of the earth? Isaiah 51:13 (NKJV)

                                             *

The spacious firmament on high,
with all the blue, ethereal sky,
and spangled heavens, a shining frame,
their great Original proclaim:
th'unwearied sun, from day to day,
does his Creators power display;
and publishes to every land
the work of an almighty hand.

## You have been born anew, not of perishable but of imperishable seed, through the living and enduring word of God. 1 Peter 1:23

                                             633

Your faithful servants bless
in all earth's varied places;
your name they all confess
among earth's many races,
until that day shall come
when multitudes untold
shall find their glorious home
in heav'n's eternal fold!

Almighty God, the entire world is under your care, but we are not in charge. Your word reminds us that you made all creation, and know our weakest, personal needs. Thank you. Amen.

*   from Favorite Hymns of Praise—public domain

## Sixth Sunday after Pentecost

**Watchword for the Week** — Jesus says, "My grace is sufficient for you, for power is made perfect in weakness." 2 Corinthians 12:9

**Sunday, July 8** — Ezekiel 2:1-5; Psalm 123
2 Corinthians 12:2-10; Mark 6:1-13

## Woe to him who piles up stolen goods and makes himself wealthy by extortion! How long must this go on? Habakkuk 2:6 (NIV)

The earth is the Lord's and its fulness,                    656*
its mystery, splendor and wealth,
its bounty, fertility, kindness,
its beauty, its reason, its health;
then who is this wise-hearted steward
who faithfully carries this trust?
The generous, gentle, obedient,
the patient, the honest, the just.

## Thieves must give up stealing; rather let them labor and work honestly with their own hands, so as to have something to share with the needy. Ephesians 4:28

All who have gone before us                    389**
Christ's victory now share!
In Christ they are established
in God's eternal care;
in Christ their pain is ended,
in Christ, death's sting is done,
in Christ, all cares forgotten,
their perfect joy begun!

This past week, we commemorate and honor the death of John Hus. We are heirs of important milestones and great blessings. Keep us conscious of these values. Amen.

**Monday, July 9** — Psalm 82:5-8
Deuteronomy 17:8-18:22; Luke 8:1-15

**I am the Lord, and there is no other. I form light and create darkness, I make weal and create woe; I the Lord do all these things. Isaiah 45:6-7**

> Early let us seek your favor;                              731
> early let us do your will;
> blessed Lord and only Savior,
> with your love our spirits fill.
> Blessed Jesus, blessed Jesus,
> you have loved us, love us still.
> Blessed Jesus, blessed Jesus,
> you have loved us, love us still.

**We give you thanks, Lord God Almighty, who are and who were, for you have taken your great power and begun to reign. Revelation 11:17**

> Jesus comes with clouds descending;                        259
> see the Lamb for sinners slain!
> Thousand, thousand saints attending
> join to sing the glad refrain:
> Alleluia!
> Alleluia!
> Christ the Lord returns to reign!

Mighty God, it is in understanding that we serve a God who is almighty and all powerful. Help us to trust you in all of life, for we live under your power and glory every day and in every way. Blessed be your name. Amen.

**Tuesday, July 10 — Psalm 83:1-8**
Deuteronomy 19:1-20:09; Luke 8:16-25

**I will recount the gracious deeds of the Lord, the praiseworthy acts of the Lord, because of all that the Lord has done for us. Isaiah 63:7**

> With your presence, Lord, our Head and Savior,     447
> bless us all, we humbly pray;
> our dear heavenly Father's love and favor
> be our comfort every day.
> May God's Spirit now in each proceeding
> favor us with his most gracious leading;
> thus shall we be truly blessed
> both in labor and in rest.

**Blessed be the God and Father of our Lord Jesus Christ! By his great mercy he has given us a new birth into a living hope through the resurrection of Jesus Christ from the dead. 1 Peter 1:3**

> Hail, the heav'n-born Prince of Peace!                    295
> Hail, the Sun of Righteousness!
> Light and life to all he brings,
> ris'n with healing in his wings.
> Mild he lays his glory by,
> born that we no more may die,
> born to raise us from the earth,
> born to give us second birth.
> Hark! The herald angels sing:
> "Glory to the newborn King!"

We are blessed by acts and deeds you have done for us. Our salvation through Jesus is such a wonderful event. We will never be able to thank you for your grace and peace. In Jesus' name. Amen.

**Wednesday, July 11 — Psalm 83:9-12**
Deuteronomy 20:10-21:23; Luke 8:26-39

## If you are returning to the Lord with all your heart, then put away the foreign gods. 1 Samuel 7:3

O Christ, by whom we come to God,       749
the life, the truth, the way!
The path of prayer you also trod;
Lord, teach us how to pray.

## Where your treasure is, there your heart will be also. Matthew 6:21

Jesus, priceless treasure,       722
source of purest pleasure,
friend to me so true,
how my heart has panted
and my soul has fainted,
thirsting after you.
Yours I am, O spotless Lamb,
I will suffer nought to hide you,
nought I ask beside you.

Our Lord, when we are tempted to compromise our relationship with you, we become confused with important parts of our faith and lose the precious values we need. Be with us. Amen.

**Thursday, July 12** — Psalm 83:13-18
Deuteronomy 22; Luke 8:40-56

**You shall not set your desire on your neighbor's
house or anything that belongs to your neighbor.
Deuteronomy 5:21 (NIV)**

> Breathe through the pulses of desire                    739
> thy coolness and thy balm;
> let sense be dumb, its heats expire;
> speak through the earthquake, wind, and fire,
> O still, small voice of calm!

**Put to death, therefore, whatever in you is
earthly: evil desire, and greed (which is idolatry).
Colossians 3:5**

> O Christ, our hope, our heart's desire,                  374
> redemption's only spring;
> creator of the world are you,
> its Savior and its King,
> its Savior and its King.

Lord, sometimes the most important relationships
with our neighbors can be spoiled by envy and
greed. Help us keep to ourselves what we desire and
give us control over that evil. We ask for escape
from idolatry. In Jesus' name. Amen.

**Friday, July 13 — Psalm 84:1-7**
Deuteronomy 23:1-24:13; Luke 9:1-11

**You sweep them away; they are like a dream, like grass, in the morning it flourishes and is renewed; in the evening it fades and withers. Psalm 90:5,6**

> We hail you as our Savior, Lord,                    267
> our refuge and our great reward;
> without your grace we waste away
> like flow'rs that wither and decay.

**What is sown is perishable, what is raised is imperishable. 1 Corinthians 15:42**

> Holy Spirit, ever dwelling                          495
> in the holiest realms of light;
> Holy Spirit, ever brooding
> o'er a world of gloom and night;
> Holy Spirit, ever raising
> those of earth to thrones on high;
> living, life-imparting Spirit,
> you we praise and magnify.

Dear Lord, give us the insight to reject those things that are temporal and select what is renewing and imperishable. Our prayer life helps us judge those things which are most valuable. Amen.

**Saturday, July 14** — Psalm 84:8-12
Deuteronomy 24:14-25:19; Luke 9:12-27

**Help me, O Lord my God! Save me according to your steadfast love. Psalm 109:26**

> Crown him the Lord of life,     405
> who triumphed o'er the grave,
> and rose victorious in the strife
> for those he came to save.
> His glories now we sing,
> who died and rose on high,
> who died, eternal life to bring
> and lives that death may die.

**Paul wrote: We were afflicted in every way—disputes without and fears within. But God, who consoles the downcast, consoled us. 2 Corinthians 7:5-6**

> Christ bids each afflicted soul     416
> "Come that I may soothe your grief.
> No one who is strong and whole
> needs a doctor for relief;
> therefore have no fear, draw nigh,
> that your want I may supply."

Your steadfast love gives us victory over fear and defeat. You console us when we need your guidance and insight. Preserve us, in your love. Amen.

### Seventh Sunday after Pentecost

**Watchword for the Week** — Surely God's salvation is at hand for those who fear him, that his glory may dwell in our land. Psalm 85:9

**Sunday, July 15** — Amos 7:7-15; Psalm 85:8-13
Ephesians 1:3-14; Mark 6:14-29

## Indeed, He loves the people. Deuteronomy 33:3 (NASB)

And in your love may we abide,                    519
estranged from none by wrath or pride,
among ourselves at unity
and with all else in charity.

## We love because he first loved us. 1 John 4:19

Upon the cross of Jesus,                          329
my eye by faith can see
the very dying form of one
who suffered there for me.
And from my contrite heart, with tears,
two wonders I confess:
the wonder of his glorious love
and my unworthiness.

Gracious God, we are grateful for your love, which always is first and deep. Your good news is always delivered in love and through love. Amen.

**Monday, July 16 — Psalm 85:1-7**
Deuteronomy 26:1-27:13; Luke 9:28-36

**O Lord, you will ordain peace for us, for indeed, all that we have done, you have done for us.
Isaiah 26:12**

> O come, Desire of Nations, bind                      274
> all peoples in one heart and mind;
> bid envy, strife and quarrels cease;
> fill the whole world with heaven's peace.

**But by the grace of God I am what I am.
1 Corinthians 15:10**

> Make me your abode,                                  608
> a temple of God,
> a vessel of grace,
> prepared for your service and formed to your praise.

Lord, because you love us, we can remain strong!
Be with us especially when we feel your grace, for
you give us all we need when we most need it. In
God's grace. Amen.

**Tuesday, July 17** — Psalm 85:8-13
Deuteronomy 27:14-28:24; Luke 9:37-50

**But you do see! Indeed you note trouble and grief, that you may take it into your hands. Psalm 10:14**

Breathe, O breathe your loving Spirit                  474
into ev'ry troubled breast;
let us all in you inherit,
let us find the promised rest.
Take away the love of sinning;
Alpha and Omega be;
end of faith, as its beginning,
set our hearts at liberty.

**Jesus saw a great crowd; and he had compassion for them, because they were like sheep without a shepherd; and he began to teach them many things. Mark 6:34**

Not your merit brings God near,                        275*
but God's great compassion
for the creature he fashioned.
He will prove his faithfulness to you
and in holy ways he will lead you.
So to God give praise which is his due.

Lord of compassion, we sense the needs of many we pass on the street but do nothing to help. Your sensitivity and concern as the great Shepherd is always at work. Hear our prayer, O Lord. Amen.

* © 1994 by Brian Henkelmann

**Wednesday, July 18 — Psalm 86:1-10**
Deuteronomy 28:25-57; Luke 9:51-62

**Come, let us go to entreat the favor of the Lord,
and to seek the Lord of hosts; I myself am going.
Zechariah 8:21**

> You are the way; to you alone                          661
> from sin and death we flee;
> and those who would the Father seek
> your followers must be.

**Some people brought a blind man to Jesus and
begged him to touch him. Mark 8:22**

> Good news! Our Christ has come!                        630*
> He heals the sad of heart.
> He sets the pris'ners free
> and helps the blind to see.
> God's Spirit works through all who love,
> through all who touch the lives of these.

O Lord, your disciples often sensed needs but
realized they could not solve them. We are also
aware of the needs of others. Your loving touch is
always able to bring relief. Amen.

*   © Sharon M. Benson (1988). Used by permission.

**Thursday, July 19** — Psalm 86:11-17
Deuteronomy 28:58-29:21; Luke 10:1-16

## God looks to the ends of the earth, and sees everything under the heavens. Job 28:24

This is our Father's world:                          456
O let us not forget
that though the wrong is often strong,
God is the ruler yet.
He trusts us with his world,
to keep it clean and fair —
all earth and trees, all skies and seas,
all creatures ev'rywhere.

## God is greater than our hearts, and he knows everything. 1 John 3:20

Alleluia! Alleluia!                                   p93
Hearts to heav'n and voices raise;
sing to God a hymn of gladness,
sing to God a hymn of praise;
he, who on the cross a victim
for the world's salvation bled,
Jesus Christ, the King of Glory,
now is risen from the dead.

Jesus, we are overwhelmed at your concerns and
resources to minister to the great needs of so many
about us. Thank you for vision and grace to meet
these needs. Amen.

Friday, July 20 — Psalm 87
Deuteronomy 29:22-31:8; Luke 10:17-24

**Daniel went home to his upstairs room where the windows opened toward Jerusalem. Three times a day he got down on his knees and prayed, giving thanks to his God. Daniel 6:10 (NIV)**

He found them in his house of prayer    396
with one accord assembled,
and so revealed his presence there;
they wept for joy and trembled.
One cup they drank, one bread they broke,
one baptism shared, one language spoke,
forgiving and forgiven.

**We are persecuted, but not forsaken; struck down, but not destroyed. 2 Corinthians 4:9**

Lead on, O King eternal!    753
The day of march has come;
henceforth in fields of conquest
your tents will be our home:
through days of preparation
your grace has made us strong,
and now, O King eternal,
we lift our battle song.

Lord, with our needs and your constant concern, we are able to be healed and work out our problems with your intervention. Keep your power and concern at work in us. In Jesus' name. Amen.

**Saturday, July 21** — Psalm 88:1-5
Deuteronomy 31:9-32:9; Luke 10:25-42

**He sent redemption to his people; he has
commanded his covenant forever. Psalm 111:9**

> O perfect redemption, the purchase of blood,      550
> to ev'ry believer the promise of God:
> the vilest offender who truly believes,
> that moment from Jesus a pardon receives.
> Praise the Lord, praise the Lord,
>     let the earth hear his voice!
> Praise the Lord, praise the Lord,
>     let the people rejoice!
> O come to the Father through Jesus the Son,
> and give him the glory—great things he has done!

**Since we are justified by faith, we have peace
with God through our Lord Jesus Christ.
Romans 5:1**

> It then reveals God's boundless grace,      509
> which justifies our sinful race,
> and gives eternal life to all
> who will accept the gospel call.

Lord Jesus, your redemption and justification bring
peace to our needs and world. Keep our faith in you
as you are always ready to help. By your grace we
are able to face our needs. Amen.

### Eighth Sunday after Pentecost

**Watchword for the Week** — So then you are no longer strangers and aliens, but you are citizens with the saints and members of the household of God. Ephesians 2:19

**Sunday, July 22** — Jeremiah 23:1-6; Psalm 23
Ephesians 2:11-22; Mark 6:30-34,53-56

## My eyes are awake before each watch of the night, that I may meditate on your promise. Psalm 119:148

Just as I am; thou wilt receive,     762
wilt welcome, pardon, cleanse, relieve;
because thy promise I believe,
O Lamb of God, I come, I come!

## You will do well to be attentive to the prophetic message as to a lamp shining in a dark place, until the day dawns and the morning star rises in your hearts. 2 Peter 1:19

Break forth, O beauteous heav'nly light,    287
and usher in the morning.
O shepherds, shudder not with fright,
but hear the angel's warning.
This child, now weak in infancy,
our confidence and joy shall be,
the pow'r of Satan breaking,
our peace eternal making.

As Charles Wesley writes in a beloved hymn, "Dayspring from on high, be near; daystar, in my heart appear." Hear our prayers and answer our desires as you minister through us. Amen.

Monday, July 23 — Psalm 88:6-12
Deuteronomy 32:10-43; Luke 11:1-13

**The people came to Moses and said, "We have sinned by speaking against the Lord and against you; pray to the Lord to take away the serpents from us." So Moses prayed for the people. Numbers 21:7**

Church, unite for the right;                    631
let your foes behold your stand;
rebuke them for their error;
inspire with hope and fervor;
declare the Savior's merit
and how the Holy Spirit
by his power, ev'ry hour,
will direct us and protect us
in a world of sin and strife.

**Jesus is able for all time to save those who approach God through him, since he always lives to make intercession for them. Hebrews 7:25**

While the prayers of saints ascend,            553
God of love, to mine attend.
Hear me, for your Spirit pleads;
hear, for Jesus intercedes.

Dear Lord, help us never to forget how much you love us and minister to our needs every day. Amen.

**Tuesday, July 24** — Psalm 88:13-18
Deuteronomy 32:44-33:17; Luke 11:14-28

**Do not be afraid, Abram. I am your shield, your very great reward. Genesis 15:1 (NIV)**

> Sun of righteousness, arise;                521*
> dawn upon our clouded skies;
> shine within your church today
> that the world may see and say,
> "Have mercy, Lord."

**If you belong to Christ, then you are Abraham's offspring, heirs according to the promise. Galatians 3:29**

> I have no help but yours, nor do I need        421
> another arm but yours to lean upon;
> it is enough, O Lord, enough indeed;
> my strength is in your might, your might alone.

Precious Lord, we worship the God of Abraham, Isaac and Jacob. We trust in the centuries of faithfulness and promise which began so long ago and continue today around the world. Amen.

* © C. Daniel Crews (1994). Used by permission.

**Wednesday, July 25** — Psalm 89:1-8
Deuteronomy 33:18-34:12; Luke 11:29-36

## O Lord my God, I cried to you for help, and you have healed me. Psalm 30:2

Praise him for his grace and favor                    529
to his people in distress.
Praise him, still the same forever,
slow to chide, and swift to bless.
Alleluia! Alleluia!
Glorious in his faithfulness!

## Christ says, "If in my name you ask me for anything, I will do it." John 14:14

My soul he doth restore again,                        720
and me to walk doth make
within the paths of righteousness,
e'en for his own name's sake;
within the paths of righteousness,
e'en for his own name's sake.

We trust in God and Jesus, his son. It requires faith
for healing and total commitment to obtain the
victory in life and death. We ask for this faith in
Jesus' name. Amen.

**Thursday, July 26** — Psalm 89:9-18
Joshua 1,2; Luke 11:37-54

## When you have eaten and are satisfied, praise the Lord your God. Deuteronomy 8:10 (NIV)

Eat and rest at this great feast,                    p206
then to serve him freely go,
as it is for pilgrims fit,
as disciples ought to do.
We, when Jesus we shall see
coming in his majesty,
shall the marriage supper share,
if we his true followers are.

## So, whether you eat or drink, or whatever you do, do everything for the glory of God. 1 Corinthians 10:31

Come, you thirsty, come and welcome,                    765
God's free bounty glorify;
true belief and true repentance,
ev'ry grace that brings you nigh.

We are fed and cared for in all of life so we can give thanks for everything large and small. Let us never forget how blessed we are and praise the Lord each day. Amen.

**Friday, July 27** — Psalm 89:19-29
Joshua 3,4; Luke 12:1-12

## "I pledged myself to you and entered into a covenant with you," says the Lord God, "and you became mine." Ezekiel 16:8

His oath, his covenant, his blood                    771
sustain me in the raging flood;
when all supports are washed away,
he then is all my hope and stay.

## Once you were not a people, but now you are God's people; once you had not received mercy, but now you have received mercy. 1 Peter 2:10

O that such may be our union                         673
as thine with the Father is,
and not one of our communion
e'er forsake the path of bliss;
may our light break forth with brightness,
from thy light reflected shine;
thus the world will bear us witness
that we, Lord, are truly thine.

We are blessed and have received a wonderful covenant with the God of Abraham. We are called by God's mercy for his people. What a beautiful blessing in Jesus' name. Amen.

**Saturday, July 28** — Psalm 89:30-37
Joshua 5,6; Luke 12:13-21

**Restore me, and I will return, because you are
the Lord my God. Jeremiah 31:18 (NIV)**

> Christ be with me, Christ within me,                    p237
> Christ behind me, Christ before me,
> Christ beside me, Christ to win me,
> Christ to comfort and restore me,
> Christ beneath me, Christ above me,
> Christ in quiet, Christ in danger,
> Christ in hearts of all that love me,
> Christ in mouth of friend and stranger.

**It is no longer I who live, but it is Christ who
lives in me. Galatians 2:20**

> No condemnation now I dread,                            773
> for Christ, and all in him, is mine!
> Alive in him, my living Head,
> and clothed in righteousness divine,
> bold I approach the eternal throne
> and claim the crown, through Christ, my own.
> Bold I approach th'eternal throne
> and claim the crown, through Christ, my own.

Lord Jesus, we are blessed both by your faith in us
and our own faith. We place our complete trust in
you. Hear our prayers. Amen.

### Ninth Sunday after Pentecost

**Watchword for the Week** — The Lord is faithful in all his words, and gracious in all his deeds. Psalm 145:13

**Sunday, July 29** — 2 Kings 4:42-44; Psalm 145:10-18
Ephesians 3:14-21; John 6:1-21

## What god in heaven or on earth can perform deeds and mighty acts like yours! Deuteronomy 3:24

> Wake your sleeping church to live,                521*
> not afraid our all to give.
> Let the mighty acts of God
> spread through all the world abroad:
> have mercy, Lord.

## Christ was revealed in flesh, vindicated in spirit, seen by angels, proclaimed among Gentiles, believed in throughout the world, taken up in glory. 1 Timothy 3:16

> Great things he has taught us,                    550
>     great things he has done,
> and great our rejoicing through Jesus the Son:
> but purer, and higher, and greater will be
> our wonder, our transport when Jesus we see.

In the whole of creation and your actions throughout the world, we are blessed from the beginning until now. May we always trust in you. Amen.

*   © C. Daniel Crews (1994). Used by permission.

**Monday, July 30** — Psalm 89:38-45
Joshua 7; Luke 12:22-34

**Position yourselves, stand still and see the
salvation of the Lord, who is with you.
2 Chronicles 20:17 (NKJV)**

> Thus may we, as your anointed,                716
> walk with you in truth and grace
> in the path you have appointed,
> till we reach your dwelling-place.

**Paul said, "To this day I have had help from God,
and so I stand here, testifying to both small and
great." Acts 26:22**

> God gave us eyes to see them,                 467
> and lips that we might tell
> how great is God Almighty,
> who has made all things well.
> All things bright and beautiful,
> all creatures great and small,
> all things wise and wonderful—
> the Lord God made them all.

Make our faith complete, Lord, when we consider
salvation. Make us aware of the small and the great
that we have in our special relationship with God.
Amen.

**Tuesday, July 31** — Psalm 89:46-52
Joshua 8:1-29; Luke 12:35-48

**For as the earth brings forth its shoots, and as a garden causes what is sown in it to spring up, so the Lord God will cause righteousness and praise to spring up before all the nations. Isaiah 61:11**

> Eternal Source, whence all did spring,                279
> almighty and all-glorious King,
> the whole creation's Head and Lord,
> by all in heav'n and earth adored;
> Lord, whom high heav'n cannot contain,
> you as a lowly infant came,
> and left your throne in heav'n above,
> O myst'ry deep, O boundless love.

**Jesus said, "The harvest is plentiful, but the laborers are few; therefore ask the Lord of the harvest to send out laborers into his harvest." Luke 10:2**

> A new creation comes to life and grows              366
> as Christ's new body takes on flesh and blood.
> The universe restored and whole will sing:
> Alleluia!

Dear Lord, you are an active part of the earth in all its righteousness and praise. You watch over us and even send laborers into the harvest. In your name we pray. Amen.

**Wednesday, August 1** — Psalm 90
Joshua 8:30-9:27; Luke 12:49-59

**Look down from heaven and see, from your holy and glorious habitation. Where are your zeal and your might? Isaiah 63:15**

To him, enthroned by filial right,     469
all pow'r in heav'n and earth proclaim,
honor, and majesty, and might;
"Worthy the Lamb, for he was slain!"

**When He had disarmed the rulers and authorities, He made a public display of them, having triumphed over them through Christ. Colossians 2:15 (NASB)**

Ride on! Ride on in majesty!     343
In lowly pomp ride on to die;
O Christ, your triumphs now begin
o'er captive death and conquered sin.

Powerful God, we know that through you all things are possible. May your will be done in our families, in our congregations, in our communities and in the world. Amen.

**Thursday, August 2** — Psalm 91:1-8
Joshua 10:1-28; Luke 13:1-17

## The Lord our God is righteous in everything he does. Daniel 9:14 (NIV)

"Fear not, I am with you; O be not dismayed,      709
for I am your God and will still give you aid;
I'll strengthen you, help you and cause you to stand
upheld by my righteous, omnipotent hand."

## God shows no partiality. Romans 2:11

This is my Father's world:                        456
he shines in all that's fair;
in rustling grass I hear him pass—
he speaks to me ev'rywhere.
This is my Father's world:
why should my heart be sad?
The Lord is King, let heaven ring!
God reigns; let earth be glad.

Holy Caregiver, help us remember that all
people are your children, regardless of their race,
nationality or political ideals. We give thanks that
you watch over all your children. Amen.

**Friday, August 3** — Psalm 91:9-16
Joshua 10:29-11:23; Luke 13:18-30

**Depart from evil, and do good; seek peace, and
pursue it. Psalm 34:14**

> From sorrow, toil, and pain,                    680
> and sin we shall be free;
> and perfect love and friendship reign
> through all eternity.

**Finally, all of you, have unity of spirit, sympathy,
love for one another, a tender heart, and a
humble mind. 1 Peter 3:8**

> One bread, one cup, one body we,                p228
> rejoicing in our unity,
> proclaim your love until you come
> to bring your scattered loved ones home.

In our families and in our church families, O holy
Mediator, help us to reflect your love. Forgive us
when we wrong those around us and restore us
to your harmony and peace, in your Son's name.
Amen.

**Saturday, August 4** — Psalm 92:1-8
Joshua 12:1-13:7; Luke 13:31-14:6

## If you seek me with all your heart, I will let you find me, says the Lord. Jeremiah 29:13-14

> Did you not bid us love you, God and King,  490
> love you with all our heart and strength and mind?
> I see the cross—there teach my heart to cling.
> O let me seek you and O let me find!

## Zacchaeus climbed a sycamore tree to see Jesus, because he was going to pass that way. When Jesus came to the place, he looked up and said to him, "Zacchaeus, hurry and come down; for I must stay at your house today." Luke 19:4-5

> Jesus calls us; o'er the tumult  600
> of our life's wild, restless sea,
> day by day his voice is sounding,
> saying, "Christian, follow me."

O Lord, sometimes it is difficult to hear your voice amid the everyday noise and distractions of our lives. Pause our lives, if only for an instant, to let us hear you clearly and know that you are still with us. Amen.

## Tenth Sunday after Pentecost

**Watchword for the Week** — Jesus says, "I am the bread of life. Whoever comes to me will never be hungry, and whoever believes in me will never be thirsty." John 6:35

**Sunday, August 5** — Exodus 16:2-4,9-15; Psalm 78:23-29
Ephesians 4:1-16; John 6:24-35

# I am watching over my word to perform it. Jeremiah 1:12

> O God, in whom our trust we place,                  509
> we thank you for your word of grace;
> help us its precepts to obey
> till we shall live in endless day.

# Heaven and earth will pass away, but my words will not pass away. Mark 13:31

> The word of God, which ne'er shall cease,           509
> proclaims free pardon, grace, and peace,
> salvation shows in Christ alone,
> the perfect will of God makes known.

O eternal Word, we thank you for the ability to learn that you have given to each of us. Bless our bishops, ministers, teachers and all those who seek to guide us as we study and interpret your teachings. Amen.

**Monday, August 6** — Psalm 92:9-15
Joshua 13:8-14:5; Luke 14:7-24

**The righteousness of the righteous shall not save them when they transgress; and as for the wickedness of the wicked, it shall not make them stumble when they turn from their wickedness. Ezekiel 33:12**

> Seek the Lord, whose willing presence                    780*
> moves your heart to make appeal.
> Turn from wickedness and evil;
> God will pardon, cleanse, and heal.

**The disciples went out and proclaimed that all should repent. Mark 6:12**

> Dear Christian friends, rejoice,                          p60**
> with heart, and soul, and voice;
> hear the news that John did cry:
> "God to us is drawing nigh;
> turn away from fear and sin,
> to let the Savior enter in."
> God is drawing nigh!
> God is drawing nigh!

O holy One, we know that we disappoint you every day, despite our efforts. Give us the strength and courage to acknowledge when we fail you, and through your grace to persevere in seeking to do your will. Amen.

**Tuesday, August 7** — Psalm 93
Joshua 14:6-15:19; Luke 14:25-35

### Create in me a clean heart, O God, and put a new and right spirit within me. Psalm 51:10

> Create in me a clean heart, O God,                    p79
> and renew a right Spirit within me.
> Cast me not away from your presence,
> and take not your Holy Spirit from me.
> Restore unto me the joy of salvation;
> anoint me with your Spirit free.
> Create in me a clean heart, O God,
> and renew a right Spirit within me.

### You were bought with a price; therefore glorify God in your body. 1 Corinthians 6:20

> Not in a temple made with hands                       512
> God the Almighty is dwelling;
> high in the heav'ns his temple stands,
> all earthly temples excelling.
> Yet he who dwells in heav'n above
> chooses to live with us in love,
> making our bodies his temple.

Heavenly Parent, help us to remember that a loving spirit, a kind heart and a caring soul demonstrate beauty much more than our physical bodies. May the world see your Spirit through us. Amen.

**Wednesday, August 8 — Psalm 94:1-11**
Joshua 15:20-63; Luke 15:1-10

## I am the Lord, who frustrates the omens of liars, and makes fools of diviners. Isaiah 44:25

Dear Lord and Father of mankind,                    739
forgive our foolish ways;
reclothe us in our rightful mind;
in purer lives thy service find,
in deeper rev'rence, praise.

## Guard what has been entrusted to you. Avoid the profane chatter and contradictions of what is falsely called knowledge. 1 Timothy 6:20

All our knowledge, sense and sight                  558
lie in deepest darkness shrouded,
till your Spirit breaks our night
with the beams of truth unclouded;
you alone to God can win us;
you must work all good within us.

Divine Guide, our world today is filled with
constant communication, information, news and
"knowledge." Help us to listen for your quiet voice
to guide us where you want us to go. Amen.

**Thursday, August 9** — Psalm 94:12-23
Joshua 16,17; Luke 15:11-32

**I will rejoice in the Lord; I will exult in the God
of my salvation. Habakkuk 3:18**

Your majesty, how vast it is,                          471
and how immense the glory,
which you, O Jesus, do possess;
the heav'ns proclaim your story;
the legions of angels exalt your great name,
your glory and might are transcendent;
and thousands of thousands your praises proclaim,
upon you gladly dependent.

**Jesus answered, "How can the guests of the
bridegroom fast while he is with them?"
Mark 2:19 (NIV)**

The watchers on the mountain                           256
proclaim the bridegroom near;
go forth as he approaches
with alleluias clear.
The marriage feast is waiting;
the gates wide open stand.
Arise, O heirs of glory;
the bridegroom is at hand.

Creator and Sustainer, you have provided such
bounty for us, your children. When we feel a lack
of earthly things, help us to trust in you to provide
for our needs, on earth and in heaven. In Christ's
name. Amen.

**Friday, August 10** — Psalm 95
Joshua 18:1-19:9; Luke 16:1-15

## When I told of my ways, you answered me; teach me your statutes. Psalm 119:26

O blessed Lord, teach me your law,     510
your righteous judgments I declare;
your testimonies make me glad,
for they are wealth beyond compare.

## Christ says, "This is my commandment, that you love one another as I have loved you." John 15:12

Grant, Lord, that with thy direction,     673
"Love each other," we comply,
aiming with unfeigned affection
thy love to exemplify;
let our mutual love be glowing;
thus the world will plainly see
that we, as on one stem growing,
living branches are in thee.

It is easy to love our friends, O Christ, but sometimes difficult to love a cranky neighbor or the driver who cuts us off in traffic. Keep reminding us to practice charity in Jesus' name. Amen.

**Saturday, August 11 — Psalm 96:1-9**
Joshua 19:10-39; Luke 16:16-31

### Does God not see my ways, and number all my steps? Job 31:4

'Tis the most blessed and needful part                    768
to have in Christ a share,
and to commit our way and heart
unto his faithful care;
this done, our steps are safe and sure,
our hearts' desires are rendered pure,
and naught can pluck us from his hand,
which leads us to the end.

### For all of us must appear before the judgment seat of Christ, so that each may receive recompense for what has been done in the body, whether good or evil. 2 Corinthians 5:10

My lasting joy and comfort here                    768
is Jesus' death and blood;
I with this passport can appear
before the throne of God.
Admitted to the realms above,
I then shall see the Christ I love,
where countless pardoned sinners meet
adoring at his feet.

We know that you are always with us, O God. Be with us today and every day as we go through life, and help us remember to live as your children, until we see you face to face. Amen.

### Eleventh Sunday after Pentecost

**Watchword for the Week** — Jesus says, "Very truly, I tell you, whoever believes has eternal life." John 6:47

**Sunday, August 12** — 1 Kings 19:4-8; Psalm 34:1-8
Ephesians 4:25-5:2; John 6:35,41-51

## The river of God is full of water. Psalm 65:9

> O, may this grace be ours:                   312
> in you always to live
> and drink of those refreshing streams
> which you alone can give.

## From his fullness we have all received, grace upon grace. John 1:16

> May your life and death supply              352
> grace to live and grace to die,
> grace to reach the home on high:
> hear us, holy Jesus.

Holy Jesus, you love us even though we have not earned it and can never be worthy of such a gift. For this grace, we give you thanks. Amen.

**Monday, August 13** — Psalm 96:10-13
Joshua 19:40-21:8; Luke 17:1-10

**August Thirteenth Festival†** — Joshua 24:16-24; Psalm 133
1 John 4:1-13; John 17:1-2,6-19

**Thus says the Lord, "I remember the devotion
of your youth, your love as a bride, how you
followed me in the wilderness, in a land not
sown." Jeremiah 2:2**

> He found them in his house of prayer            396
> with one accord assembled,
> and so revealed his presence there;
> they wept for joy and trembled.
> One cup they drank, one bread they broke,
> one baptism shared, one language spoke,
> forgiving and forgiven.

**Be faithful until death, and I will give you the
crown of life. Revelation 2:10**

> Stand up, stand up for Jesus;                   752
> the fight will not be long—
> this day the noise of battle,
> the next the victor's song.
> To ev'ryone who conquers,
> a crown of life shall be;
> we with the King of glory
> shall reign eternally.

Holy Spirit, on this anniversary day we remember
how you spoke to our ancestors in faith 285 years
ago. Continue to speak to us and speak through us
as we share your love with the world. Amen.

---

† At the conclusion of a Holy Communion service in the church at Berthelsdorf,
   Germany, on August 13, 1727, the residents of Herrnhut were united into the Renewed
   Brethren's Church through the Spirit of God.

**Tuesday, August 14** — Psalm 97:1-6
Joshua 21:9-45; Luke 17:11-19

**Sing for joy, O heavens, and exult, O earth;
break forth, O mountains, into singing! For the
Lord has comforted his people, and will have
compassion on his suffering ones. Isaiah 49:13**

> O sing, choirs of angels,                          283
> sing in exultation,
> sing, all ye citizens of heav'n above:
> glory to God, glory in the highest;
> O come, let us adore him,
> O come, let us adore him,
> O come, let us adore him, Christ, the Lord.

**Paul wrote: I am confident about all of you, that
my joy would be the joy of all of you.
2 Corinthians 2:3**

> Jesus is my joy,                                    594
> therefore blessed am I;
> O his mercy is unbounded,
> all my hope on him is grounded;
> Jesus is my joy,
> therefore blessed am I.

It may not feel like Christmas outside, heavenly
Father, but we remember with joy that you have
given us the gift of salvation through your Son.
We give you thanks and praise. Amen.

**Wednesday, August 15** — Psalm 97:7-12
Joshua 22; Luke 17:20-25

**See, you shall call nations that you do not know, and nations that do not know you shall run to you, because of the Lord your God. Isaiah 55:5**

> Long before our proclamation 684*
> you announced God's liberty,
> seeding hope in ev'ry nation
> of unending jubilee.
> Thus the Kingdom spreads its branches,
> grows in all humanity.

**Paul wrote: I came to you in weakness and in fear and in much trembling. My speech and my proclamation were not with plausible words of wisdom, but with a demonstration of the Spirit and of power. 1 Corinthians 2:3-4**

> Spirit of God, who dwells within my heart, p224
> wean it from sin, through all its pulses move.
> Stoop to my weakness, mighty as you are,
> and make me love you as I ought to love.

Heavenly Inspiration, we want to share your love with all the world, but we are just one person. Show us that whatever we do in your name, no matter how small, will help to bring your kingdom on earth. Amen.

* by Ted Wilde (1984)

**Thursday, August 16** — Psalm 98
Joshua 23:1-24:13; Luke 17:26-37

## Lift up your voice like a trumpet! Announce to my people their rebellion. Isaiah 58:1

Stand up, stand up for Jesus,                           752
the trumpet call obey;
then join the mighty conflict
in this, his glorious day.
Be strong in faith and serve him
against unnumbered foes;
let courage rise with danger,
and with God's strength oppose.

## If we are faithless, he remains faithful—for he cannot deny himself. 2 Timothy 2:13

O God, my faithful God,                                 615
O fountain ever flowing,
without whom nothing is,
all perfect gifts bestowing,
grant me a faithful life,
and give me, Lord, within,
commitment free from strife,
a soul unhurt by sin.

Sometimes it is difficult to obey you, holy One, and often we just stop trying. Even though we do not always have faith in you, you always have faith in us. Thank you for your constant presence. Amen.

**Friday, August 17** — Psalm 99
Joshua 24:14-Judges 1:16; Luke 18:1-17

## As for me, I shall behold your face in righteousness; when I awake I shall be satisfied, beholding your likeness. Psalm 17:15

Christ, whose glory fills the skies,                     475
Christ, the true and only light,
Sun of righteousness, arise,
triumph o'er the shades of night;
dayspring from on high, be near;
daystar, in my heart appear.

## The Word became flesh and lived among us, and we have seen his glory. John 1:14

Yea, Lord, we greet thee,                                283
born that happy morning;
Jesus, to thee be all glory giv'n;
Word of the Father, now in flesh appearing!
O come, let us adore him,
O come, let us adore him,
O come, let us adore him, Christ, the Lord.

We see your face, risen Savior, in the smile of a loved one, in the eyes of one we have helped, in the hands of one who offers aid. May they also see your face in us as we perform our daily tasks. Amen.

Saturday, August 18 — Psalm 100
Judges 1:17-2:23; Luke 18:18-30

**Do not be afraid, for I am with you to deliver you, says the Lord. Jeremiah 1:8**

> Lord, if your arm support us still          p106
> with its eternal strength,
> we shall o'ercome the mightiest ill,
> and conquer'rs prove at length.

**You did not receive the spirit of bondage again to fear, but you received the Spirit of adoption by whom we cry out, "Abba, Father." Romans 8:15 (NKJV)**

> Bless your own truth, dear Lord,          502
> to me, to me,
> as when you blessed the bread
> by Galilee.
> Then shall all bondage cease,
> all fetters fall;
> and I shall find my peace,
> my All in All!

You are our strength, supporting Lord, who enables us to live without fear. Remind us daily that because of Christ and his death, we live as your children. Amen.

## Twelfth Sunday after Pentecost

**Watchword for the Week** — Lay aside immaturity, and live, and walk in the way of insight. Proverbs 9:6

**Sunday, August 19** — Proverbs 9:1-6; Psalm 34:9-14
Ephesians 5:15-20; John 6:51-58

# I will lead the blind by a road they do not know, by paths they have not known I will guide them. Isaiah 42:16

Lead on, O King eternal;                         753
we follow, not with fears,
for gladness breaks like morning
where'er your face appears:
your cross is lifted o'er us;
we journey in its light;
the crown awaits the conquest;
lead on, O God of might!

# God is light and in him there is no darkness at all. 1 John 1:5

Savior, you came to give                         380
those who in darkness live
healing and sight,
health to the sick in mind,
sight to the inward blind:
now to all humankind
let there be light!

Heavenly Guide, we think we know where we are going and how to get there on our own. Our route is so much clearer when we listen for your directions. Lead us in the way you would have us go. Amen.

Monday, August 20 — Psalm 101
Judges 3; Luke 18:31-43

**The Lord God will not fail you or forsake you, until all the work for the service of the house of the Lord is finished. 1 Chronicles 28:20**

> But poor, in weakness, comes the Christ;      p58*
> his glory gone, no king we see;
> a servant, Lord, no praise he seeks.
> Thus comes God's power to you and me.

**Our Lord Jesus Christ will keep you strong to the end, so that you will be blameless on the day of our Lord Jesus Christ. 1 Corinthians 1:8 (NIV)**

> Not in our own strength, Lord, we move;      p58*
> your kingdom falls not when we fall,
> but forward presses day by day
> until your truth is known to all.

There is so much to do in your service, Lord, and we despair of accomplishing anything. Give us strength to continue and to know that all will be done in your time, not ours. Be with us in our work today. Amen.

\* © by Hermann I. Weinlick

**Tuesday, August 21†** — Psalm 102:1-11
Judges 4; Luke 19:1-10

**Bless the Lord, all his works, in all places of his dominion. Bless the Lord, O my soul.**
**Psalm 103:22**

> Blessed be the day when I must roam          794
> far from my country, friends, and home,
> an exile, poor and mean;
> my fathers' God will be my Guide,
> will angel guards for me provide,
> my soul, my soul in danger screen.

**Christ says, "Go therefore and make disciples of all nations." Matthew 28:19**

> "Go forth in all the earth," —          633
> your word to us is given:
> "Proclaim salvation's worth
> to people under heaven."
> This holy task, O Lord,
> your church must quite fulfill;
> to us your grace afford,
> and mold us to your will.

We hear the call to share your Gospel with all nations, our Redeemer, but we cannot always go ourselves. Remind us that sharing the Gospel with our neighbors or those in need in our own communities also answers your call. In Jesus' name. Amen.

† On this day in 1732, the first missionaries departed from Herrnhut bound for St. Thomas.

**Wednesday, August 22** — Psalm 102:12-22
Judges 5; Luke 19:11-27

**Help, O Lord, for there is no longer anyone who is godly; the faithful have disappeared from humankind. Psalm 12:1**

> Lo! The hosts of evil round us                751
> scorn the Christ, assail his ways!
> From the fears that long have bound us,
> free our hearts to faith and praise.
> Grant us wisdom, grant us courage,
> for the living of these days,
> for the living of these days.

**The gate is narrow and the road is hard that leads to life, and there are few who find it. Matthew 7:14**

> Be with me, Lord, where'er I go;               733
> teach me what you would have me do;
> suggest whate'er I think or say;
> direct me in the narrow way.

Lord, often it feels that many have forgotten you or have never known you at all. Lead us to others who are faithful, so together we can share your joy with each other and with those who do not know of your love. Amen.

**Thursday, August 23** — Psalm 102:23-28
Judges 6; Luke 19:28-44

**These people draw near with their mouths and honor me with their lips, while their hearts are far from me. Isaiah 29:13**

Lord God, with shame I now confess          p32
I've turned away from you;
forgive me all my sin today,
my heart and soul renew.

**Jesus said, "Whoever does the will of God is my brother and sister and mother." Mark 3:35**

By love's closest bonds united,          515
as the Lord's own family,
be to serve his name excited,
be to him a fruitful tree.

Too often, we are alienated from the people to whom we should be the closest: family members, friends, spouse or partner. Heavenly Mediator, heal these broken relationships, we pray. Amen.

**Friday, August 24** — Psalm 103:1-5
Judges 7; Luke 19:45-20:8

## Make haste to help me, O Lord, my salvation. Psalm 38:22

> O Master, from the mountain side                581
> make haste to heal these hearts of pain;
> among these restless throngs abide;
> O tread the city's streets again.

**The prayer of faith will save the sick, and the Lord will raise them up. James 5:15**

> O Lord, who through this holy week                348
> did suffer for us all,
> the sick to heal, the lost to seek,
> to raise up them that fall.

There are many in our fellowship and in our community who are sick or lost, divine Physician. Be with those whom we name, and with those we do not know. Lay your hand upon them to bring healing, wholeness and new life. Amen.

**Saturday, August 25** — Psalm 103:6-18
Judges 8; Luke 20:9-19

**Jacob called the place where God had spoken
with him Bethel. Genesis 35:15**

> Lord, speak to me, that I may speak                    646
> in living echoes of your tone.
> As you have sought, so let me seek
> your erring children lost and lone.

**Christ was faithful over God's house as a
son, and we are his house if we hold firm the
confidence and the pride that belong to hope.
Hebrews 3:6**

> We are God's house of living stones,                   512
> built for his own habitation;
> he fills our hearts, his humble thrones,
> granting us life and salvation.
> Yet to this place, an earthly frame,
> we come with thanks to praise his name;
> God grants his people true blessing.

We are your lips, we are your hands, we are your
feet, Lord, but you are the one who gives direction.
Help us to listen as you speak to us, and then to
share that good news with others. In Jesus' name.
Amen.

## Thirteenth Sunday after Pentecost

**Watchword for the Week** — Jesus says, "The words that I have spoken to you are spirit and life." John 6:63

**Sunday, August 26** — Joshua 24:1-2a,14-18; Psalm 34:15-22
Ephesians 6:10-20; John 6:56-69

# Moreover, it is God's gift that all should eat and drink and take pleasure in all their toil. Ecclesiastes 3:13

> Eat and rest at this great feast,                    p206
> then to serve him freely go,
> as it is for pilgrims fit,
> as disciples ought to do.
> We, when Jesus we shall see
> coming in his majesty,
> shall the marriage supper share,
> if we his true followers are.

# Day by day, as they spent much time together in the temple, they broke bread at home and ate their food with glad and generous hearts. Acts 2:46

> Lord Jesus Christ, we humbly pray                    p228
> that we may feast on you today;
> beneath these forms of bread and wine
> enrich us with your grace divine.

Too often we forget that all we have comes from you, Heavenly Provider. For everything you have given us—our food, our life on earth, our eternal life in Heaven—we give you thanks. Amen.

**Monday, August 27** — Psalm 103:19-22
Judges 9:1-33; Luke 20:20-26

**O give thanks to the Lord of lords, who alone does great wonders, for his steadfast love endures forever. Psalm 136:3,4**

The church on earth, in humble strain,     471
exalts the Christ, our Savior,
and sings, "The Lamb for us was slain,
our foe is lost forever;
for Christ has redeemed us with his precious blood
out of ev'ry nation and kindred,
and made us thereby kings and priests unto God.
To him thanksgiving be rendered."

**Every good thing given and every perfect gift is from above, coming down from the Father of lights. James 1:17 (NASB)**

Lord, when you look on us in love,     p188*
at once there falls from God above
a ray of purest pleasure.
Your Word and Spirit, flesh and blood
refresh our souls with heav'nly food.
You are the dearest treasure!
Let your mercy
warn and cheer us!
O, draw near us!
for you teach us
God's own love through
you has reached us.

O God of love, we are in awe that you look on us as your children. We praise your goodness towards us, and we thank you for your constant love. Amen.

**Tuesday, August 28** — Psalm 104:1-9
Judges 9:34-10:18; Luke 20:27-40

**I praised and honored the one who lives forever.
For his sovereignty is an everlasting sovereignty,
and his kingdom endures from generation to
generation. All the inhabitants of the earth are
accounted as nothing. Daniel 4:34-35**

Worship, honor, glory, blessing,                          p1
Lord, we offer unto you;
young and old, your praise expressing,
sing your mercies ever new.
All the saints in heav'n adore you;
we would bow before your throne.
As your angels serve before you,
so on earth your will be done.

**We proclaim Christ the power of God and the
wisdom of God. For God's weakness is stronger
than human strength. 1 Corinthians 1:23-24**

The Father's equal, God the Son,                          471
with him is ever reigning;
you are partaker of his throne,
and all things are sustaining;
both heaven and earth view their Maker as man,
with joy that is past all expression;
O happy, unspeakably happy, who can
in Jesus find life and salvation.

Divine Teacher, we ask your blessing on all
students, teachers, administrators and all those who
have a hand in education. Grant them and all of us
wisdom, learning and understanding. Amen.

**Wednesday, August 29** — Psalm 104:10-18
Judges 11:1-27; Luke 20:41-21:4

## Fools say in their hearts, "There is no God." Psalm 14:1

> We long for mighty signs of God—                    p58*
> cathedral, miracle, and sword,
> his pow'r and glory written plain—
> so none may doubt that he is Lord.

## God chose what is foolish in the world to shame the wise. 1 Corinthians 1:27

> Freedom, wealth, regard and beauty                    715**
> come to nothing good unless—
> gentle children, bound in duty—
> we are blessed with simpleness.

We yearn for proof of your existence, O God, for a clear, unmistakable sign, so we often overlook the many small clues that you are with us. Open our eyes to see the daily reminders of your presence in our lives. Amen.

\*   © by Hermann I. Weinlick

\*\*  © 1994 by Madeleine Forell Marshall

**Thursday, August 30** — Psalm 104:19-23
Judges 11:28-12:15; Luke 21:5-28

## O Lord, do not rebuke me in your anger, or discipline me in your wrath. Psalm 6:1

> He will not always chide;                                546
> he will with patience wait;
> his wrath is ever slow to rise
> and ready to abate.

## Christ died for all, so that those who live might live no longer for themselves, but for him who died and was raised for them. 2 Corinthians 5:15

> Who can condemn, since Christ was dead,               364
> and ever lives to God?
> Now our whole debt is fully paid;
> he saves us by his blood.
> The ransomed hosts in earth and heav'n
> through countless choirs proclaim,
> "He has redeemed us; praise be giv'n
> to God and to the Lamb."

O Lord, we continually fall short of your
expectations of us, and we deserve your anger.
But because your Son died for us, we know only
your love. May we ever live with thanks. Amen.

**Friday, August 31** — Psalm 104:24-30
Judges 13; Luke 21:29-38

**The people who walked in darkness have seen
a great light; those who lived in a land of deep
darkness—on them light has shined. Isaiah 9:2**

> Behold, a great, a heavenly light,                            62r
> from Bethlehem's manger shining bright,
> around those who in darkness dwell,
> the night of evil to dispel.

**For once you were darkness, but now in the
Lord you are light. Live as children of light.
Ephesians 5:8**

> Come, Holy Spirit, come                                       p21
> let your bright beams arise;
> dispel the darkness from our minds,
> and open now our eyes.

The days grow shorter, the time of darkness
approaches. Yet we rejoice, Light of the world,
because we know that when our world is darkest,
you come again to bring hope and salvation.
Shine on us, O Lord. Amen.

**Saturday, September 1 — Psalm 104:31-35**
Judges 14,15; Luke 22:1-13

# I will thank you in the great congregation; in the mighty throng I will praise you. Psalm 35:18

O that with yonder sacred throng                403
we at his feet may fall;
we'll join the everlasting song,
and crown him Lord of all!
We'll join the everlasting song,
and crown him Lord of all!

# Let your light shine before others, so that they may see your good works and give glory to your Father in heaven. Matthew 5:16

O that such may be our union                    673
as thine with the Father is,
and not one of our communion
e'er forsake the path of bliss;
may our light break forth with brightness,
from thy light reflected shine;
thus the world will bear us witness
that we, Lord, are truly thine.

Father, glorify yourself in the midst of your people. Holy Spirit, empower us to live in ways that when others see us, they see Jesus. Lord Jesus, thank you for modeling and perfecting our faith through your life and atoning death. Amen.

## Fourteenth Sunday after Pentecost

**Watchword for the Week** — Let everyone be quick to listen, slow to speak, slow to anger. James 1:19

**Sunday, September 2** — Deuteronomy 4:1-2,6-9; Psalm 15
James 1:17-27; Mark 7:1-8,14-15,21-23

## You shall not make for yourself an image in the form of anything. Deuteronomy 5:8 (NIV)

> Forth in your name, O Lord, I go        638
> my daily labor to pursue—
> you only, Lord, resolved to know
> in all I think or speak or do.

## No one has ever seen God; if we love one another, God lives in us, and his love is perfected in us. 1 John 4:12

> Blessed are the pure in heart,        584
> for they shall see their God.
> The secret of the Lord is theirs;
> their soul is Christ's abode.

Help us keep our eyes upon you, Lord Jesus, so nothing can come between us. Empower us to love one another and let your Spirit speak through us. Your love is perfect and far above the idols of our own making. Come live in us, gracious God, for your glory and for the benefit of your people. Amen.

**Monday, September 3** — Psalm 105:1-7
Judges 16,17; Luke 22:14-23

# I will remove the heart of stone from their flesh and give them a heart of flesh, so that they may keep my ordinances and obey them. Ezekiel 11:19,20

I, the Lord of snow and rain,　　　　　　641*
I have born my people's pain.
I have wept for love of them,
they turn away.
I will break their hearts of stone,
give them hearts for love alone.
I will speak my word to them.
Whom shall I send?

# Now that you have purified your souls by your obedience to the truth so that you have genuine mutual love, love one another deeply from the heart. 1 Peter 1:22

Grant, Lord, that with thy direction,　　　673
"Love each other," we comply,
aiming with unfeigned affection
thy love to exemplify;
let our mutual love be glowing;
thus the world will plainly see
that we, as on one stem growing,
living branches are in thee.

Come replace our hearts with whole hearts devoted to you, Lord Jesus. Take away our love of sinning and burn away the impurities of our minds. Help us bring every thought, word and deed into captivity through our mutual love and ministry. Amen.

Tuesday, September 4 — Psalm 105:8-15
Judges 18; Luke 22:24-38

**The earth is full of the steadfast love of the Lord.
Psalm 33:5**

> We covenant in church and home                    p121
> this peace to show each other,
> to represent your steadfast love
> as sister and as brother.
> O, may we through each other know
> your grace which fails us never,
> and find at last our true abode
> within your house forever. Amen.

**You know the generous act of our Lord Jesus
Christ, that though he was rich, yet for your
sakes he became poor, so that by his poverty you
might become rich. 2 Corinthians 8:9**

> Lord, be ever my protector;                    568
> with me stay, all the day,
> ever my director.
> Holy, holy, holy giver
> of all good, life and food,
> reign adored forever.

How unshakeable are your ways of love and truth,
O God. The earth abounds with your goodness and
grace. As beggars we come, as kings we depart;
richly blessed and filled with all good things from
your hand. Amen.

Wednesday, September 5 — Psalm 105:16-22
Judges 19; Luke 22:39-51

## Noah did all that God commanded him. Genesis 6:22

God, grant me strength to do            615
with ready heart and willing,
whatever you command,
my calling here fulfilling;
and do it when I ought,
with zeal and joyfulness;
and bless the work I've wrought,
for you must give success.

## You were taught, with regard to your former way of life, to put off your old self, which is being corrupted by its deceitful desires; to be made new in the attitude of your minds. Ephesians 4:22-23 (NIV)

And now, O God, our Father,           433
we pledge ourselves anew
by work and prayer and worship
to serve your kingdom too.
With grateful hearts we praise you
and pray, O Lord, that we
who are your church at present,
may serve you faithfully.

Give us the courage to obey you, Lord, even when others don't understand. Wash away the filth of this world in us, refreshing us with newness of life and purpose. As we put away our old selves, renew our minds by your presence and power, living joyfully in your grace. Amen.

**Thursday, September 6** — Psalm 105:23-36
Judges 20:1-31; Luke 22:52-62

## The angel of the Lord encamps around those who fear him, and delivers them. Psalm 34:7

You have cancelled my transgression,                    p202
Jesus, by your precious blood;
may I find therein salvation,
happiness, and peace with God;
and since you, for sinners suff'ring
on the cross were made an off'ring,
from all sin deliver me,
that I wholly yours may be.

## Suddenly an angel of the Lord appeared and a light shone in the cell. He tapped Peter on the side and woke him, saying, "Get up quickly." And the chains fell off his wrists. Acts 12:7

Blessings abound where'er he reigns,                    404
the pris'ners leap to lose their chains,
the weary find eternal rest,
and all who suffer want are blessed.

Mighty Deliverer, protect us in our hour of need.
Bring us out of bondage and into peace. Break the
chains of our sin and call us to action as we witness
to your power and enjoy the freedom of life in you.
Redeem our trials so others may find faith in theirs.
Amen.

**Friday, September 7** — Psalm 105:37-45
Judges 20:32-21:25; Luke 22:63-71

## In the path of your judgments, O Lord, we wait for you. Isaiah 26:8

Still will I wait, O Lord, on you,                    721
till in your light I see anew;
till you in my behalf appear,
to banish ev'ry doubt and fear.

## When we are judged by the Lord, we are disciplined so that we may not be condemned along with the world. 1 Corinthians 11:32

Rejoice in glorious hope;                    372
for Christ, the Judge, shall come
to gather all his saints
to their eternal home.
We soon shall hear the archangel's voice;
the trump of God shall sound, rejoice!

When you see fit to judge us, God, help us to remember your love and grace. Call to our minds the redemptive purposes of your discipline and the promise of eternal life. Thank you for training us so we shall forever be your children. Amen.

**Saturday, September 8** — Psalm 106:1-5
Ruth 1; Luke 23:1-12

**For me it is good to be near God; I have made
the Lord God my refuge, to tell of all your works.
Psalm 73:28**

> We hail you as our Savior, Lord,     267
> our refuge and our great reward;
> without your grace we waste away
> like flow'rs that wither and decay.

**Those who serve well gain a good standing for
themselves and great boldness in the faith that is
in Christ Jesus. 1 Timothy 3:13**

> In all our world—     629*
>     in fact'ry, shop or schoolroom,
> in kitchen, boardroom, market, office, mill,
> we each must make our witness
>     known with boldness —
> God's Spirit works through mortal mind and will.

Let us be strong and courageous as we witness to
your truth and grace, O God. No matter where
we find ourselves, may we always abide in you.
Jesus, as you went boldly to the cross, send us with
confidence into the everyday places of life. Grow
our faith as we serve and share. Amen.

### Fifteenth Sunday after Pentecost

**Watchword for the Week** — I will praise the Lord as long as I live; I will sing praises to my God all my life long. Psalm 146:2

**Sunday, September 9** — Isaiah 35:4-7a; Psalm 146
James 2:1-10,(11-13),14-17; Mark 7:24-37

## "I will surely save you, and you shall not fall by the sword; but you shall have your life as a prize of war, because you have trusted in me," says the Lord. Jeremiah 39:18

Make me a captive, Lord,                604
and then I shall be free;
force me to render up my sword,
and I shall conquer'r be.
I sink in life's alarms
when by myself I stand;
imprison me within your arms,
and strong shall be my hand.

## Christ says, "Everyone who lives and believes in me will never die." John 11:26

Here is a pasture, rich and never failing,                593
here living waters in abundance flow;
none can conceive the grace with them prevailing,
who Jesus' shepherd-voice obey and know.
He banishes all fear and strife,
and leads them gently on to everlasting life.

Lord Jesus, you have saved us from sin and unbelief. Set us free from doubt through simple faith and the joy of eternal life. What an awesome truth that by your death we may forever live. Hallelujah! Amen.

**Monday, September 10** — Psalm 106:6-12
Ruth 2,3; Luke 23:13-31

## He who keeps Israel will neither slumber nor sleep. Psalm 121:4

What God's almighty pow'r has made,                    537
in mercy he is keeping;
by morning glow or evening shade
his eye is never sleeping.
And where he rules in kingly might,
there all is just and all is right:
to God all praise and glory!

## The night is far gone, the day is near. Let us then lay aside the works of darkness and put on the armor of light. Romans 13:12

Stand up, stand up for Jesus,                          752
stand in his strength alone;
the arm of flesh will fail you,
you dare not trust your own.
Put on the gospel armor,
each piece put on with prayer;
where duty calls, or danger,
be ever faithful there.

By the light of day we serve you who never slumbers, O God. Shaking off the darkness of sin and doubt, we clothe ourselves with your Holy Spirit. May we never grow weary in our ministry, fighting the powers and principalities that would lull us into the sleepiness of indifference. Equip your saints, Lord Jesus, for the battles ahead. Amen.

**Tuesday, September 11** — Psalm 106:13-23
Ruth 4; Luke 23:32-43

## Even before a word is on my tongue, O Lord, you know it completely. Psalm 139:4

Have we trials and temptations?                    743
Is there trouble anywhere?
We should never be discouraged;
take it to the Lord in prayer!
Can we find a friend so faithful
who will all our sorrows share?
Jesus knows our ev'ry weakness;
take it to the Lord in prayer!

## The good works of some are clearly evident, and those that are otherwise cannot be hidden. 1 Timothy 5:25 (NKJV)

The task your wisdom has assigned                  638
here let me cheerfully fulfill,
in all my work your presence find
and prove your good and perfect will.

Lord, in you alone we are an unstoppable force. Even when we think you are far away, you are so close. Even when we have hidden from you or run away, you are always there. We will not deny you any longer, but spread the word of your glory and goodness. Let our works magnify you among the peoples. Amen.

**Wednesday, September 12** — Psalm 106:24-31
1 Samuel 1:1-2:11; Luke 23:44-56

**The steadfast love of the Lord is from everlasting to everlasting on those who fear him, and his righteousness to children's children, to those who keep his covenant. Psalm 103:17-18**

> Thus may our lips your praises sound,                519
> our hearts in steadfast hope abound;
> till you to heaven our steps shall bring
> where saints and angels hail you King.

**Continue securely established and steadfast in the faith, without shifting from the hope promised by the gospel that you heard, which has been proclaimed to every creature under heaven. Colossians 1:23**

> Consecrate me now to thy service, Lord,                607
> by the pow'r of grace divine;
> let my soul look up with a steadfast hope
> and my will be lost in thine.

What a treasure it is to love one another, Lord, just as you have loved us. May that love be shared from generation to generation among your people. Cast aside our fear and doubt, proclaiming through us the good news of hope to all whom you put in our path. Amen.

**Thursday, September 13** — Psalm 106:32-39
1 Samuel 2:12-36; Luke 24:1-12

**The days of our life are seventy years, or perhaps eighty, if we are strong; even then their span is only toil and trouble. Psalm 90:10**

> Jesus, yourself to us reveal.                          p204
> Grant that we may not only feel
> some drawings of your grace,
> but in communion with you live,
> and daily from your death derive
> the needful strength to run our race.

**What can be seen is temporary, but what cannot be seen is eternal. 2 Corinthians 4:18**

> He comes to us as one unknown,                          478*
> a breath unseen, unheard;
> as though within a heart of stone,
> or shriveled seed in darkness sown,
> a pulse of being stirred,
> a pulse of being stirred.

Our love for you, Lord Jesus, shall never die; nor shall we fall again under the curse of the enemy. Though now we see only in part, one day we shall see and know in the fullness of eternity. Through our belief, we live now and forever in your sustaining presence. Amen.

**Friday, September 14** — Psalm 106:40-48
1 Samuel 3,4; Luke 24:13-27

**Surely his salvation is at hand for those who fear him. Steadfast love and faithfulness will meet; righteousness and peace will kiss each other. Psalm 85:9,10**

Blessed Jesus, at your word                    558
we are gathered all to hear you;
let our hearts and souls be stirred
now to seek and love and fear you;
by your teachings true and holy,
drawn from earth to love you solely.

**Therefore, beloved, while you are waiting for these things, strive to be found by him at peace, without spot or blemish. 2 Peter 3:14**

Finish, then, your new creation,                    p218
pure and spotless, gracious Lord;
let us see your great salvation
perfectly in you restored.
Changed from glory into glory,
till in heav'n we take our place,
till we sing before th'Almighty
lost in wonder, love, and praise.

You are our salvation, righteousness and peace, O Christ. While we await your coming, fulfill in us your holiness so others may see and know that you are God. The time is now for faith and a holy fear that binds us resolutely to you. O spotless Lamb, take away the sin in us as you have taken away the sin of the world. Amen.

**Saturday, September 15** — Psalm 107:1-9
1 Samuel 5:1-7:1; Luke 24:28-35

## The Lord lives! Blessed be my rock. Psalm 18:46

Blessed name! the rock on which we build,                    487
our shield and resting place,
our never-failing comfort, filled
with blessings of his grace.
O Jesus, Shepherd, Guardian, Friend,
our Prophet, Priest, and King,
our Lord, our Life, our Way, our End,
accept the praise we bring.

## Come to Jesus Christ, a living stone, though rejected by mortals yet chosen and precious in God's sight. 1 Peter 2:4

Christ is our cornerstone,                                    517
on him alone we build;
with his true saints alone
the courts of heav'n are filled;
on his great love our hopes we place
of present grace and joys above.

Lead us to the rock that is higher than us, O Lord!
Let our lives be forever in you. We come to you
Jesus, our foundation and strength. Upon you we
will build our lives. May we be steadfast in faith
and the assurance of life unending. Amen.

### Sixteenth Sunday after Pentecost
### Ministers' Covenant Day†

**Watchword for the Week** — Jesus asks, "But who do you say that I am?" Mark 8:29

**Sunday, September 16** — Isaiah 50:4-9a; Psalm 116:1-9
James 3:1-12; Mark 8:27-38

**The Lord says, "I desire steadfast love and not sacrifice, the knowledge of God rather than burnt-offerings." Hosea 6:6**

> To God and to the Lamb I will sing, I will sing,     328
> to God and to the Lamb I will sing!
> To God and to the Lamb, who is the great "I Am,"
> while millions join the theme, I will sing, I will sing;
> while millions join the theme, I will sing!

**"To love him with all the heart, and with all the understanding, and with all the strength," and "to love one's neighbor as oneself,"—this is much more important than all whole burnt offerings and sacrifices. Mark 12:33**

> Did you not bid us love you, God and King,     490
> love you with all our heart and strength and mind?
> I see the cross—there teach my heart to cling.
> O let me seek you and O let me find!

May our love for you be without reservation, O Lord. Immovable and unshaken, let our faith in you ever be. We covenant again to follow and to love you and one another. Let our lives be an offering sweetened by your grace and enriched by your ministry among us. Amen.

---

† During a synodal conference in London, Jesus Christ was recognized as chief elder of the Brethren's Church. The day is observed as a covenanting day for servants of the church.

**Monday, September 17** — Psalm 107:10-16
1 Samuel 7:2-8:22; Luke 24:36-53

## When the wicked turn away from the wickedness they have committed and do what is lawful and right, they shall save their life. Ezekiel 18:27

Seek the Lord, whose willing presence            780*
moves your heart to make appeal.
Turn from wickedness and evil;
God will pardon, cleanse, and heal.

## Regard the patience of our Lord as salvation. 2 Peter 3:15

Teach me your patience; share with me            735
a closer, dearer company.
In work that keeps faith sweet and strong,
in trust that triumphs over wrong.

How patient you are with us, O God. Even while we were yet sinners, your salvation was won according to the fullness of time through our repentance and faith. Help us to be patient with one another and with the world, knowing that by your grace others will turn away from evil and come to you, good Lord. Amen.

**Tuesday, September 18** — Psalm 107:17-22
1 Samuel 9; John 1:1-13

**Let us come into his presence with thanksgiving;
let us make a joyful noise to him with songs of
praise! For the Lord is a great God. Psalm 95:2-3**

Thanks we give and adoration                    559
for your gospel's joyful sound.
May the fruits of your salvation
in our hearts and lives abound.
Ever faithful, ever faithful
to your truth may we be found.

**Jesus said, "Give to God what is God's."
Mark 12:17 (NIV)**

We give you but your own                    657
in any gifts we bring;
all that we have is yours alone,
a trust from you, our King.

You alone are good, O God. We give you all
thanksgiving and praise! You alone are great, O
Christ. We bow before you in humble adoration!
May the joyous sound of grateful hearts never end
as the strains of truth and trust resound in you, our
Savior. Amen.

Wednesday, September 19 — Psalm 107:23-32
1 Samuel 10; John 1:14-28

## I the Lord will speak the word that I speak, and it will be fulfilled. Ezekiel 12:25

> In his temple now behold him,      314
> see the long-expected Lord;
> ancient prophets had foretold him,
> God has now fulfilled his word.
> Now to praise him, his redeemed
> shall break forth with one accord.

## The centurion said to Jesus, "Only speak the word, and my servant will be healed." Matthew 8:8

> Plenteous grace with thee is found,      724
> grace to cover all my sin;
> let the healing streams abound;
> make and keep me pure within.
> Thou of life the fountain art,
> freely let me take of thee;
> spring thou up within my heart,
> rise to all eternity.

Speak Lord, your servants are listening. Let your voice resound, fulfilling all your purposes in the world today. Just as you spoke light into darkness and healing into pain, speak your word of truth again to an unbelieving world. Whisper your compassion and mercy, giving us ears of faith to hear. Amen.

**Thursday, September 20** — Psalm 107:33-43
1 Samuel 11,12; John 1:29-42

**Out of Zion, the perfection of beauty, God shines forth. Our God comes and does not keep silence. Psalm 50:2-3**

> Hushed was the evening hymn,                    609
> the temple courts were dark,
> the lamp was burning dim
> before the sacred ark,
> when suddenly a voice divine
> rang through the silence of the shrine.

**Jesus was baptized by John in the Jordan. And just as he was coming up out of the water, he saw the heavens torn apart and the Spirit descending like a dove on him. And a voice came from heaven, "You are my Son, the Beloved; with you I am well pleased." Mark 1:9-11**

> There as the Lord, baptized and praying          315*
> rose from the stream, the sinless one,
> a voice was heard from heaven saying,
> "This is my own beloved Son."
> There as the Father's word was spoken,
> not in the pow'r of wind and flame,
> but of his love and peace the token,
> seen as a dove, the Spirit came.

Lord God, you shine forth your word and call us to express ourselves in worship to you. Cleanse us and bless us as we offer our lives in dedication to you. We love you Lord and are grateful for your unconditional love. We lift our voices to you and sing your wondrous grace. Your word amazes us, verse after verse baptizing us into your truth. With a thankful heart, we pray. Amen.

**Friday, September 21** — Psalm 108:1-5
1 Samuel 13; John 1:43-51

## You are my hope; O Lord God, You are my confidence from my youth. Psalm 71:5 (NASB)

If you but trust in God to guide you                    712
and place your confidence in him,
you'll find him always there beside you
to give you hope and strength within;
for those who trust God's changeless love
build on the rock that will not move.

## Guard the good treasure entrusted to you, with the help of the Holy Spirit living in us. 2 Timothy 1:14

O let that faith which you have taught                    703
be treasured in our breast,
the evidence of unseen joys,
the substance of our rest.

Lord, we place all our trust in you. Thank you for guidance in days past and for the help of your Spirit in the days to come. As we live according to the treasure of your truth, may your word be a light unto our feet and a light unto our path. Amen.

**Saturday, September 22** — Psalm 108:6-13
1 Samuel 14:1-40; John 2:1-11

## The Lord is my stronghold and my refuge, my savior; you save me from violence. 2 Samuel 22:3

Now we bring ourselves to you;                    741
cleanse us, Lord, we humbly pray;
undeserving though we be,
draw us closer ev'ry day.
Lord, our refuge, hope, and strength!
Keep, O keep us safe from harm,
shield us through our earthly life
by your everlasting arm.

## Be strong in the Lord and in the strength of his power. Ephesians 6:10

I have no help but yours, nor do I need              421
another arm but yours to lean upon;
it is enough, O Lord, enough indeed;
my strength is in your might, your might alone.

Strength and righteousness flow from your throne,
O God! Salvation and power abound in your
presence. We are weak and frail apart from you.
Be ever near us as we travel the perilous road of
life. In the knowledge of your saving grace and the
stronghold of your steadfast love let us live forever,
O Christ. Amen.

## Seventeenth Sunday after Pentecost

**Watchword for the Week** — Jesus says, "Whoever wants to be first must be last of all and servant of all." Mark 9:35

**Sunday, September 23** — Jeremiah 11:18-20; Psalm 54 James 3:13-4:3,7-8a; Mark 9:30-37

## See, I am the Lord, the God of all flesh; is anything too hard for me? Jeremiah 32:27

> May the God of hope go with us ev'ry day,    708
> filling all our lives with love and joy and peace.
> May the God of justice speed us on our way,
> bringing light and hope to ev'ry land and race.
> Praying, let us work for peace, singing,
>    share our joy with all.
> Working for a world that's new, faithful
>    when we hear Christ's call.

## "I am the Alpha and the Omega," says the Lord God, who is and who was and who is to come, the Almighty. Revelation 1:8

> Of the Father's love begotten    483
> ere the worlds began to be,
> he is Alpha and Omega—
> he the source, the ending he
> of the things that are, that have been,
> and that future years shall see
> evermore and evermore.

Father in heaven, we recognize that you are the Alpha and Omega, you are the beginning and the end. We also know that you have no ending and will be with us forever. You who are, who were and are to come, be all power and glory in Christ our Almighty Savior. Amen.

Monday, September 24 — Psalm 109:1-7
1 Samuel 14:41-15:23; John 2:12-25

## Just like the clay in the potter's hand, so are you in my hand. Jeremiah 18:6 (NASB)

His sov'reign pow'r without our aid                    455
formed us of clay and gave us breath;
and when like wand'ring sheep we strayed,
he saved us from the pow'r of death.

## It is God who is at work in you, enabling you both to will and to work for his good pleasure. Philippians 2:13

All our knowledge, sense and sight                    558
lie in deepest darkness shrouded,
till your Spirit breaks our night
with the beams of truth unclouded;
you alone to God can win us;
you must work all good within us.

Work in us, dear Lord. Shape us into the vessel of
your will as we do your works of grace. Bend us into
your likeness, Lord Jesus and may the Holy Spirit
complete in us all your gifts. Amen.

**Tuesday, September 25** — Psalm 109:8-20
1 Samuel 15:24-16:13; John 3:1-15

## My thoughts are not your thoughts, nor are your ways my ways, says the Lord. Isaiah 55:8

> "For my thoughts are not like your thoughts,"      780*
> says the Lord, "nor your ways mine.
> Farther still than earth from heaven
> are things human from divine."

## Jesus said to Simon and Andrew, "Follow me and I will make you fish for people." And immediately they left their nets and followed him. Mark 1:17-18

> Two fishermen, who lived along                      611**
> the Sea of Galilee,
> stood by the shore to cast their nets
> into an ageless sea.
> Now Jesus watched them from afar,
> then called them each by name;
> it changed their lives, these simple men—
> they'd never be the same.

Help us to continue to follow you, O Lord. Restore our hearts and renew our minds so that each action and motive may be of service in spreading your good news. Bless the casting of our nets upon the waters of this world, bringing to shore the bounty and beauty of your will. Amen.

**Wednesday, September 26** — Psalm 109:21-31
1 Samuel 16:14-17:31; John 3:16-26

**Therefore I will allot him a portion with the great, and he shall divide the spoil with the strong; because he poured out himself to death. Isaiah 53:12**

And can it be that I should gain                    773
an int'rest in the Savior's blood?
Died he for me, who caused his pain—
for me, who caused his bitter death?
Amazing love! How can it be
that you, my Lord, should die for me?
Amazing love! How can it be
that you, my Lord, should die for me?

**Christ says, "All things have been handed over to me by my Father; and no one knows the Son except the Father, and no one knows the Father except the Son and anyone to whom the Son chooses to reveal him." Matthew 11:27**

One our Master, one alone,                    525
none but Christ as Lord we own;
"brethren of his law" are we—
"As I loved you, so love ye."
Branches we in Christ, the Vine,
living by his life divine;
as the Father with the Son,
so, in Christ, we all are one.

You are Lord over all, O Christ! We know you are the only begotten, sent to show us the Father. Without you we would forever wander. All praise to you who gave himself for us by the will of God in the power of the Holy Spirit. Amen.

**Thursday, September 27** — Psalm 110
1 Samuel 17:32-58; John 3:27-36

## Give us life, and we will call on your name. Psalm 80:18

> Good news is ours to tell!                    p138*
> Let no one fail to hear!
> God gives us life; God conquers death!
> There's nothing we must fear.

## Jesus said to Bartimaeus, "Go; your faith has made you well." Immediately he regained his sight and followed him on the way. Mark 10:52

> Savior, you came to give                       380
> those who in darkness live
> healing and sight,
> health to the sick in mind,
> sight to the inward blind:
> now to all humankind
> let there be light!

Into the world we go, Lord, telling of your tender mercy and healing power. Life is granted by your death alone—empower us to share what you have done. Like people with a new lease on life, let us dance and sing to you our king. Alleluia! Amen.

---

*   © 1980 by Jane Parker Huber

**Friday, September 28** — Psalm 111
1 Samuel 18:1-19:7; John 4:1-26

## He does not deal with us according to our sins, nor repay us according to our iniquities. Psalm 103:10

He pardons all our sins,                                        546
prolongs our feeble breath;
he heals all our infirmities
and ransoms us from death.

## In this is love, not that we loved God but that he loved us and sent his Son to be the atoning sacrifice for our sins. 1 John 4:10

To God be the glory—great things he has done!   550
So loved he the world that he gave us his Son,
who yielded his life an atonement for sin,
and opened the lifegate that all may go in.

How can we begin to understand your grace
Lord Jesus? May we never seek to earn anything
from you, but simply rest in your finished work
of salvation. Thank you for paying the price so
that we might live and move and have our being.
Amen.

**Saturday, September 29 — Psalm 112**
1 Samuel 19:8-20:17; John 4:27-38

## Even the stork in the heavens knows its times; and the turtledove, swallow, and crane observe the time of their coming; but my people do not know the ordinance of the Lord. Jeremiah 8:7

Praise the Lord! You heav'ns, adore him,          454
praise him, angels in the height;
sun and moon, rejoice before him;
praise him, all you stars and light.
Praise the Lord! For he has spoken;
worlds his mighty voice obeyed;
laws which never shall be broken
for their guidance he has made.

## Jesus said, "Why do you call me 'Lord, Lord,' and do not do what I tell you?" Luke 6:46

To you our vows with sweet accord,          677
head of your church, we pay;
we and our house will serve you, Lord;
your word we will obey.
Grant us and all our children grace
in word and deed your name to praise,
and in each family, your will
and purpose to fulfill.

How often do we give mere lip service to you rather than simply obeying and trusting you, Lord Jesus? Before you come in power and glory, grant us the wisdom to seek your face and to do your will. Serving you all the days of life, may we be found ready on that great day. Amen.

## Eighteenth Sunday after Pentecost

**Watchword for the Week** — The precepts of the Lord are right, rejoicing the heart; the commandment of the Lord is clear, enlightening the eyes. Psalm 19:8

**Sunday, September 30** — Numbers 11:4-6,10-16,24-29; Psalm 19:7-14 James 5:13-20; Mark 9:38-50

## Do not, O Lord, withhold your mercy from me; let your steadfast love and your faithfulness keep me safe forever. Psalm 40:11

O God, in whom our trust we place,                    509
we thank you for your word of grace;
help us its precepts to obey
till we shall live in endless day.

## The Lord is faithful; he will strengthen you and guard you from the evil one. 2 Thessalonians 3:3

O most wholesome balm of healing,                    419
all our debt to sins repealing,
feed us; set us free from evil;
lead us in your light primeval.

Jesus, you have promised to never leave nor forsake us. Earnestly we call out to you for the faith and courage needed to walk in your wondrous light. Bless us with your mercy and love, fulfilling in us the promise we made to you long ago. Amen.

**Monday, October 1** — Psalm 113
1 Samuel 20:18-21:9; John 4:39-42

## I believe that I shall see the goodness of the Lord in the land of the living. Psalm 27:13

> We come to you, our Father,                                    433
> with thoughts of thanks and praise,
> for your abundant mercy,
> and all your love and grace;
> we praise you for your goodness
> and for your loving care,
> for daily show'rs of blessing,
> for answers to our prayers.

## See, now is the acceptable time; see, now is the day of salvation! 2 Corinthians 6:2

> And now, O God, our Father,                                    433
> we pledge ourselves anew
> by work and prayer and worship
> to serve your kingdom too.
> With grateful hearts we praise you
> and pray, O Lord, that we
> who are your church at present,
> may serve you faithfully.

We thank you for your goodness, mercy, love
and grace. May we embody our gratitude in our
interactions with others! How may we and how
have we served you today? Grant us an ever-present
sense of gratitude that we may respond faithfully to
the love shown us in Christ. Amen.

**Tuesday, October 2** — Psalm 114
1 Samuel 21:10-22:23; John 4:43-54

**The Lord has sent me to proclaim the year of the Lord's favor, and the day of vengeance of our God. Isaiah 61:1-2**

Lord, for thy coming us prepare;                    p8
may we to meet thee without fear,
at all times ready be;
in faith and love preserve us sound;
O let us day and night be found
waiting with joy to welcome thee.

**When Jesus came to Nazareth, he went to the synagogue on the Sabbath day, as was his custom. Then he began to say to them, "Today this scripture has been fulfilled in your hearing." Luke 4:16,21**

Hail to the Lord's Anointed,                    p49
great David's greater Son!
hail in the time appointed
his reign on earth begun!
He comes to break oppression
to set the captive free,
to take away transgression,
and rule in equity.

God with us, we are not often mindful of the present moment, unaware of your presence or the breaking forth of your Kingdom. Let us once again be reminded of the life-changing gift of your incarnation; may we live as people transformed by your love. Amen.

**Wednesday, October 3** — Psalm 115:1-8
1 Samuel 23; John 5:1-15

## O Lord, be gracious to me; heal me, for I have sinned against you. Psalm 41:4

> Lord God, with shame I now confess                    p32
> I've turned away from you;
> forgive me all my sin today,
> my heart and soul renew.

## Then some people came, bringing to Jesus a paralyzed man, carried by four of them. When Jesus saw their faith, he said to the paralytic, "Son, your sins are forgiven." Mark 2:3,5

> Father, now your sinful child                          779
> through your love is reconciled.
> By your pard'ning grace I live;
> daily still I cry, forgive.

We pause now to become aware of the many ways in which we sin, both by our actions and inactions. Forgive us, heal us and grant us your peace. In Christ's name. Amen.

**Thursday, October 4** — Psalm 115:9-18
1 Samuel 24:1-25:17; John 5:16-30

## The Lord was with Joseph; and whatever he did, the Lord made it prosper. Genesis 39:23

Praise to the Lord, who will prosper your work      530
  and defend you;
surely his goodness and mercy
  shall daily attend you.
Ponder anew
what the almighty can do
if with his love he befriend you.

## Paul wrote: I planted, Apollos watered, but God gave the growth. 1 Corinthians 3:6

Father, we praise you;                              535*
Jesus, we love you;
Spirit, we thank you,
for these new days;
help us to know, Lord;
help us to grow, Lord;
help us to sow, Lord,
your love always.

You are with us, Lord, and again this day we pledge our love and commitment to you. We pray our service may bear fruit to your name's glory. Amen.

* © 1993 by C. Daniel Crews

**Friday, October 5** — Psalm 116:1-7
1 Samuel 25:18-44; John 5:31-47

## The Lord has made his salvation known and revealed his righteousness to the nations. Psalm 98:2 (NIV)

Your majesty, how vast it is,                     471
and how immense the glory,
which you, O Jesus, do possess;
the heav'ns proclaim your story;
the legions of angels exalt your great name,
your glory and might are transcendent;
and thousands of thousands your praises proclaim,
upon you gladly dependent.

## Let it be known to you then that this salvation of God has been sent to the Gentiles; they will listen. Acts 28:28

But not for us alone this news                    543
was brought by Christ our Lord.
'Twas meant for all the world to hear
and thus with one accord
with all God's children everywhere
his name and sign with pride we bear.
To us, to us, this task is giv'n:
to spread God's word. Amen.

You call us all, Christ, and we hear your voice.
We praise you, we thank you, we rejoice in your
name. Strengthen us, embolden us and inspire us to
share your good news beyond our church walls. In
Christ's name. Amen.

Saturday, October 6 — Psalm 116:8-14
1 Samuel 26,27; John 6:1-15

**Declare this with a shout of joy, proclaim it, send it forth to the end of the earth; say, "The Lord has redeemed his servant Jacob!" Isaiah 48:20**

> O my soul, bless God, the Father;                     458
> all within me bless his name;
> bless the Father, and forget not
> all his mercies to proclaim.

**God was pleased to have all his fullness dwell in him, and through him to reconcile to himself all things, whether things on earth or things in heaven, by making peace through his blood, shed on the cross. Colossians 1:19-20 (NIV)**

> Proclaim to ev'ry people, tongue, and nation     618
> that God, in whom they live and move, is love;
> tell how he stooped to save his lost creation,
> and died on earth that we might live in love.
> Publish glad tidings, tidings of peace,
> tidings of Jesus, redemption, and release.

Great and loving God, you bring us redemption and reconciliation and we respond in joy to your great faithfulness. Thousand, thousand thanks to thee, dear Lord. Amen.

### Nineteenth Sunday after Pentecost

**Watchword for the Week** — I will proclaim your name to my brothers and sisters, in the midst of the congregation I will praise you. Hebrews 2:12

**Sunday, October 7** — Genesis 2:18-24; Psalm 8
Hebrews 1:1-4,2:5-12; Mark 10:2-16

## God has power to help or to overthrow.
2 Chronicles 25:8

> Lord of all being, throned afar,                                   p159
> your glory flames from sun and star;
> center and soul of ev'ry sphere,
> yet to each loving heart how near!

## You say, "Today or tomorrow we will go to such and such a town and spend a year there, doing business and making money." Yet you do not even know what tomorrow will bring.
James 4:13-14

> Abide with me; fast falls the eventide;                          807
> the darkness deepens; Lord, with me abide.
> When other helpers fail and comforts flee,
> help of the helpless, O abide with me.

Gracious God, we do not know what tomorrow may bring. Grant us the comfort of your presence, and the faith that you are with us unfailingly. In the name of your precious Son we pray. Amen.

**Monday, October 8** — Psalm 116:15-19
1 Samuel 28,29; John 6:16-24

**If you will only obey the Lord your God: Blessed shall you be when you come in, and blessed shall you be when you go out. Deuteronomy 28:1,6**

> Upon your precepts and your ways                    510
> my heart will meditate with awe;
> your word shall be my chief delight,
> and I will not forget your law.

**Let anyone with ears to hear listen! Mark 4:9**

> In simple trust like theirs who heard,              739
> beside the Syrian sea,
> the gracious calling of the Lord,
> let us, like them, without a word
> rise up and follow thee.

Obedience, trust, following your lead: all these are based on studying your Word and listening for your voice. Ever-present God, still our busy minds that we may hear your voice today. Amen.

**Tuesday, October 9** — Psalm 117
1 Samuel 30,31; John 6:25-42

## I will sing to the Lord, for he has triumphed gloriously. Exodus 15:1

Sing praise to God who reigns above,                537
the God of all creation,
the God of pow'r, the God of love,
the God of our salvation.
My soul with comfort rich he fills,
and ev'ry grief he gently stills:
to God all praise and glory!

## He destined us for adoption as his children through Jesus Christ, according to the good pleasure of his will, to the praise of his glorious grace. Ephesians 1:5-6

Lord, your praise we sing,                          542*
our glad thanks we bring,
for your favor, gracious Savior.
Lord, your praise we sing.

Too often we are blinded by mindless focus on the tasks and routines we have set for ourselves. Let us stop now and pause in gratitude, for we are your beloved children through the grace and mercy of Jesus Christ. Blessed be your name! Amen.

**Wednesday, October 10** — Psalm 118:1-9
2 Samuel 1; John 6:43-51

**You shall not pervert the justice due to your poor in their lawsuits. Exodus 23:6**

When the church of Jesus                              651*
shuts its outer door,
lest the roar of traffic
drown the voice of prayer:
may our prayers, Lord, make us
ten times more aware
that the world we banish
is our Christian care.

**Whatever is true, whatever is honorable, whatever is just... think about these things. Philippians 4:8**

Minds to think and hearts to love—                   649
God's good gifts to me and you;
minds and hearts he gave to us
to help each other the whole day through.

What is just, true and honorable in your eyes, O God? Are we doing all we can to see and serve the least of these in our midst? Transform us to love and serve you and others this day, compassionate One, with our full hearts and minds. Amen.

**Thursday, October 11** — Psalm 118:10-14
2 Samuel 2; John 6:52-59

## Wash your heart clean of wickedness so that you may be saved. How long shall your evil schemes lodge within you? Jeremiah 4:14

O God of grace, we come to you                    750
with broken, contrite hearts;
give what your eye delights to view,
truth in the inward parts.

## Do you not know that a little yeast leavens the whole batch of dough? Clean out the old yeast so that you may be a new batch, as you really are unleavened. 1 Corinthians 5:6-7

O Breath of Love, come, breathe within us,        p47
renewing thought and will and heart.
Come, love of Christ, afresh to win us;
revive your church in ev'ry part.

God of grace and hope, lead us to look within and confess the ways we fall short of your glory and your call. Forgive and renew us that we may rise to serve you faithfully. Amen.

**Friday, October 12 — Psalm 118:15-21**
2 Samuel 3:1-34; John 6:60-71

**I, the Lord your God, hold your right hand; it is I who say to you, "Do not fear, I will help you." Isaiah 41:13**

> "Fear not, I am with you; O be not dismayed,     709
> for I am your God and will still give you aid;
> I'll strengthen you, help you and cause you to stand
> upheld by my righteous, omnipotent hand.

**Jesus took her by the hand and said to her, "Talitha cum," which means, "Little girl, get up!" Mark 5:41**

> Stretch forth your hand, our health restore,     267
> and make us rise to fall no more;
> O let your face upon us shine
> and fill the world with love divine.

Great Physician, you speak to us in many ways, bringing both comfort and challenge. Healing God, comfort us, heal us and encourage us. May we share your blessing with others this day. Amen.

**Saturday, October 13** — Psalm 118:22-29
2 Samuel 3:35-5:16; John 7:1-13

**I am going to gather them from the farthest parts of the earth, among them the blind and the lame, those with child and those in labor, together; a great company, they shall return here. Jeremiah 31:8**

> O Master, from the mountain side          581
> make haste to heal these hearts of pain;
> among these restless throngs abide;
> O tread the city's streets again.

**Jesus spoke to them in parables: "The king said to his slaves, 'Go into the main streets, and invite everyone you find to the wedding banquet.'" Matthew 22:9**

> Till all the world shall learn your love,          581
> and follow where your feet have trod;
> till glorious from your heav'n above
> shall come the city of our God.

O loving God, your reach and invitation extend to everyone, both near and far. Remind us each day to extend that invitation in your name. Amen.

### Twentieth Sunday after Pentecost

**Watchword for the Week** — Since we have a great high priest who has passed through the heavens, Jesus, the Son of God, let us hold fast to our confession. Hebrews 4:14

**Sunday, October 14** — Amos 5:6-7,10-15; Psalm 90:12-17 Hebrews 4:12-16; Mark 10:17-31

## Better is a little with righteousness than large income with injustice. Proverbs 16:8

When simplicity we cherish,                          717
then the soul is full of light;
but that light will quickly vanish,
when of Jesus we lose sight.

## There is great gain in godliness combined with contentment. 1 Timothy 6:6

Only be still and wait his pleasure                   712
in cheerful hope with heart content.
He fills your needs to fullest measure
with what discerning love has sent;
doubt not our inmost wants are known
to him who chose us for his own.

God of wisdom and justice, we are tempted by the lure of the new, and we do not always have our priorities in righteous order. Grant us the gift of contentment grounded in your love and service. Amen.

**Monday, October 15 — Psalm 119:1-8**
2 Samuel 5:17-6:23; John 7:14-24

## He will bring me out to the light; I shall see his vindication. Micah 7:9

Spirit of truth and love,                                          380
lifegiving, holy dove,
speed on your flight!
Move on the water's face
bearing the lamp of grace,
and in earth's darkest place
let there be light!

## Sin will have no dominion over you, since you are not under law but under grace. Romans 6:14

For God, in grace and tenderness,                          519
regarded us in our distress;
yea, to our aid himself he came;
let all adore God's holy name.

Light of the world, when we sit mired in darkness or distress, come again to us. Come to our aid, grant us your grace anew and be our morning star, our cheering sight! Amen.

**Tuesday, October 16** — Psalm 119:9-16
2 Samuel 7; John 7:25-44

**I am with you to save you and deliver you, says
the Lord. Jeremiah 15:20**

> Spirit of God, who dwells within my heart,                490
> wean it from sin, through all its pulses move.
> Stoop to my weakness, mighty as you are,
> and make me love you as I ought to love.

**Where two or three are gathered in my name,
I am there among them. Matthew 18:20**

> The Lord is here!                                         p227*
> His promised word
> is evermore the same,
> Himself to be
> where two or three
> are gathered in his Name.

God, you bring us deliverance and you give us
awareness of your presence. Where there are only
two gathered in your name, you promise to be
there among us. We pray either in solitude or in the
company of others, remind us of those who pray in
your name at that moment in time. Amen.

\*   © by Hope Publishing Company

**Wednesday, October 17 — Psalm 119:17-24**
2 Samuel 8,9; John 7:45-52

## O Lord, open my lips, that my mouth may declare your praise. Psalm 51:15 (NASB)

Stand up, and bless the Lord,                    531
you people of his choice!
Stand up and bless the Lord your God,
with heart and soul and voice.

## Praise our God, all you his servants, and all who fear him, small and great. Revelation 19:5

As a mother looks with favor                     659
on the new life in her arms,
searching ev'ry small expression,
sav'ring moments filled with charm,
so God smiles on ev'ry person,
so God takes such keen delight
in the praises that we offer;
we are precious in God's sight.

Holy One, we thank you for blessings each day
and we lift our voices to sing your praises. May our
praise be acceptable to you, O God! Amen.

**Thursday, October 18** — Psalm 119:25-32
2 Samuel 10,11; John 8:1-11

**The word of the Lord is upright, and all his work is done in faithfulness. Psalm 33:4**

> In heav'nly love abiding,                              732
> no change my heart shall fear;
> and safe is such confiding,
> for nothing changes here.
> The storm may roar around me,
> my heart may low be laid,
> but God is round about me,
> and can I be dismayed?

**By faith even Sarah herself received ability to conceive, even beyond the proper time of life, since she considered Him faithful who had promised. Hebrews 11:11 (NASB)**

> If you but trust in God to guide you                   712
> and place your confidence in him,
> you'll find him always there beside you
> to give you hope and strength within;
> for those who trust God's changeless love
> build on the rock that will not move.

Steadfast God, we strive to believe but pray for help in our unbelief! Move close to us on those days when we do not feel your presence. We claim your promise that you will be with us to the end. Strengthen our faith. Amen.

**Friday, October 19** — Psalm 119:33-40
2 Samuel 12; John 8:12-30

## The day of the Lord is coming, it is near. Joel 2:1

Come, O long-expected Jesus,                    262
born to set your people free;
from our fears and sins release us;
O, in you our rest shall be.
Israel's strength and consolation,
hope to all the earth impart,
dear desire of ev'ry nation,
joy of ev'ry longing heart.

## Christ says, "Keep awake and pray that you may not come into the time of trial; the spirit indeed is willing, but the flesh is weak." Mark 14:38

Hear then, dear Lord Jesus,                      746
hear our earnest prayer,
grant your loving mercy,
keep us in your care.
All that is displeasing
unto you, forgive;
more to your name's glory
may we henceforth live.

Save us from the time of trial, Lord, and forgive
us when we falter. Enable us the wisdom and
generosity to forgive those who have hurt us or hurt
others. Have mercy on us, and renew us for service
in your name. Amen.

Saturday, October 20 — Psalm 119:41-48
2 Samuel 13:1-33; John 8:31-41

## There is no Holy One like the Lord, no one besides you. 1 Samuel 2:2

God is my strong salvation,                        769
no enemy I fear;
he hears my supplication,
dispelling all my care;
if he, my head and master,
defend me from above,
what pain or what disaster
can part me from his love?

## No one can lay any foundation other than the one that has been laid; that foundation is Jesus Christ. 1 Corinthians 3:11

How firm a foundation, you saints of the Lord,   709
is laid for your faith in his excellent world!
What more can he say than to you he has said,
to you who for refuge to Jesus have fled?

You are the one God in whom we live and move
and have our being. You are our Rock and our
Foundation. Our trust is in you; your grace is
sufficient for all. May we share our joy in our
interactions with each person we meet today.
Amen.

### Twenty-First Sunday after Pentecost

**Watchword for the Week** — For the Son of Man came not to
be served but to serve, and to give his life a ransom for many.
Mark 10:45

**Sunday, October 21** — Isaiah 53:4-12; Psalm 91:9-16
Hebrews 5:1-10; Mark 10:35-45

## Moses stood in the gate of the camp, and said, "Who is on the Lord's side? Come to me!" Exodus 32:26

O Jesus, I have promised                      603
to serve you to the end;
be now and ever near me,
my master and my friend.
I shall not fear the battle
if you are by my side,
nor wander from the pathway
if you will be my guide.

## Examine yourselves to see whether you are living in the faith. Test yourselves. 2 Corinthians 13:5

By love's closest bonds united,              515
as the Lord's own family,
be to serve his name excited,
be to him a fruitful tree.

Holy One, every day we make decisions that define
who, and whose, we are. Have those decisions
brought us closer to you? We examine ourselves
now: have we been open to your love? Have we
shared that love with others? Guide us to make wise
decisions today, gracious God. Amen.

Monday, October 22 — Psalm 119:49-56
2 Samuel 13:34-14:33; John 8:42-59

**It was not because you were more numerous than any other people that the Lord set his heart on you and chose you—for you were the fewest of all peoples. It was because the Lord loved you. Deuteronomy 7:7-8**

> For the beauty of the earth,                    538
> for the glory of the skies,
> for the love which from our birth
> over and around us lies,
> Lord of all, to you we raise
> this our hymn of grateful praise.

**God chose what is low and despised in the world, things that are not, to reduce to nothing things that are. 1 Corinthians 1:28**

> Because the Lord our God is good,               539
> his mercy is forever sure.
> His truth at all times firmly stood,
> and shall from age to age endure.

O God of wisdom, God of love, you have chosen us and we are your people. Enduring God, may the world see that we are yours by the love we spread into our communities. Amen.

**Tuesday, October 23 — Psalm 119:57-64**
2 Samuel 15:1-29; John 9:1-12

## The Lord said to Moses, "You shall speak all that I command you." Exodus 7:1-2

Lord, speak to me, that I may speak    646
in living echoes of your tone.
As you have sought, so let me seek
your erring children lost and lone.

## For it is not you who speak, but the Spirit of your Father speaking through you. Matthew 10:20

Called by Christ, redeemed, accepted,    624*
we are blessed with work to do.
By the Spirit we're empowered:
"Tell the good news, life renew."
Our lives now reveal Christ's presence;
we will show God's love and grace.
Faith in action, ever, always,
while on earth we run our race.

Compassionate God, speak through us today that we might share your love with all we meet. Open our eyes to see the stranger passing by and offer welcome and blessing in your name. Amen.

* © 1988 by W. Thomas Stapleton

**Wednesday, October 24** — Psalm 119:65-72
2 Samuel 15:30-16:23; John 9:13-34

## I will seek the lost, and I will bring back the strayed. Ezekiel 34:16

My Shepherd will supply my need;                    730
the Lord God is his name.
In pastures fresh he makes me feed,
beside the living stream.
He brings my wand'ring spirit back
when I forsake his ways,
and leads me for his mercy's sake
in paths of truth and grace.

## Christ says, "This is the will of him who sent me, that I should lose nothing of all that he has given me, but raise it up on the last day." John 6:39

Give of your own to bear the message glorious;      618
give of your wealth to speed them on their way;
pour out your soul for them in prayer victorious,
till God shall bring his kingdom's joyful day.

O gentle Shepherd, you do not lose sight of even
one lost sheep. Help us to see the lonely, hidden
and quiet ones within our midst. Whom have
we overlooked this week, even within our own
congregations? Increase our awareness and open
our hearts. Amen.

**Thursday, October 25** — Psalm 119:73-80
2 Samuel 17; John 9:35-41

**The Israelites will return and seek the Lord their God. They will come trembling to the Lord and to his blessings in the last days. Hosea 3:5 (NIV)**

> Here we kneel to seek your presence,                 557*
> share our sin, confess our shame,
> touch the joy whose very essence
> cleanses, strengthens, cancels blame.
> Grace invited, faith united,
> fellowship of love set free.

**Paul wrote: I am confident of this, that the one who began a good work among you will bring it to completion by the day of Jesus Christ. Philippians 1:6**

> Jesus, Prince of Peace, be near us;                 556
> fix in all our hearts your home;
> with your gracious presence cheer us;
> let your sacred kingdom come;
> raise to heav'n our expectation,
> give our favored souls to prove
> glorious and complete salvation
> in the realms of bliss above.

Compassionate God, we come to you with both sadness and joy. We are filled with sadness by the many ways that we fall short: by our hard-heartedness and by unhealthy self-preoccupation. Yet we are filled with joy, because we trust you will complete your work within us by your mercy and grace. Strengthen us! Amen.

* © 1988 by Ralph E. Freeman

Friday, October 26 — Psalm 119:81-88
2 Samuel 18:1-30; John 10:1-10

## With righteousness he shall judge the poor, and decide with equity for the meek of the earth. Isaiah 11:4

His righteous government and power 320
shall over all extend;
on judgment and on justice based,
his reign shall have no end.

## The grace of God has appeared, bringing salvation to all. Titus 2:11

O, to grace how great a debtor 782
daily I'm constrained to be!
Let that grace, Lord, like a fetter,
bind my wand'ring heart to thee.
Prone to wander, Lord, I feel it,
prone to leave the God I love,
here's my heart, O take and seal it;
seal it for thy courts above.

O God our help and hope, speak to and through
us this day. Judgment and righteousness are yours.
You offer salvation and grace and we thank you for
these gifts. May we be faithful servants and friends.
Amen.

**Saturday, October 27** — Psalm 119:89-96
2 Samuel 18:31-19:30; John 10:11-21

**All who forsake you shall be put to shame; for they have forsaken the fountain of living water, the Lord. Jeremiah 17:13**

> O Lord, have mercy on us all;                    p2
> have mercy on us when we call;
> Lord, we have put our trust in you;
> grant us your word of grace anew.

**Take care that none of you may have an evil, unbelieving heart that turns away from the living God. Hebrews 3:12**

> Therefore I pray, while here I stay              596
> and look to him with yearning:
> fixed in him may I abide,
> kept from ever turning.

Lead us to search our hearts, gracious God, that we may fully open ourselves to you and your love. Save us from the temptation of cynicism and breathe new life into us again. Amen.

### Twenty-Second Sunday after Pentecost

**Watchword for the Week** — The Lord has done great things for us.
Psalm 126:3

**Sunday, October 28** — Jeremiah 31:7-9; Psalm 126
Hebrews 7:23-28; Mark 10:46-52

## He spoke and it came to be; he commanded, and it stood firm. Psalm 33:9

> His sov'reign pow'r without our aid          455
> formed us of clay and gave us breath;
> and when like wand'ring sheep we strayed,
> he saved us from the pow'r of death.

## Jesus said to the deaf man, "Ephphatha," that is, "Be opened." And immediately his ears were opened, his tongue was released, and he spoke plainly. Mark 7:34-35

> Lord Jesus, for our call of grace,          437
> to praise your name in fellowship
> we humbly meet before your face
> and in your presence love-feast keep.
> Shed in our hearts your love abroad,
> your Spirit's blessing now impart;
> grant we may all, O Lamb of God,
> in you be truly one in heart.

Worship, honor, glory, blessing—you are worthy to receive! Great Creator and great Healer, we thank you for the gift of life. Open our ears and enable us to speak plainly the words of love and grace you would have us share with others. Amen.

**Monday, October 29** — Psalm 119:97-104
2 Samuel 19:31-20:26; John 10:22-33

## Thus far the Lord has helped us. 1 Samuel 7:12

They who Jesus' mercy know                416
are from wrath and envy freed;
love unto our neighbor shows
that we are his flock indeed;
thus we may in all our ways
show forth our Redeemer's praise.

## The Lord stood by me and gave me strength, so that through me the message might be fully proclaimed. 2 Timothy 4:17

If dangers gather round,                  615
still keep me calm and fearless;
help me to bear the cross
when life is bleak and cheerless,
to overcome my foes
with words and actions kind;
O God, your will disclose,
your counsel let me find.

You are with us always—guiding, comforting
and challenging us to continue our journey with
and to you. May our steps today bring us closer to
you. We pause before you now in gratitude and
supplication. Amen.

**Tuesday, October 30** — Psalm 119:105-112
2 Samuel 21; John 10:34-42

**The Lord has proclaimed to the end of the earth:
Say to daughter Zion, "See, your salvation
comes." Isaiah 62:11**

Jesus' name, Jesus' name,                                324
source of life and happiness!
In this name true consolation
mourning sinners may possess;
here is found complete salvation.
Blessed Jesus, we your name will praise
all our days, all our days.

**Christ was destined before the foundation of the
world, but was revealed at the end of the ages for
your sake. 1 Peter 1:20**

God with us, God with us,                                324
God made known in human frame;
in his name rejoice with gladness,
since to save the lost he came;
none need sink in hopeless sadness,
for Immanuel is now with us,
God with us, God with us.

Holy Christ, you are the Alpha and the Omega, the
Beginning and the End. In you we find consolation,
salvation and joy. We pause now to thank you for
your graciousness and pray for a daily sense of
gratitude. In Christ's name. Amen.

**Reformation Day**

**Wednesday, October 31** — Psalm 119:113-120
2 Samuel 22:1-25; John 11:1-16

**Like an eagle that stirs up its nest and hovers over its young, as it spreads its wings, takes them up, and bears them aloft on its pinions, the Lord alone guided him. Deuteronomy 32:11,12**

> When I walk through the shades of death,          730
> your presence is my stay;
> one word of your supporting breath
> drives all my fears away.
> Your hand, in sight of all my foes,
> shall still my table spread;
> my cup with blessings overflows;
> your oil anoints my head.

**Through faith you are shielded by God's power until the coming of the salvation that is ready to be revealed in the last time. 1 Peter 1:5 (NIV)**

> The sure provisions of my God          730
> attend me all my days;
> O may your house be my abode
> and all my work be praise.
> There would I find a settled rest,
> while others go and come—
> no more a stranger or a guest,
> but like a child at home.

O Holy Comforter, we once again thank you for your guidance and support. We thank you for the ways you breathe new life into your church. God, may we be part of that new life and not cling to comfortable ways of doing things only because they are comfortable. Amen.

## All Saints Day

**Watchword for All Saints Day** — Salvation belongs to our God who is seated on the throne, and to the Lamb! Revelation 7:10

**Thursday, November 1** — Psalm 119:121-128
2 Samuel 22:26-23:17; John 11:17-30

**All Saints Day** — Isaiah 25:6-9; Psalm 24
Revelation 21:1-6a; John 11:32-44

# Hatred stirs up strife, but love covers all offenses. Proverbs 10:12

Much forgiven, may I learn 779
love for hatred to return;
then my heart assured shall be
you, my God, have pardoned me.

# If I speak in the tongues of mortals and of angels, but do not have love, I am a noisy gong or a clanging cymbal. 1 Corinthians 13:1

Though I may speak with bravest fire, 590*
and have the gift to all inspire,
and have not love: my words are vain
as sounding brass, and hopeless gain.

Lord, help us to love first always, as you first loved us. All other work we do for you comes from the love you give us. Amen.

* © 1972 by Hope Publishing Company. All rights reserved. Used by permission.

**Friday, November 2** — Psalm 119:129-136
2 Samuel 23:18-24:25; John 11:31-44

## It is good that one should wait quietly for the salvation of the Lord. Lamentations 3:26

Rejoice, rejoice, the kingdom comes;     260*
be glad, for it is near.
It comes with joy surprising us;
it triumphs o'er our fears.
Give thanks, for as the kingdom comes
it brings God's own shalom,
a state of peace and justice
where all with God are one.

## Stand firm, and you will win life. Luke 21:19 (NIV)

Rejoice, rejoice, God's will stands firm     260*
throughout all time and space.
It is a quiet, steady force
pervading ev'ry place.
It snaps the brittleness of hate,
unties the bonds of greed.
It holds out love abundant
which never fails our need.

God, we are still and silent and know that you are God. Strong in your assurance, we loudly rejoice your unyielding presence. Be our firm and guiding light. Amen.

* © 1987 by M. Lynnette Delbridge

**Saturday, November 3** — Psalm 119:137-144
1 Kings 1:1-27; John 11:45-57

## I am the Lord your God, the Holy One of Israel, your Savior. Isaiah 43:3

> The God of Abraham praise,                    468
> who reigns enthroned above,
> the Ancient of eternal days,
> the God of love!
> The Lord, the great I Am,
> by earth and heav'n confessed—
> we bow before his holy name
> forever blessed.

## Grow in the grace and knowledge of our Lord and Savior Jesus Christ. 2 Peter 3:18

> Mighty God, we humbly pray,                    586
> let your pow'r now lead the way
> that in all things we may show
> that we in your likeness grow.

Lord, we know you are our Savior. Help us to grow in our faith to understand what it means that we are saved. Let us share that message and grow in numbers. Amen.

### Twenty-Third Sunday after Pentecost

**Watchword for the Week** — Hear, O Israel: The Lord is our God, the Lord alone. You shall love the Lord your God with all your heart, and with all your soul, and with all your might. Deuteronomy 6:4,5

**Sunday, November 4** — Deuteronomy 6:1-9; Psalm 119:1-8
Hebrews 9:11-14; Mark 12:28-34

# What are human beings that you are mindful of them, mortals that you care for them? Psalm 8:4

And when these failing limbs grow numb,         422
and mind and memory flee,
when thou shalt in thy kingdom come,
Jesus, remember me.

# God proves his love for us in that while we still were sinners Christ died for us. Romans 5:8

What wondrous love is this,         328
   O my soul, O my soul!
What wondrous love is this, O my soul!
What wondrous love is this
   that caused the Lord of bliss
to bear the dreadful curse for my soul, for my soul,
to bear the dreadful curse for my soul?

Father, you give us so much more than we deserve. Show us the way to live like you; to give to others more than we think they deserve and more than we think we can afford. Amen.

**Let the unrighteous forsake their thoughts; let
them return to the Lord, for he will abundantly
pardon. Isaiah 55:7**

> How can your pardon reach and bless                   777
> the unforgiving heart
> that broods on wrongs and will not let
> old bitterness depart,
> old bitterness depart?

**Christ says, "There will be more joy in heaven
over one sinner who repents than over ninety-
nine righteous persons who need no repentance."
Luke 15:7**

> Come, you thirsty, come and welcome,                  765
> God's free bounty glorify;
> true belief and true repentance,
> ev'ry grace that brings you nigh.

We claim your presence in our lives, but time and
again we turn to other things for comfort and find
ourselves lost. As we return again to you, thank you
for your welcoming arms. Amen.

**Tuesday, November 6 — Psalm 119:153-160**
1 Kings 2:1-38; John 12:12-19

## We have heard with our ears, O God, our ancestors have told us, what deeds you performed in their days, in the days of old. Psalm 44:1

> We listen to your word on this, your holy day;      563
> bless all that we have heard on this, your holy day.
> Go with us when we part, and to each longing heart
> your saving grace impart on this, your holy day.

## Though you have not seen Him, you love Jesus Christ, obtaining as the outcome of your faith the salvation of your souls. As to this salvation, the prophets who prophesied of the grace that would come to you made careful searches and inquiries. 1 Peter 1:8,9-10 (NASB)

> May we in service to our God                    696*
> act out the living word,
> and walk the road the saints have trod
> till all have seen and heard.
> As stewards of the earth may we
> give thanks in one accord
> to God who calls us all to be
> disciples of the Lord.

Lord, it is by faith that we know and that we are called. May we follow your call as strongly as those who walked side by side with you. We hear of your works and are led to do your work as well. Amen.

* © 1989 by H. Kenn Carmichael

**Wednesday, November 7** — Psalm 119:161-168
1 Kings 2:39-3:28; John 12:20-36

**The bows of the mighty are broken, but the feeble gird on strength. 1 Samuel 2:4**

> Hail to the Lord's anointed!                    263
> Great David's greater Son!
> Hail, in the time appointed,
> his reign on earth begun!
> He comes to break oppression,
> to set the captive free,
> to take away transgression,
> and rule in equity.

**Paul wrote: I will boast all the more gladly of my weaknesses, so that the power of Christ may dwell in me. 2 Corinthians 12:9**

> Restrain me lest I harbor pride,               733
> lest I in my own strength confide;
> though I am weak, show me anew
> I have my pow'r, my strength from you.

Almighty God, we are strong when our strength comes from you. Help us in moments of weakness to remember that we can call on you and all that works against you shall be broken while we will be made whole. Amen.

**Thursday, November 8** — Psalm 119:169-176
1 Kings 4:1-28; John 12:37-50

## You say, "The way of the Lord is unfair." Hear now, O house of Israel: Is my way unfair? Is it not your ways that are unfair? Ezekiel 18:25

> You are the way, the truth, the life;                              661
> grant us that way to know;
> that truth to keep, that life to win,
> whose joys eternal flow.

## Humble yourselves therefore under the mighty hand of God, so that he may exalt you in due time. 1 Peter 5:6

> Straight shall be what long was crooked,                          264
> and the rougher places plain!
> Let your hearts be true and humble,
> as befits his holy reign!
> For the glory of the Lord
> now on earth is shed abroad,
> and all flesh shall see the token
> that God's word is never broken.

Lord, you are our guide. Help us to humble ourselves enough to trust you and your way, the truth and life you place before us. Amen.

**Friday, November 9** — Psalm 120
1 Kings 4:29-5:18; John 13:1-17

**Into your hand I commit my spirit; you have redeemed me, O Lord, God of truth. Psalm 31:5 (NKJV)**

> Other refuge have I none;                724
> hangs my helpless soul on thee;
> leave, ah, leave me not alone,
> still support and comfort me.
> All my trust on thee is stayed,
> all my help from thee I bring;
> cover my defenseless head
> with the shadow of thy wing.

**All belong to you, and you belong to Christ, and Christ belongs to God. 1 Corinthians 3:22-23**

> Jesus loves me! This I know,             726
> for the Bible tells me so.
> Little ones to him belong;
> they are weak but he is strong.
> Yes, Jesus loves me, yes, Jesus loves me,
> yes, Jesus loves me, the Bible tells me so.

Jesus, we put all of our eggs in your basket, all our trust in you because we know you love us. Help us to live a life that shows we always trust in you. Amen.

**Saturday, November 10** — Psalm 121
1 Kings 6; John 13:18-30

**There are glad songs of victory in the tents of
the righteous: "The right hand of the Lord
is exalted; the right hand of the Lord does
valiantly." Psalm 118:15,16**

> Manifest in making whole                    313
> palsied limbs and fainting soul;
> manifest in valiant fight,
> quelling all the devil's might;
> manifest in gracious will,
> ever bringing good from ill;
> anthems be to you addressed,
> God in flesh made manifest.

**Thanks be to God, who in Christ always leads us
in triumphal procession. 2 Corinthians 2:14**

> Lead on, O King eternal;                    753
> we follow, not with fears,
> for gladness breaks like morning
> where'er your face appears:
> your cross is lifted o'er us;
> we journey in its light;
> the crown awaits the conquest;
> lead on, O God of might!

Our Lamb, you have conquered! Let us follow you
and sing in loud voices of all the blessings you give
us. Amen.

### Twenty-Fourth Sunday after Pentecost

**Watchword for the Week** — The Lord lifts up those who are bowed down; the Lord loves the righteous. Psalm 146:8

**Sunday, November 11** — 1 Kings 17:8-16; Psalm 146
Hebrews 9:24-28; Mark 12:38-44

# I will give them a heart to know that I am the Lord. Jeremiah 24:7

> Jesus is my joy,                                       594
> therefore blessed am I;
> O his mercy is unbounded,
> all my hope on him is grounded;
> Jesus is my joy,
> therefore blessed am I.

# Now it is God who makes both us and you stand firm in Christ. He anointed us, set his seal of ownership on us, and put his Spirit in our hearts as a deposit, guaranteeing what is to come. 2 Corinthians 1:21-22 (NIV)

> Take my life, O Lord, renew,                           610
> consecrate my heart to you.
> Take my self, and I will be
> yours for all eternity,
> yours for all eternity.

God, our Savior, our Lord, to you be all glory and power, and may you bring us to stand in your joyful presence. We sing your praises as we await your promises. Amen and Amen.

**Monday, November 12** — Psalm 122
1 Kings 7:1-33; John 13:31-38

## Mortals look on the outward appearance, but the Lord looks on the heart. 1 Samuel 16:7

Blessed are the pure in heart,                    584
for they shall see their God.
The secret of the Lord is theirs;
their soul is Christ's abode.

## As he who called you is holy, be holy yourselves in all your conduct. 1 Peter 1:15

Follow with rev'rent steps the great example    p151
of him whose holy work was doing good;
so shall the wide earth seem our father's temple,
each loving life a psalm of gratitude.

Lord, you find that little spark inside of us that
grows into a burning flame for you. We want to
work for you, the one who knows us inside and out.
We know you have given us everything we need to
complete the tasks you call us to. Amen.

### Chief Elder Festival

**Tuesday, November 13** — Psalm 123
1 Kings 7:34-8:16; John 14:1-14

**Chief Elder Festival†** — Ezekiel 34:11-16,23-24; Psalm 8
Hebrews 4:14-16; John 10:1-10

**For as the heavens are higher than the earth, so are my ways higher than your ways and my thoughts than your thoughts. Isaiah 55:9**

> Great things he has taught us,                               550
>     great things he has done,
> and great our rejoicing through Jesus the Son:
> but purer, and higher, and greater will be
> our wonder, our transport when Jesus we see.

**Now I know only in part; then I will know fully, even as I have been fully known. 1 Corinthians 13:12**

> O yes, having found in the Lord our delight,              675
> he is our chief object by day and by night;
> this knits us together; no longer we roam;
> we all have one Father, and heav'n is our home.

Chief Elder, we elect you each day to be the guiding force in our lives—your ways are so much better than our ways. Help us to trust that you know fully, and if we seek to be like you we will be living life to the fullest. Amen.

† On November 13, 1741, announcement was made to the congregations of the Brethren's Church of the Chief Eldership of Jesus Christ.

**Wednesday, November 14** — Psalm 124
1 Kings 8:17-53; John 14:15-24

## My tongue shall tell of your righteousness and of your praise all day long. Psalm 35:28

> Blessed assurance, Jesus is mine!                     714
> O what a foretaste of glory divine!
> Heir of salvation, purchase of God,
> born of his Spirit, washed in his blood.

## If any think they are religious, and do not bridle their tongues but deceive their hearts, their religion is worthless. James 1:26

> Your bountiful care what tongue can recite?          566
> It breathes in the air; it shines in the light;
> it streams from the hills; it descends to the plain,
> and sweetly distills in the dew and the rain.

Lord, as we sing your praises, we know our silent actions, done for you, speak so much louder than our words. Help us walk humbly as we carry out your work, bringing glory not to us or our church brand, but to you. Amen.

**Thursday, November 15 — Psalm 125**
1 Kings 8:54-9:19; John 14:25-15:8

## You show me the path of life. Psalm 16:11

O come, O wisdom from on high,    274
and order all things far and nigh;
to us the path of knowledge show,
and teach us in her ways to go.

**Simon Peter answered him, "Lord, to whom can we go? You have the words of eternal life. We have come to believe and know that you are the Holy One of God." John 6:68-69**

Hail, all hail victorious Lord and Savior;    p82
you have burst the bonds of death,
grant us, as to Mary, the great favor
to embrace your feet in faith:
you have in our stead the curse endured,
and for us eternal life procured;
joyful, we with one accord
hail you as our risen Lord.

Our guide, we come to you because you know so well the paths we must take to eternal life. You give us signs each day and plead for us to walk in your footsteps. So often we turn away. Help us to always find our way back to your path and the truth you provide of everlasting life. Amen.

**Friday, November 16 — Psalm 126**
1 Kings 9:20-10:29; John 15:9-17

**It is my pleasure to tell you about the miraculous signs and wonders that the Most High God has performed for me. Daniel 4:2 (NIV)**

Now thank we all our God 533
with heart and hands and voices,
who wondrous things has done,
in whom his world rejoices;
who, from our mother's arms,
has blessed us on our way
with countless gifts of love,
and still is ours today.

**He answered, "The man called Jesus made mud, spread it on my eyes, and said to me, 'Go to Siloam and wash.' Then I went and washed and received my sight." John 9:11**

Amazing grace! How sweet the sound 783
that saved a wretch like me!
I once was lost, but now am found,
was blind, but now I see.

Giver of grace, how amazing it is that you love us so much to give us as we ask — through miracles in our everyday lives. Don't let us take your presence for granted. We wish to see the role you play in our lives and tell others that they may see you at work too. Amen.

Saturday, November 17 — Psalm 127
1 Kings 11:1-25; John 15:18-16:4

**God, you know my folly; the wrongs I have done are not hidden from you. Psalm 69:5**

> For he, my soul,                                    p72
> has sent his Son
> to die for wrongs
> which you have done;
> he paid the ransom,
> and forgives
> the hourly follies of our lives.

**God forgave us all our trespasses, erasing the record that stood against us with its legal demands. He set this aside, nailing it to the cross. Colossians 2:13-14**

> My sin, O, the bliss of this glorious thought!        754
> My sin—not in part, but the whole—
> is nailed to his cross and I bear it no more,
> praise the Lord, praise the Lord, O my soul!

Redemptive Savior, forgive us this day our sins as we try so hard to forgive those who have hurt and wronged us. Remind us that we are not perfect. Just as you show us grace and understanding, so should we do the same to others. Amen.

### Twenty-Fifth Sunday after Pentecost

**Watchword for the Week** — Let us hold fast to the confession of our hope without wavering, for God who has promised is faithful. Hebrews 10:23

**Sunday, November 18** — Daniel 12:1-3; Psalm 16
Hebrews 10:11-14,(15-18),19-25; Mark 13:1-8

## Then we your people, the flock of your pasture, will give thanks to you forever; from generation to generation we will recount your praise. Psalm 79:13

Jesus makes my heart rejoice,    662
I'm his sheep and know his voice;
he's a Shepherd, kind and gracious,
and his pastures are delicious;
constant love to me he shows,
yea, my very name he knows.

## Everything created by God is good, and nothing is to be rejected, provided it is received with thanksgiving. 1 Timothy 4:4

We plow the fields, and scatter    453
the good seed on the land,
but it is fed and watered
by God's almighty hand;
he sends the snow in winter,
the warmth to swell the grain,
the breezes and the sunshine
and soft refreshing rain.

God, you are good! Help us to be the creatures you created us to be—to help make the world as it was when you said, "It is good." Amen.

**Monday, November 19** — Psalm 128
1 Kings 11:26-12:24; John 16:5-16

**There is none like you, O Lord; you are great, and your name is great in might. Jeremiah 10:6**

My hope is built on nothing less                          771
than Jesus' blood and righteousness;
no merit of my own I claim
but wholly lean on Jesus' name.
On Christ the solid rock, I stand;
all other ground is sinking sand,
all other ground is sinking sand.

**Every tongue should confess that Jesus Christ is Lord, to the glory of God the Father. Philippians 2:11**

At the name of Jesus                                      480
ev'ry knee shall bow,
ev'ry tongue confess him
King of glory now;
'tis the Father's pleasure
we should call him Lord,
who from the beginning
was the mighty Word.

Lord, we build our lives upon you, our solid ground and cornerstone. Living in this way is a witness to you, and the way, the truth and life that comes to us when we turn to you. Keep us steady on solid ground. Amen.

**Tuesday, November 20** — Psalm 129
1 Kings 12:25-13:22; John 16:17-33

## Do as the occasion demands; for God is with you. 1 Samuel 10:7 (NKJV)

> Be thou my wisdom, and thou my true word;      719
> I ever with thee and thou with me, Lord;
> thou my great Father, I thy true son;
> thou in me dwelling, and I with thee one.

## Do not seek your own advantage, but that of the other. 1 Corinthians 10:24

> Hands to work and feet to run—      649
> God's good gifts to me and you;
> hands and feet he gave to us
> to help each other the whole day through.

Lord, help us to seize the day! Help us to see how we can put the gifts you give us to work now in the ways you ask us to. Let there be no waiting. Amen.

**Wednesday, November 21** — Psalm 130
1 Kings 13:23-14:20; John 17:1-19

**Happy are those whose help is the God of Jacob, whose hope is in the Lord their God. Psalm 146:5**

Alleluia! Heav'nly High Priest,    373
here on earth our help, our stay;
alleluia! Hear the sinful
cry to you from day to day.
Intercessor, Friend of sinners,
earth's Redeemer, hear our plea,
where the songs of all the sinless
sweep across the crystal sea.

**For to this end we toil and struggle, because we have our hope set on the living God, who is the Savior of all people. 1 Timothy 4:10**

Fulfiller of the past    326
and hope of things to be,
we hail your body glorified
and our redemption see.

Giver of hope, in times of struggle and pain that we all feel at times; when the world is so heavy; and when we try to be strong for others but feel bitter and weak within—give us hope. Amen.

**Thursday, November 22** — Psalm 131
1 Kings 14:21-15:8; John 17:20-26

## Show me your glory, I pray. Exodus 33:18

We long for mighty signs of God— p58*
cathedral, miracle, and sword,
his pow'r and glory written plain—
so none may doubt that he is Lord.

## Jesus revealed his glory; and his disciples believed in him. John 2:11

Christ, whose glory fills the skies, 475
Christ, the true and only light,
Sun of righteousness, arise,
triumph o'er the shades of night;
dayspring from on high, be near;
daystar, in my heart appear.

Lord, we admit that it is often personal glory that
we seek. Today let us seek your glory; for when we
see it fully we will be blessed. That blessing is far
greater reward than any personal achievement.
Together we look both outward and inward to see
your presence. Amen.

* © by Hermann I. Weinlick

**Friday, November 23** — Psalm 132
1 Kings 15:9-16:14; John 18:1-11

**God said, "I have set my bow in the clouds, and it shall be a sign of the covenant between me and the earth." Genesis 9:13**

> Water has held us,                                          408
> moved by creation.
> Out of dark chaos,
> broke forth the light.
> Up from the deluge,
> showing God's promise,
> has come a rainbow,
> gladdening sight.

**Then Jesus took a cup, and after giving thanks he gave it to the disciples, and all of them drank from it. He said to them, "This is my blood of the covenant, which is poured out for many." Mark 14:23-24**

> O Lord, your feast we celebrate:                            355*
> we show your death, we sing your name
> till you return, when we shall eat
> the marriage supper of the Lamb.

Father, you give us signs of your promises each day. Help us to be aware of the signs you show us today. Amen.

**Saturday, November 24** — Psalm 133
1 Kings 16:15-17:24; John 18:12-24

**O my God, I cry by day, but you do not answer;
and by night, but find no rest. Psalm 22:2**

> Dark midnight was my cry,                          573
> dark midnight was my cry,
> dark midnight was my cry,
> give me Jesus.

**Do not worry about anything, but in everything
by prayer and supplication with thanksgiving
let your requests be made known to God.
Philippians 4:6**

> Gentle Jesus, hear our prayer.                     574
> Keep us in your loving care;
> and when evening shadows fall,
> casting darkness over all,
> loving Jesus, then be near,
> for with you we have no fear.

Gentle Jesus, hear our prayer. With honest hearts,
our greatest fear is that our prayers go unheard.
Give us assurance that our joy, pain, needs and
passions are heard and felt by you. Amen.

### Reign of Christ (Christ the King Sunday)

**Watchword for the Week** — "I am the Alpha and the Omega," says the Lord God, who is and who was and who is to come, the Almighty. Revelation 1:8

**Sunday, November 25** — Daniel 7:9-10,13-14; Psalm 93
Revelation 1:4b-8; John 18:33-37

## O sing to the Lord a new song, for he has done marvelous things. Psalm 98:1

Sing a new song to the Lord,      547*
he to whom wonders belong!
Rejoice in his triumph
and tell of his pow'r—
O sing to the Lord a new song!

## Sing psalms and hymns and spiritual songs among yourselves, singing and making melody to the Lord in your hearts. Ephesians 5:19

Your hallelujahs loud,      786
your clear hosannas raise!
Send forth your sturdy hymns of old,
the psalms of ancient days.
Rejoice, rejoice, rejoice,
give thanks and sing!

Father, we make a joyful noise to you! When we think of all you do for us each day, we cannot be silent. Let our songs and praises be a joy unto you. Amen.

Monday, November 26 — Psalm 134
1 Kings 18; John 18:25-40

## The fear of the Lord is hatred of evil.
## Proverbs 8:13

> The years have all been crowded                    p13
> with tokens of your love;
> and many who have sought you
> now worship you above.
> But we, O Lord, still need you,
> our pilgrim feet to stay,
> for evil often triumphs
> as faith to fear gives way.

## God did not call us to impurity but in holiness.
## Therefore whoever rejects this rejects not human
## authority but God, who also gives his Holy Spirit
## to you. 1 Thessalonians 4:7-8

> While a helpless infant still,                    336*
> he had to flee his foes,
> and, in time, rejected by
> the people whom God chose;
> yet he came to seek and serve
> the wayward and the lost,
> faithful to his Father's will
> and heedless of the cost.

Redeemer, time and again we reject and deny you.
Still, it is amazing how you love us so much. We
receive so much more than we deserve. Let us give
from those blessings we are given. Amen.

*    © 1989 by Jaroslav Vajda

**Tuesday, November 27** — Psalm 135:1-12
1 Kings 19; John 19:1-11

**You must therefore be careful to do as the Lord your God has commanded you; you shall not turn to the right or to the left. Deuteronomy 5:32**

> Unto such as keep God's cov'nant          458
> and are steadfast in his way,
> unto those who still remember
> the commandments and obey.

**Jesus answered, "The first is, 'Hear, O Israel: the Lord our God, the Lord is one; you shall love the Lord your God with all your heart, and with all your soul, and with all your mind, and with all your strength.' The second is this, 'You shall love your neighbor as yourself.' There is no other commandment greater than these." Mark 12:29-31**

> They who Jesus' mercy know          416
> are from wrath and envy freed;
> love unto our neighbor shows
> that we are his flock indeed;
> thus we may in all our ways
> show forth our Redeemer's praise.

Lord, we debate, discuss and overcomplicate what you call faith. We try to make it an organization of exclusion through rules and our own commandments. You tell us simply, "love each other." Help us to complete this task and keep this commandment. Amen.

**Wednesday, November 28** — Psalm 135:13-21
1 Kings 20:1-21; John 19:12-24

## In your days I will speak the word and fulfill it, says the Lord God. Ezekiel 12:25

> In his temple now behold him,                   314
> see the long-expected Lord;
> ancient prophets had foretold him,
> God has now fulfilled his word.
> Now to praise him, his redeemed
> shall break forth with one accord.

## Jesus said to Martha, "Did I not tell you that if you believed, you would see the glory of God?" John 11:40

> 'Twas grace that taught my heart to fear          783
> and grace my fears relieved;
> how precious did that grace appear
> the hour I first believed.

Promise Keeper, each day our anticipation grows as we grow closer to you, and know in our hearts that the promises you make to us will be fulfilled. We believe we will see your glory. We shall be blessed. Amen.

**Thursday, November 29 — Psalm 136**
1 Kings 20:22-21:16; John 19:25-37

**You have delivered my soul from death, and
my feet from falling, so that I may walk before
God in the light of life. Psalm 56:13**

> Then with delight may I employ                    638
> all that your bounteous grace has giv'n,
> and run my earthly course with joy,
> and closely walk with you to heav'n.

**God is faithful, and he will not let you be tested
beyond your strength, but with the testing he
will also provide the way out so that you may be
able to endure it. 1 Corinthians 10:13**

> Sometimes I feel discouraged,                    500
> and think my work's in vain,
> but then the Holy Spirit
> revives my soul again.
> There is a balm in Gilead
> to make the wounded whole,
> there is a balm in Gilead
> to heal the sin-sick soul.

Lord, though we are scared of tests, we know that
they are our opportunity to live up to your calling
for us. You give us everything we need to pass the
test. We will stand strong in all our tests today.
Amen.

**Friday, November 30** — Psalm 137
1 Kings 21:17-22:28; John 19:38-20:9

# I will sing to the Lord as long as I live; I will sing praise to my God while I have being.
**Psalm 104:33**

> Sing praise to God who reigns above,          537
> the God of all creation,
> the God of pow'r, the God of love,
> the God of our salvation.
> My soul with comfort rich he fills,
> and ev'ry grief he gently stills:
> to God all praise and glory!

**The Lord will rescue me from every evil attack and will bring me safely to his heavenly kingdom. To him be glory for ever and ever.**
**2 Timothy 4:18 (NIV)**

> To God be the glory—great things he has done!   550
> So loved he the world that he gave us his Son,
> who yielded his life an atonement for sin,
> and opened the lifegate that all may go in.

Our Protector, when we find ourselves frustrated or stressed by the long day we find ourselves in, help us to remember that you will lead and guide us to a place that will never seem long. We cannot wait for the day when all we have to do is sing your praise! Amen.

**Saturday, December 1** — Psalm 138:1-5
1 Kings 22:29-53; John 20:10-23

## Jonathan went to David and helped him find strength in God. 1 Samuel 23:16 (NIV)

I have no help but yours, nor do I need          421
another arm but yours to lean upon;
it is enough, O Lord, enough indeed;
my strength is in your might, your might alone.

## Encourage one another and build up each other. 1 Thessalonians 5:11

As you, Lord, have lived for others,             648
so may we for others live;
freely have your gifts been granted;
freely may your servants give.
Yours the gold and yours the silver,
yours the wealth of land and sea;
we but stewards of your bounty
held in solemn trust will be.

O God of humanity, we are not separated one from another, for you have knit us together. Today, when we see the person sitting before us in need of your care, may we be ready to encourage them. Amen.

### First Sunday of Advent

**Watchword for the Week** — Jesus says, "Heaven and earth will pass away, but my words will not pass away." Luke 21:33

**Sunday, December 2** — Jeremiah 33:14-16; Psalm 25:1-10
1 Thessalonians 3:9-13; Luke 21:25-36

## Know that the Lord is God. Psalm 100:3

The God of Abraham praise, 468
who reigns enthroned above,
the Ancient of eternal days,
the God of love!
The Lord, the great I Am,
by earth and heav'n confessed—
we bow before his holy name
forever blessed.

## Those who went ahead and those who followed were shouting, "Hosanna! Blessed is the one who comes in the name of the Lord!" Mark 11:9

Hosanna! Blessed is he that comes! p239
Hosanna! Hosanna!
Blessed is he that comes,
he that comes in the name of the Lord!
Hosanna! Blessed is he that comes!
Hosanna in the highest!

Hosanna God, Jesus of Nazareth, come into our lives. May we rejoice and shout with thanksgiving and praise. May our joy be unavoidable; our laughter, holy; and our worship, pleasing to you. Amen.

**Monday, December 3** — Psalm 138:6-8
2 Kings 1:1-2:18; John 20:24-31

**You are the God of my salvation; for you I wait all day long. Psalm 25:5**

> How shall I meet my Savior?                    269
> How shall I truly welcome thee?
> What manner of behavior
> is by thy love required of me?
> I wait for thy salvation;
> grant me, O Lord, thy Spirit's light;
> and may my preparation
> be well accepted in thy sight.

**Christ says, "Ask, and it will be given you; search, and you will find; knock, and the door will be opened for you." Matthew 7:7**

> Ask and it shall be given unto you,            605
> seek and you shall find,
> knock and the door shall be opened unto you—
> Allelu, alleluia!

O God of our salvation, eternal hope and source of strength, let our lives be a response to your steadfast love and grace. Amen.

**Tuesday, December 4** — Psalm 139:1-6
2 Kings 2:19-3:27; John 21:1-14

**If you obey the Lord your God: Blessed shall you be in the city, and blessed shall you be in the field. Deuteronomy 28:2-3**

> You have kindly led us                                    p205
> through our joys and tears;
> now accept our praises
> and remove our fears.
> Grant us all with gladness
> to obey your voice;
> let your will and pleasure
> be our only choice.

**Jesus said, "Blessed rather are those who hear the word of God and obey it!" Luke 11:28**

> O word of God incarnate,                                  505
> O wisdom from on high,
> O truth unchanged, unchanging,
> O light of our dark sky:
> we praise you for the radiance
> that from the scripture's page,
> a lantern to our footsteps,
> shines on from age to age.

Dear Jesus, you came to fulfill the law, to give the commandments a human body. You obeyed the law and infused it with love. May we know the freedom and joy of obedience. Amen.

**Wednesday, December 5** — Psalm 139:7-12
2 Kings 4:1-37; John 21:15-25

## The Lord will fulfill his purpose for me. Psalm 138:8

> Blessed are the strong but gentle,                    595
> trained to served a higher will,
> wise to know th'eternal purpose
> which their Father shall fulfill.
> Blessed are they who with true passion
> strive to make the right prevail,
> for the earth is God's possession
> and his purpose will not fail.

## Who will bring any charge against God's elect? It is God who justifies. Romans 8:33

> Stand up, stand up for Jesus,                    752
> the trumpet call obey;
> then join the mighty conflict
> in this, his glorious day.
> Be strong in faith and serve him
> against unnumbered foes;
> let courage rise with danger,
> and with God's strength oppose.

O Lord and God, as we encounter the unbelief of those we love, let us stand firm in our love and in our faith, knowing that each of us is your son or your daughter. Amen.

**Thursday, December 6** — Psalm 139:13-16
2 Kings 4:38-5:14; Acts 1:1-14

## The path of the righteous is like the light of dawn, which shines brighter and brighter until full day. Proverbs 4:18

When morning gilds the skies,                    552
my heart awaking cries:
may Jesus Christ be praised!
In all my work and prayer
I ask his loving care:
may Jesus Christ be praised!

## We are not of the night or of darkness. So then let us not fall asleep as others do, but let us keep awake and be sober. 1 Thessalonians 5:5-6

"Wake, awake, for night is flying,"              258
the watchmen on the heights are crying;
"Awake, Jerusalem, arise!"
Midnight hears the welcome voices
and at the thrilling cry rejoices:
"Where are the virgins, pure and wise?
The bridegroom comes, awake!
Your lamps with gladness take!
Alleluia!
With bridal care and faith's bold prayer,
to meet the bridegroom, come, prepare!"

Dear Jesus, as we awaken from our sleep and the light of day streams into our window, may you be our first thought. Before we even stand, Lord, may we praise you. Amen.

Friday, December 7 — Psalm 139:17-24
2 Kings 5:15-6:23; Acts 1:15-26

## Good and upright is the Lord; therefore he instructs sinners in the way. Psalm 25:8

Lord Jesus, think on me,    764
nor let me go astray;
through darkness and perplexity
point out your chosen way.

## Through Jesus forgiveness of sins is proclaimed to you. Acts 13:38

Here would I feed upon the bread of God,    421
here drink with you the royal wine of heav'n;
here would I lay aside each earthly load,
here taste afresh the calm of sin forgiv'n.

O God, we sin, we speak too quickly, we give in to anger, we hold hate in our hearts, but you stand calm. May we feel the calmness of sin forgiven and may we be made clean now, today. Amen.

**Saturday, December 8** — Psalm 140:1-5
2 Kings 6:24-7:20; Acts 2:1-13

## He is a shield for all who take refuge in him. Psalm 18:30

Blessed name! the rock on which we build,          487
our shield and resting place,
our never-failing comfort, filled
with blessings of his grace.
O Jesus, Shepherd, Guardian, Friend,
our Prophet, Priest, and King,
our Lord, our Life, our Way, our End,
accept the praise we bring.

## Jesus said to his disciples, "Therefore I tell you, do not worry about your life, what you will eat, or about your body, what you will wear. For life is more than food, and the body more than clothing." Luke 12:22-23

As a mother feeds her baby,                         659
with the milk from her own breast,
giving nourishment and nurture,
loving touch and calming rest,
so God feeds us through communion,
holy presence, blessed food,
loving touch of the Eternal;
hope and wonder are renewed.

Jesus, you are the bread of life. Let us be fed with
strength and grace and no longer hunger for that
which we do not need. Let us drink from the river of
life and be satisfied. Amen.

## Second Sunday of Advent

**Watchword for the Week** — Blessed be the Lord God of Israel, for he has looked favorably on his people and redeemed them. Luke 1:68

**Sunday, December 9** — Malachi 3:1-4; Luke 1:68-79
Philippians 1:3-11; Luke 3:1-6

# The Lord kills and brings to life; he brings down to Sheol and raises up. 1 Samuel 2:6

You, Christ, are the king of glory,                    p235
the eternal Son of the Father.
When you took our flesh to set us free,
you humbly chose the virgin's womb.
You overcame the sting of death
and opened the kingdom of heaven to all believers.
You are seated at God's right hand in glory.
We believe that you will come to be our judge.
Come, then, Lord, and help your people,
bought with the price of your own blood,
and bring us with your saints to glory everlasting.

# The powers of the heavens will be shaken. Then they will see the Son of Man coming in a cloud with power and great glory. Now when these things begin to take place, stand up and raise your heads, because your redemption is drawing near. Luke 21:26-28

Jesus comes with clouds descending;                    259
see the Lamb for sinners slain!
Thousand, thousand saints attending
join to sing the glad refrain:
Alleluia!
Alleluia!
Christ the Lord returns to reign!

O Christ, you have conquered death. We are not afraid. We beg you to come again so we may see you face to face. May our worship prepare us to see you today. Let us live ready. Amen.

**Monday, December 10** — Psalm 140:6-13
2 Kings 8; Acts 2:14-28

# My tears have been my food day and night, while people say to me continually, "Where is your God?" Psalm 42:3

> Prayer is the burden of a sigh,                 749
> the falling of a tear,
> the upward glancing of an eye,
> when none but God is near.

# In the days of his flesh, Jesus offered up prayers and supplications, with loud cries and tears, to the one who was able to save him from death, and he was heard because of his reverent submission. Hebrews 5:7

> Jesus in Gethsemane,                            347*
> you kept watch in agony,
> pouring out your soul in love
> that we all might live above,
> and as you that vigil kept,
> Peter, James, and John all slept.

Dear Jesus, you prayed to God in agony. Let us never forget that we can come to you with every pain, every burden, every secret angst. We can pour ourselves at your feet and we can be reborn, thank God. Amen.

* © 1992 by Albert H. Frank

Tuesday, December 11 — Psalm 141:1-4
2 Kings 9; Acts 2:29-47

**Even the sparrow finds a home, and the swallow a nest for herself, where she may lay her young, at your altars, O Lord of hosts, my King and my God. Psalm 84:3**

> The church is God's abiding place,     439
> his altar is within,
> and here by faith we see God's face,
> are cleansed from stain of sin.
> A sanctuary for the soul,
> where love can cast out fear,
> where broken spirits are made whole,
> for God himself is here.

**So then, a Sabbath rest still remains for the people of God. Hebrews 4:9**

> O Sabbath rest by Galilee!     739
> O calm of hills above,
> where Jesus knelt to share with thee
> the silence of eternity,
> interpreted by love!

O God, when we are weary, you invite us to rest. In our anxiety and busyness, let us take your invitation seriously today. Make us stop. Let us rest in your embrace from our labors and be renewed. Amen.

**Wednesday, December 12** — Psalm 141:5-10
2 Kings 10; Acts 3:1-10

## As a shepherd looks after his scattered flock when he is with them, so will I look after my sheep. Ezekiel 34:12 (NIV)

The Lord's my shepherd; I'll not want.    720
He makes me down to lie
in pastures green; he leadeth me
the quiet waters by;
he leadeth me, he leadeth me
the quiet waters by.

## Christ says, "I am the good shepherd. I know my own and my own know me." John 10:14

Jesus makes my heart rejoice,    662
I'm his sheep and know his voice;
he's a Shepherd, kind and gracious,
and his pastures are delicious;
constant love to me he shows,
yea, my very name he knows.

Jesus, sometimes we are so far away we can't hear your voice. When we are scattered, distracted by plenty or by want, you come looking for us. You, indeed, are our shepherd. Amen.

**Thursday, December 13** — Psalm 142
2 Kings 11; Acts 3:11-26

## Know then in your heart that as a parent disciplines a child so the Lord your God disciplines you. Deuteronomy 8:5

Be with me, Lord, where'er I go;                733
teach me what you would have me do;
suggest whate'er I think or say;
direct me in the narrow way.

## While the son was still far off, his father saw him and was filled with compassion; he ran and put his arms around him and kissed him. Luke 15:20

And now at length discerning                763*
the evil that I do,
behold me, Lord, returning
with hope and trust to you.
In haste you come to meet me
and home rejoicing bring,
in gladness there to greet me
with calf and robe and ring.

Parent God, our teacher and protector, let us learn from our mistakes. Help us be open to correction as we receive your forgiveness. Amen.

**Friday, December 14** — Psalm 143:1-6
2 Kings 12,13; Acts 4:1-12

## This people I have formed for myself; they shall declare my praise. Isaiah 43:21 (NKJV)

To God all glory, praise, and love            548
be now and ever giv'n
by saints below and saints above,
the church in earth and heav'n.

## Now God has reconciled you by Christ's physical body through death to present you holy in his sight, without blemish and free from accusation. Colossians 1:22 (NIV)

Most loving Jesus, only child            776*
of God, your bloodshed reconciled
our fallen world to God above:
we praise and bless you for this love.

O Christ, you wash us clean and present us to God
as his children, brothers and sisters through you,
dear Jesus. Our joy is profound; we find our family
in you. Amen.

* © 1994 by Madeleine Forell Marshall

**Saturday, December 15** — Psalm 143:7-12
2 Kings 14; Acts 4:13-22

## Do not be afraid, but let your hands be strong. Zechariah 8:13

Fear not, I am with you; O be not dismayed,        709
for I am your God and will still give you aid;
I'll strengthen you, help you and cause you to stand
upheld by my righteous, omnipotent hand.

## You are the light of the world. Matthew 5:14

Light of the world, we worship you;        p68
our gifts to you we bring;
accept our sinful hearts, O Lord,
while praise to you we sing.

Dear Jesus, we are afraid of the dark and in this
holiday season sometimes our spirits cloud over. Be
a light for us, shine for us, that we may glimpse the
joy that is ours. Amen.

**Third Sunday of Advent**

**Watchword for the Week** — Bear fruits worthy of repentance.
Luke 3:8

**Sunday, December 16** — Zephaniah 3:14-20; Isaiah 12:2-6
Philippians 4:4-7; Luke 3:7-18

# I have loved you, says the Lord. Malachi 1:2

Jesus loves me! This I know,                      726
for the Bible tells me so.
Little ones to him belong;
they are weak but he is strong.
Yes, Jesus loves me, yes, Jesus loves me,
yes, Jesus loves me, the Bible tells me so.

# May the Lord direct your hearts to the love of God and to the steadfastness of Christ. 2 Thessalonians 3:5

Church, unite for the right;                      631
let your foes behold your stand;
rebuke them for their error;
inspire with hope and fervor;
declare the Savior's merit
and how the Holy Spirit
by his power, ev'ry hour,
will direct us and protect us
in a world of sin and strife.

O faithful and steadfast God, you are unmoved.
You are rooted to us and bound to us by a divine
love and we humbly offer you our worship and
praise. Amen.

**Monday, December 17** — Psalm 144:1-4
2 Kings 15; Acts 4:23-37

**Job answered the Lord: "See, I am of small account; what shall I answer you? I lay my hand on my mouth." Job 40:3,4**

God reveals his presence;                    554
let us now adore him
and with awe appear before him.
God is in his temple;
all in us keep silence
and before him bow with reverence.
Him alone God we own;
he's our Lord and Savior.
Praise his name forever.

**Just as we have been approved by God to be entrusted with the message of the gospel, even so we speak, not to please mortals, but to please God who tests our hearts. 1 Thessalonians 2:4**

"Go forth in all the earth," —                633
your word to us is given:
"Proclaim salvation's worth
to people under heaven."
This holy task, O Lord,
your church must quite fulfill;
to us your grace afford,
and mold us to your will.

Gracious God, at times we feel unable and unworthy
to speak on your behalf. We feel ashamed or afraid.
Instead, Lord, fill us with your words and your
power and strength and we will speak. Amen.

**Tuesday, December 18 — Psalm 144:5-8**
2 Kings 16:1-17:6; Acts 5:1-11

He stands at the right hand of the needy, to save
them from those who would condemn them to
death. Psalm 109:31

> While we, deeply humbled,                      746
> own we're oft to blame,
> this remains our comfort,
> you are still the same.
> In you all the needy
> have a friend most dear,
> whose love and forbearance
> unexampled are.

The one who sanctifies and those who are
sanctified all have one Father. For this reason
Jesus is not ashamed to call them brothers and
sisters. Hebrews 2:11

> Always giving and forgiving,                    544
> ever blessing, ever blessed,
> wellspring of the joy of living,
> ocean depth of happy rest!
> Loving Father, Christ our brother,
> let your light upon us shine;
> teach us how to love each other,
> lift us to the joy divine.

O Christ, you stand among us, you direct our
hands. You take our hands and clasp them to
another: to the stranger who will save us, to the
doctor who will heal us, to our sister and our
brother. Amen.

**Wednesday, December 19** — Psalm 144:9-15
2 Kings 17:7-41; Acts 5:12-16

**The Lord will be your everlasting light, and your God will be your glory. Isaiah 60:19**

> Glorious Lord, yourself impart!     558
> Light of light, from God proceeding,
> open now our ears and heart,
> help us by your Spirit's pleading;
> hear the cry that we are raising;
> hear, and bless our prayers and praising.

**John, the Baptist, came as a witness to testify to the light, so that all might believe through him. John 1:7**

> Dear Christian Friends, rejoice,     p60*
> with heart, and soul, and voice;
> hear the news that John did cry:
> "God to us is drawing nigh;
> turn away from fear and sin,
> to let the Savior enter in."
> God is drawing nigh!
> God is drawing nigh!

O holy Child, we know of your arrival, your mother's pondering heart, your guests of shepherds, kings and angels. We imagine ourselves there with you, O Christ. May the joy of this thought warm us this day. Amen.

**Thursday, December 20** — Psalm 145:1-7
2 Kings 18; Acts 5:17-40

## Unless the Lord guards the city, the guard keeps watch in vain. Psalm 127:1

O God, our help in ages past,                    461
our hope for years to come,
remain our guard while life shall last,
and our eternal home.

## Not that we are competent in ourselves to claim anything for ourselves, but our competence comes from God. 2 Corinthians 3:5

Restrain me lest I harbor pride,                  733
lest I in my own strength confide;
though I am weak, show me anew
I have my pow'r, my strength from you.

O Lord, you know we act as if we can do all things
and be all things. But deep down, Lord, we know
our strength, our wisdom, our competence all
comes from you. Let us give thanks. Amen.

**Friday, December 21** — Psalm 145:8-16
2 Kings 19:1-28; Acts 5:41-6:7

**And afterward, I will pour out my Spirit on all people. Joel 2:28 (NIV)**

May ev'ry heart receive his loving spirit                671
and know the truth that makes life truly free;
then, in that spirit may we live united,
and find in God our deep security.

**Jesus said, "The Advocate, the Holy Spirit, whom the Father will send in my name, will teach you everything, and remind you of all that I have said to you." John 14:26**

The young, the old inspire                               376
with wisdom from above,
and give us hearts and tongues of fire
to pray and praise and love.

O God of light, on this the darkest day may our hearts find lightness of being in the gift of your Son and the Advocate, the Holy Spirit, who attends to our darkness and who offers a way. Amen.

Saturday, December 22 — Psalm 145:17-21
2 Kings 19:29-20:21; Acts 6:8-7:3

## Do not take the word of truth utterly out of my mouth. Psalm 119:43

> Because the Lord our God is good,　　　539
> his mercy is forever sure.
> His truth at all times firmly stood,
> and shall from age to age endure.

## Think of us in this way, as servants of Christ and stewards of God's mysteries. 1 Corinthians 4:1

> Lord, have mercy, Lord, have mercy　　　636
> on each land and place
> where your servants, where your servants
> preach the word of grace;
> life and pow'r on them bestow,
> them with needful strength endow,
> that with boldness, that with boldness
> they may you confess.

O Master God, we are your servants. As Christ served this world, we strive to do the same. Lord, be patient as we try to honor you and speak your truth to all you call us to discover. Amen.

## Fourth Sunday of Advent

**Watchword for the Week** — God has brought down the powerful from their thrones, and lifted up the lowly. Luke 1:52

**Sunday, December 23** — Micah 5:2-5a; Luke 1:46b-55
Hebrews 10:5-10; Luke 1:39-45,(46-55)

**Do not turn to mediums or wizards; do not seek them out, to be defiled by them: I am the Lord your God. Leviticus 19:31**

> Lord God of hosts!         p31
> O may our praise
> your courts with grateful incense fill;
> still may we stand
> before your face,
> still hear and do your sovereign will.

**He has rescued us from the power of darkness and transferred us into the kingdom of his beloved Son. Colossians 1:13**

> Ye servants of God, your Master proclaim,    565
> and publish abroad his wonderful name;
> the name all-victorious of Jesus extol;
> his kingdom is glorious, he rules over all.

O Lord and God, may our worship recognize you as One, the One we worship today, the One who defines us as a body. May we be transferred to the embrace of your beloved. Amen.

## Christmas Eve

**Monday, December 24** — Psalm 146
2 Kings 21:1-22:10; Acts 7:4-16

## Those who oppress the poor insult their Maker. Proverbs 14:31

Why lies he in such mean estate 305
where ox and ass are feeding?
Good Christian, fear; for sinners here
the silent Word is pleading.
This, this is Christ the King,
whom shepherds guard and angels sing.
Haste, haste to bring him laud,
the babe, the son of Mary!

## Let your gentleness be known to everyone. The Lord is near. Philippians 4:5

Softly the night is sleeping 284
on Bethlehem's peaceful hill;
silent the shepherds watching,
the gentle flocks are still.
But hark! The wondrous music
falls from the op'ning sky;
valley and cliff re-echo,
"Glory to God on high!"

O Christ, tonight we light the candles, pour the coffee, share the bun, play the music and tell your story. Gentle Jesus, you are here. Amen.

### Nativity of the Lord (Christmas Day)

**Watchword for Christmas Day** — And the Word became flesh and lived among us, and we have seen his glory, the glory as of a father's only son, full of grace and truth. John 1:14

**Nativity of the Lord** — Isaiah 52:7-10; Psalm 98
Hebrews 1:1-4,(5-12); John 1:1-14

**Tuesday, December 25** — Psalm 147:1-6
2 Kings 22:11-23:20; Acts 7:17-29

## No resident will say, "I am sick"; The people who dwell there will be forgiven their iniquity. Isaiah 33:24 (NASB)

> Thus if we have known him,                    273
> not ashamed to own him,
> nor have spurned him coldly,
> but will trust him boldly,
> he will then receive us,
> heal us, and forgive us.

## The angel said, "Do not be afraid; for see—I am bringing you good news of great joy for all the people: to you is born this day in the city of David a Savior, who is the Messiah, the Lord." Luke 2:10-11

> Hark! The herald angels sing:                 295
> "Glory to the newborn King!
> Peace on earth and mercy mild,
> God and sinners reconciled!"
> Joyful, all you nations, rise,
> join the triumph of the skies;
> with th'angelic host proclaim:
> "Christ is born in Bethlehem!"

O humble God, on this singular morning, this day of feasting and family, steal us away for a moment, so we might give you our love and receive your love. Renewed, send us out to be a blessing, a Christmas gift. Amen.

Wednesday, December 26 — Psalm 147:7-14
2 Kings 23:21-24:20; Acts 7:30-43

**Do not be afraid, stand firm, and see the deliverance that the Lord will accomplish for you today. Exodus 14:13**

> Come, Almighty to deliver;                              p218
> let us all your life receive;
> suddenly return, and never,
> nevermore your temples leave.
> Lord, we would be always blessing,
> serve you as your hosts above,
> pray, and praise you without ceasing,
> glory in your precious love.

**The shepherds returned, glorifying and praising God for all they had heard and seen, as it had been told them. Luke 2:20**

> While shepherds watched their flocks by night,   296
> all seated on the ground,
> the angel of the Lord came down,
> and glory shown around,
> and glory shown around.

O Lord and God, may we have the outspoken joy the shepherds carried with them as they told the story of all they had seen and heard. May our lives in you be a story worthy of proclamation. Amen.

**Thursday, December 27** — Psalm 147:15-20
2 Kings 25; Acts 7:44-60

**Do not be exceedingly angry, O Lord, and do not remember iniquity for ever. Now consider we are all your people. Isaiah 64:9**

> He will not always chide;                        546
> he will with patience wait;
> his wrath is ever slow to rise
> and ready to abate.

**Whoever believes in the Son has eternal life; whoever disobeys the Son will not see life, but must endure God's wrath. John 3:36**

> For God so loved us, he sent the Savior:          775
> for God so loved us, and loves me too.

Patient and steadfast God, you so loved the world you sent your Son who embodied love and radical forgiveness. In your wide embrace you bring us all home to you. Amen.

**Friday, December 28 — Psalm 148**
1 Chronicles 1:1-37; Acts 8:1-8

**Truly the day of the Lord is great; terrible indeed—who can endure it? Yet even now, says the Lord, return to me with all your heart. Joel 2:11,12**

> Much forgiven, may I learn     779
> love for hatred to return;
> then my heart assured shall be
> you, my God, have pardoned me.

**May the Lord make you increase and abound in love for one another and for all, and may he so strengthen your hearts in holiness that you may be blameless before our God and Father at the coming of our Lord Jesus. 1 Thessalonians 3:12-13**

> Grant, Lord, that with thy direction,     673
> "Love each other," we comply,
> aiming with unfeigned affection
> thy love to exemplify;
> let our mutual love be glowing;
> thus the world will plainly see
> that we, as on one stem growing,
> living branches are in thee.

God of love, let us learn love, profound and defining, that gathers us when we are scattered. Anchor us in a loving and faithful community of believers that we may be at home in you. Amen.

**Saturday, December 29** — Psalm 149
1 Chronicles 1:38-2:17; Acts 8:9-25

**You shall not bear false witness against your
neighbor. Exodus 20:16**

> Lord, grant that we impelled by love                643
> in smallest things may faithful prove;
> till we depart, our lives be true,
> devoted wholly unto you.

**Let no evil talk come out of your mouths, but
only what is useful for building up, as there is
need, so that your words may give grace to those
who hear. Ephesians 4:29**

> As we are taught of Jesus                          434*
> we celebrate the faith
> built up by those before us
> and passed through us today.
> Thus our lives are established
> in time and history.
> We know who we are called to be:
> The church, empow'red in ministry
> to serve all people lovingly.
> Alleluia!

O God of community, we are built, shaped and
formed by those you call into our lives. Let us be
the church and know our responsibility to and our
hope for your body. Amen.

* © 1991 by John T. Hicks

### First Sunday after Christmas

**Watchword for the Week** — Let them praise the name of the Lord, for his name alone is exalted; his glory is above earth and heaven. Psalm 148:13

**Sunday, December 30** — 1 Samuel 2:18-20,26; Psalm 148 Colossians 3:12-17; Luke 2:41-52

## Do not withhold good from those to whom it is due, when it is in your power to do it. Proverbs 3:27

> Had I the grace to seek his face                    596
> in any trying hour!
> Help from none will he withhold
> who implores his power.

## Be doers of the word, and not merely hearers who deceive themselves. James 1:22

> Hands to work and feet to run—                    649
> God's good gifts to me and you;
> hands and feet he gave to us
> to help each other the whole day through.

Gracious and giving Savior, forgive us when we withhold our power. Forgive us when we act on the behalf of a brother or a sister. Let us be fed by worship this day and go out to be your hands and feet. Amen.

**Monday, December 31** — Psalm 150
1 Chronicles 2:18-55; Acts 8:26-40

## My eyes fail with watching for your promise; I ask, "When will you comfort me?" Psalm 119:82

O come, O bright and morning star,                274
and bring us comfort from afar!
Dispel the shadows of the night,
and turn our darkness into light.

## May our Lord Jesus Christ himself and God our Father, who loved us and through grace gave us eternal comfort and good hope, comfort your hearts. 2 Thessalonians 2:16-17

Breathe, O breathe your loving Spirit             474
into ev'ry troubled breast;
let us all in you inherit,
let us find the promised rest.
Take away the love of sinning;
Alpha and Omega be;
end of faith, as its beginning,
set our hearts at liberty.

God of endings and beginnings, may we bring glory tonight as we close this year and begin another. May our faith in your promise remain strong as you breathe your spirit upon us. Amen.

# DIRECTORY
# AND STATISTICS

Moravian Church in North America
Northern and Southern Provinces

# 2012

# THE MORAVIAN CHURCH IN NORTH AMERICA

1021 Center Street, Bethlehem, PA 18018
459 South Church Street, Winston-Salem, NC 27101

*Published by the Interprovincial Board of Communication
Moravian Church in North America*

**www.moravian.org**

Printed in the U.S.A.

# CONTENTS

## ADDRESSES OF CHURCHES

Churches are listed alphabetically by state and then alphabetically by city of physical location.

**NP** = Northern Province
**SP** = Southern Province

**CD** = Canadian District
**ED** = Eastern District
**WD** = Western District

### ALBERTA, CANADA (NP, CD):

**BRUDERHEIM -**
**Bruderheim Church**
Highway 45
*Mail:* Box 208
Bruderheim AB T0B 0S0
Canada
O: 780.796.3775
F: 780.796.9736
email:
admin.bruderheimmoravian@shaw.ca
www.bruderheimmoravian.org

**CALGARY -**
**Christ Church**
600 Acadia Drive SE
Calgary AB T2J 0B8
Canada
O: 403.271.2700
F: 403.271.2810
email: moravian@nucleus.com
www.christmoravian.com

**Good Shepherd Community Church**
6311 Norfolk Drive NW
Calgary AB T2K 5J8
Canada
O: 403.274.4888
F: 403.451.1556
email:
admin@goodshepherdmoravian.org
www.goodshepherdmoravian.org

**EDMONTON -**
**Edmonton Church**
9540 83 Avenue
Edmonton AB T6C 1B9
Canada
O: 780.439.1063
F: 780.756.7898
email: edmontonmoravian@shaw.ca
www.edmontonmoravian.com

**Millwoods Church**
2304 38th Street
Edmonton AB T6L 4K9
Canada
O: 780.463.7427
F: 780.461.3058
email: office@mcchurch.ca
www.mcchurch.ca

**Rio Terrace Church**
15108 76 Avenue
Edmonton AB T5R 2Z9
Canada
O/F: 780.487.0211
email: rioterracechurch@shaw.ca
www.rioterracemoravianchurch.ca

**SHERWOOD PARK -**
**Good News Church**
2 Primrose Boulevard
Sherwood Park AB T8H 1G2
Canada
O: 780.467.0337
email: goodnewschurch@yahoo.com
www.goodnewschurch.ca

SOUTH EDMONTON -
**Heimtal Church**
RR 3
South Edmonton AB T6H 4N7
Canada
O: 780.955.7305
F: 780.955.7988
email: heimtal@telus.net
www.heimtal.com

**CALIFORNIA (NP, WD):**
BANNING -
**Morongo Church**
11440 Potrero Road
Banning CA 92220
*Mail:* PO Box 352
Banning CA 92220-0352
O: 951.849.3067
email: morongomoravian@verizon.net

DOWNEY-
**Downey Church**
10337 Old River School Road
Downey CA 90241-2057
O: 562.927.0718
F: 562.927.0858
email: office@downeymoravian.org
www.downeymoravian.org

**DISTRICT OF COLUMBIA
(NP, ED):**
WASHINGTON -
**Faith Church**
405 Riggs Road NE
Washington DC 20011-2515
O: 202.635.9012
F: 202.635.9014
www.faithmoravianchurch.org

**FLORIDA (SP):**
LONGWOOD-
**Rolling Hills Church**
1525 State Road 434 W
Longwood FL 32750-3877
O: 407.332.8380
email: rhmcoffice@centurylink.net
www.rhmoravian.org

MIAMI-
**King of Kings Church**
1880 NW 183rd Street
Miami FL 33056
email: kokmoravian@att.net

**New Hope Church**
6001 SW 127th Avenue
Miami FL 33183-1427
O/F: 305.273.4047
email: nhmiami@yahoo.com

**Prince of Peace Church**
1880 NW 183rd Street
Miami FL 33056
O: 305.628.2061
F: 305.625.5365
email: pop@bellsouth.net

WEST PALM BEACH -
**Palm Beach Church**
297 27th Street
West Palm Beach FL 33407
O: 561.832.1363
F: 561.832.1363 (call first)
email: pbmoravian@yahoo.com

**GEORGIA (SP):**
STONE MOUNTAIN -
**First Church of Georgia**
4950 Hugh Howell Road
Stone Mountain GA 30087
O: 770.491.7250
F: 770.414.5678
www.gamoravian.org

**ILLINOIS (NP, WD):**
**WEST SALEM -**
**West Salem Church**
PO Box 27
West Salem IL 62476-0027
O: 618.456.8532
email: wsmor1@frontier.com
www.westsalemmoravian.org

**INDIANA (NP, WD):**
**HOPE -**
**Hope Church**
202 Main Street
Hope IN 47246
O: 812.546.4641
email: pastor@hopemoravianchurch.org
www.hopemoravianchurch.org

**MARYLAND (NP, ED):**
**NEW CARROLLTON -**
**Trinity Church**
7011 Good Luck Road
New Carrollton MD 20784
O: 301.441.1814
email: trinitymoravian@aol.com
www.trinitymoravianchurch.org

**THURMONT -**
**Graceham Church**
8231-A Rocky Ridge Road
Thurmont MD 21788
O: 301.271.2379
F: 301.271.4241
www.gracehammoravian.org

**UPPER MARLBORO -**
**St. Paul's Church**
8505 Heathermore Boulevard
Upper Marlboro MD 20772
O: 301.627.4200
F: 301.627.4204
email: spmoravian@aol.com
www.spmoravian.org

**MICHIGAN (NP, WD):**
**DAGGETT -**
**Daggett Church**
102 Old US Highway 41
Daggett MI 49821
O: 906.753.6995
email: daggett@new.rr.com

**UNIONVILLE-**
**Unionville Church**
2711 Cass Street
Unionville MI 48767
O: 989.674.8686
F: 989.674.0115
email: moravian@airadv.net

**WESTLAND -**
**Grace Church**
31133 Hively Avenue
Westland MI 48185
O/F: 734.721.9290
email: gracemoravian@gmail.com

**MINNESOTA (NP, WD):**
**ALTURA -**
**Our Savior's Church**
PO Box 161
Altura MN 55910-0161
O: 507.796.5612
email: manyds@embarqmail.com
www.oursaviorsmoravian.org

**CHASKA -**
**Chaska Church**
115 E 4th Street
Chaska MN 55318
O: 952.448.4000
F: 952.448.6016
email: chaskamoravian@embarqmail.com
www.chaskamoravian.org

**MAPLE GROVE -**
**Christ's Community Church**
13250 93rd Avenue
Maple Grove MN 55369
O: 763.420.7187
email: office@ccc-mg.org
www.ccc-mg.org

**NORTHFIELD -**
**Northfield (Main Street) Church**
713 Division Street
Northfield MN 55057
O: 507.645.7566
www.mainstreetmoravian.org

**SAINT CHARLES -**
**Berea Church**
1270 Berea Dr.
St. Charles MN 55972
*Mail:* PO Box 402
Saint Charles MN 55972-0402
O: 507.932.3584
www.bereamoravian.org

**VICTORIA -**
**Lake Auburn Church**
7460 Victoria Drive
PO Box 160
Victoria MN 55386
O/F: 952.443.2051
email:
lakeauburnchurch@centurylink.net
www.lakeauburnchurch.embarqspace.com

**WACONIA -**
**Waconia Church**
209 East 2nd Street
Waconia MN 55387
O: 952.442.2920
email: wmoravian@gmail.com
www.waconiamoravian.org

**NEW JERSEY (NP, ED):**
**CINNAMINSON -**
**Palmyra Church**
1921 Cinnaminson Avenue
Cinnaminson NJ 08077
O: 856.829.2886
email: palmyramoravian@verizon.net
www.palmyramoravian.org

**EGG HARBOR -**
**Egg Harbor City Church**
235 Boston Avenue
Egg Harbor City NJ 08215
O: 609.965.1920
www.moravianchurchehc.org

**RIVERSIDE -**
**First Church**
228 East Washington Street
Riverside NJ 08075-3629
*Mail:* PO Box 214
Riverside NJ 08075-0214
O: 856.461.0132
F: 856.764.7032
email:
riversidemoravian@verizon.net
www.riversidemoravian.org

**UNION -**
**Battle Hill Church**
777 Liberty Avenue
Union NJ 07083
O: 908.686.5262
email: bhmoravian@verizon.net

**NEW YORK (NP, ED):**
**BRONX -**
**Tremont Terrace Church**
1621 Pilgrim Avenue
Bronx NY 10461
O: 718.829.2156
F: 718.829.0044
email: tremontterrace@verizon.net

**BROOKLYN -**
**Fellowship Church** (Meeting at
Church of the Evangel U.C.C.)
1950 Bedford Avenue
Brooklyn NY 11225
O: 718.287.7200

**John Hus Church**
153 Ocean Avenue
Brooklyn NY 11225
O: 718.856.2200
F: 718.856.2201
email: johnhusmoravian@optonline.net
www.johnhusmoravianchurch.com

**NEW YORK -**
**First Church**
154 Lexington Avenue
New York NY 10016
*Mail:* PO Box 1874
Murray Hill Station
New York NY 10156-0609
O: 212.683.4219
F: 212.683.9734
email: firstmoravian@verizon.net

**United Church**
200 East 127th Street
New York NY 10035
*Mail:* PO Box 90
New York NY 10035-0090
O: 212.722.2109
F: 212.987.2818
email: unitedmoravian@gmail.com

**QUEENS -**
**Grace Church**
178-38 137th Avenue
Springfield Gardens
Queens NY 11434
O: 718.723.2681
F: 718.723.4288
email: gracemoravian@verizon.net

**STATEN ISLAND -**
**Castleton Hill Church**
1657 Victory Boulevard
Staten Island NY 10314
O: 718.442.5215 or 718.442.5309
F: 718.442.5211
email: officechmc@si.rr.com
www.castletonhill.org

**Great Kills Church**
74 Hillside Terrace
Staten Island NY 10308
O: 718.317.7788
F: 718.356.2826
email: pastorgkmc@si.rr.com
www.greatkillsmoravianchurch.org

**New Dorp Church**
2205 Richmond Road
Staten Island NY 10306-2557
O: 718.351.0090
F: 718.351.0290
email:
ndmcthree.moravian@verizon.net
www.newdorpmoravian.org

**Vanderbilt Avenue Church**
285 Vanderbilt Avenue
Staten Island NY 10304
O: 718.447.2966
www.simoravians.org

**NORTH CAROLINA (SP):**
**ADVANCE -**
**Macedonia Church**
700 NC Highway 801 N
Advance NC 27006
O: 336.998.4394
F: 336.940.5317
email: macedonia@yadtel.net
www.macedoniamoravianchurch.org

**BETHANIA -**
**Bethania Church**
5545 Main Street
Bethania NC 27010
*Mail:* PO Box 170
Bethania NC 27010-0170
O: 336.922.1284
F: 336.922.1294
email: bethaniaoffice@windstream.net
www.bethaniamoravian.org

**CHARLOTTE -**
**Little Church on the Lane**
522 Moravian Lane
Charlotte NC 28207
O: 704.334.1381
F: 704.333.2281 (call first)
www.littlechurchonthelane.com

**Peace Church**
4418 Rea Road
Charlotte NC 28226
O: 704.759.9939
F: 704.927.1688
email: general@peacemoravian.com
www.peacemoravian.com

**CLEMMONS -**
**Clemmons Church**
3560 Spangenberg Avenue
Clemmons NC 27012
*Mail:* PO Box 730
Clemmons NC 27012
O: 336.766.6273
F: 336.766.3794
email: Office@clemmonsmoravian.org
www.clemmonsmoravian.org

**DURHAM -**
**Christ the King Church**
4405 Hope Valley Road
Durham NC 27707
O: 919.489.1711
F: 919.419.0032
email: office@ctkhome.org
www.ctkhome.org

**EDEN -**
**Leaksville Church**
712 McConnell Street
Eden NC 27288
*Mail:* PO Box 35
Eden NC 27289
O: 336.623.9440
email:
leaksvillemoravian@embarqmail.com
www.leaksvillemoravian.org

**GREENSBORO -**
**First Church**
304 South Elam Avenue
Greensboro NC 27403
O: 336.272.2196
F: 336.275.7800
email: office@greensboromoravian.org
www.greensboromoravian.org

**HUNTERSVILLE -**
**New Beginnings Church**
201 Seagle Street
Huntersville NC 28078
*Mail:* PO Box 2278
Huntersville NC 28070-2278
O: 704.992.2003
F: 704.992.2002
email:
newbeginnings100@bellsouth.net
www.newbeginningsmoravian.org

**KERNERSVILLE -**
**Good Shepherd Church**
1474 Kerner Road
Kernersville NC 27284
O: 336.993.6633
F: 336.993.6633 (call first)
email:
secretary@goodshepherdmoravian.com
www.goodshepherdmoravian.com

**Kernersville Church**
504 South Main Street
Kernersville NC 27284
O: 336.993.3620
F: 336.993.7052
email: kmchurch@embarqmail.com
www.kernersvillemoravian.org

**King -**
**King Church**
228 West Dalton Road
King NC 27021
O: 336.983.2710
F: 336.983.7045 (call first)
email: office@kingmoravianchurch.org
www.kingmoravian.org

**Lewisville -**
**Unity Church**
8300 Concord Church Road
Lewisville NC 27023
O: 336.945.3801 or 336.945.3877
email: unitymc@windstream.net
www.unitymoravian.org

**Lexington -**
**Enterprise Church**
2733 Enterprise Church Road
Lexington NC 27295-9233
O: 336.764.1281
email: emcpastor@bellsouth.net

**Mayodan -**
**Mayodan Church**
104 South 3rd Avenue
Mayodan NC 27027
Mail: PO Box 245
Mayodan NC 27027-0245
O: 336.548.2645
F: 336.548.2645 (call first)
email:
mayodanmoravian@embarqmail.com
www.mayodanmoravian.org

**Mt. Airy -**
**Grace Church**
1401 North Main Street
Mt. Airy NC 27030
O: 336.786.5627
F: 336.786.2896
email:
office@gracemoravianchurch.org
www.gracemoravianchurch.org

**Newton -**
**New Hope Church**
2897 Sandy Ford Road
Newton NC 28658
O: 828.294.4802
F: 828.294.1237
email:
newhopemoravian@gmail.com

**Oak Ridge -**
**Moravia Church**
2920 Oak Ridge Road
Oak Ridge NC 27310
O/F: 336.643.5166
email: moraviamoravian@att.net

**Raleigh -**
**Raleigh Church**
1816 Ridge Road
Raleigh NC 27607
O: 919.787.4034
F: 919.787.4250
email: office@raleighmoravian.org
www.raleighmoravian.org

**Rural Hall -**
**Mizpah Church**
3165 Mizpah Church Road
Rural Hall NC 27045
O: 336.924.1661
email:
mizpahmoravianchurch@windstream.net

**Rural Hall Church**
7939 Broad Street
Rural Hall NC 27045
*Mail:* PO Box 487
Rural Hall NC 27045-0487
O: 336.969.9488
F: 336.969.1819
email: secretary@rhmc.org
www.rhmc.org

**WALNUT COVE -
Fulp Church**
1556 US 311 Highway South
Walnut Cove NC 27052
O/F: 336.591.7940
email:
fulpmoravian@embarqmail.com

**WILMINGTON -
Covenant Church**
4126 South College Road
Wilmington NC 28412
O/F: 910.799.9256
email: office@covenantmoravian.org
www.covenantmoravian.org

**WINSTON-SALEM -
Advent Church**
1514 West Clemmonsville Road
Winston-Salem NC 27127
O: 336.788.4951
F: 336.788.0739
email: amchurch@triad.rr.com
www.adventmoravian.org

**Ardmore Church**
2013 West Academy Street
Winston-Salem NC 27103
O: 336.723.3444
F: 336.723.5710
email: officeamc@triad.rr.com
www.ardmoremoravian.org

**Bethabara Church**
2100 Bethabara Road
Winston-Salem NC 27106
O/F: 336.924.8789
email: bethabaraoffice@windstream.net
www.bethabara.org

**Bethesda Church**
740 Bethesda Road
Winston-Salem NC 27103
O: 336.765.1357
F: 336.768.6977

**Calvary Church**
600 Holly Avenue
Winston-Salem NC 27101
O: 336.722.3703
F: 336.724.1956 (call first)
email: ncalvarymoravia@triad.rr.com
www.calvarymoravian.org

**Christ Church**
919 West Academy Street
Winston-Salem NC 27101-5103
O: 336.722.2007
F: 336.724.1704
email: office@christmoravianchurch.org
www.christmoravianchurch.org

**Fairview Church**
6550 Silas Creek Parkway
Winston-Salem NC 27106
O: 336.768.5629
F: 336.768.5637
email:
fmc@fairviewmoravianchurch.org
www.fairviewmoravianchurch.org

**Friedberg Church**
2178 Friedberg Church Road
Winston-Salem NC 27127-9073
O: 336.764.1830
F: 336.764.4524
email: info@friedbergmoravian.org
www.friedbergmoravian.org

**Friedland Church**
2750 Friedland Church Road
Winston-Salem NC 27107
O: 336.788.2652
F: 336.788.0305
email: lindalyons2@triad.rr.com
www.friedlandmoravian.org

**Fries Memorial Church**
251 North Hawthorne Road NW
Winston-Salem NC 27104
O: 336.722.2847
F: 336.722.2132
email: frieschurch@aol.com
www.friesmoravian.org

**Home Church**
529 South Church Street
Winston-Salem NC 27101
O: 336.722.6171
F: 336.723.5085
email: home1771@homemoravian.org
www.homemoravian.org

**Hope Church**
2759 Hope Church Road
Winston-Salem NC 27127
O: 336.765.8017
www.hopemoraviannc.org

**Hopewell Church**
701 Hopewell Church Road
Winston-Salem NC 27127
O: 336.788.2289
email: hmc701@triad.rr.com

**Immanuel-New Eden Church**
3680 Old Lexington Road
Winston-Salem NC 27127
O: 336.788.1561
email:
immanuelneweden@bellsouth.net

**Konnoak Hills Church**
3401 Konnoak Drive
Winston-Salem NC 27127
O: 336.788.9321
F: 336.785.0211
email: khmc3401@bellsouth.net
www.khmoravian.org

**Messiah Church**
1401 Peace Haven Road
Winston-Salem NC 27104-1397
O: 336.765.5961
F: 336.659.6642
email: messiah1@clearwire.net
www.messiahmoravian.org

**New Philadelphia Church**
4440 Country Club Road
Winston-Salem NC 27104
O: 336.765.2331
O: 336.768.5961
F: 336.765.5536
email: pastor@newphilly.org
www.newphilly.org

**Oak Grove Church**
120 Hammock Farm Road
Winston-Salem NC 27105
O: 336.595.8167
email:
oakgrovemoravian@embarqmail.com

**Olivet Church**
2205 Olivet Church Road
Winston-Salem NC 27106
O: 336.924.8063
F: 336.922.9005
email: olivet@windstream.net
www.olivetmoravian.org

**Pine Chapel**
324 Goldfloss Street
Winston-Salem NC 27127
O: 336.723.7118
email: pinechapelmoravian@att.net

**Providence Church**
929 Old Hollow Road
Winston-Salem NC 27105
O/F: 336.767.8234

**St. Philips Church**
3002 Bon Air Avenue
Winston-Salem NC 27105
O: 336.722.3933
email: office@stphilipsmoravian.org
www.stphilipsmoravian.org

**Trinity Church**
220 East Sprague Street
Winston-Salem NC 27127
O: 336.724.5541 or 336.724.5542
F: 336.724.1246
email: office@trinitymoravian.org
www.trinitymoravian.org

**Union Cross Church**
4295 High Point Road
Winston-Salem NC 27107
O: 336.769.2411
email: ucmc@unioncrossmoravian.org
www.unioncrossmoravian.org

**NORTH DAKOTA (NP, WD):**
DAVENPORT -
**Canaan Church**
4465 159th Avenue SE
Davenport ND 58021
O: 701.347.4730
www.moravian.nd.com

DURBIN -
**Goshen Church**
4201 153rd Avenue SE
Durbin ND 58059
*Mail:* PO Box 336
Leonard ND 58052
O: 701.645.2466
www.bethelgoshen.com

FARGO -
**Shepherd of the Prairie**
6151 25th Street South
Fargo ND 58104
O: 701.235.5711 or 701.645.2466
email: office@shepherdfargo.org
www.shepherdfargo.org

LEONARD -
**Bethel Church**
State Highway 18
Leonard ND 58052
*Mail:* PO Box 336
Leonard ND 58052
O: 701.645.2466
www.bethelgoshen.com

**OHIO (NP, ED):**
DOVER -
**First Church**
319 North Walnut Street
Dover OH 44622
O: 330.364.8831
F: 330.602.6711
email:
pastor@firstmoravianchurch.org
www.firstmoravianchurch.org

DUBLIN -
**Church of the Redeemer**
3883 Summitview Road
Dublin OH 43016-8426
O: 614.766.5030
or 614.766.5032
email: redeemerdublin@yahoo.com
www.redeemermoravian.org

**GNADENHUTTEN -**
**Gnadenhutten Church**
145 South Walnut Street
Gnadenhutten OH 44629
*Mail:* PO Box 126
Gnadenhutten OH 44629-0126
O: 740.254.4374
F: 740.254.4437
email: gnadenmor2@yahoo.com
http://web.tusco.net/gnadenmoravian

**LEWIS CENTER—**
**The Promise**
9012 Cotter Street
Lewis Center OH 43035
O: 740.549.1716
email: pastor@thepromisechurch.net
www.thepromisechurch.net

**NEW PHILADELPHIA -**
**Fry's Valley Church**
594 Fry's Valley Road SW
New Philadelphia OH 44663-7830
O: 740.254.9373
email: frysvalleymc@yahoo.com

**Schoenbrunn Community Church**
2200 East High Avenue
New Philadelphia OH 44663
O: 330.339.1940
F: 216.274.9998
email:
pastor@schoenbrunnmoravian.org
www.schoenbrunnmoravian.org

**Sharon Church**
4776 Moravian Church Road SE
New Philadelphia OH 44663
*Mail:* PO Box 385
Tuscarawas OH 44682-0385
O: 740.922.5507
F: 740.922.0895
email: sharonsec@roadrunner.com
www.sharonmoravian.org

**UHRICHSVILLE -**
**First Church**
315 North Water Street
Uhrichsville OH 44683
O: 740.922.0886
email: uhrichsvillemoravian.gmail.com
www.uhrichsvillemoravian.blogspot.com

**ONTARIO, Canada (NP, ED):**
**TORONTO -**
**New Dawn Church**
7 Glenora Avenue
Toronto ON M6C 3Y2
Canada
O: 416.656.0473
email: newdawnmoravian@bellnet.ca

**PENNSYLVANIA (NP, ED):**
**ALLENTOWN -**
**Calvary Church**
948 North 21st Street
Allentown PA 18104-3785
O: 610.435.6881
email: calvarym@ptd.net
www.calvarymoravian.net

**BETHLEHEM -**
**Advent Church**
3730 Jacksonville Road
Bethlehem PA 18017
O: 610.866.1402 or 610.868.0477
F: 610.868.0507
email: adventmoravian@verizon.net
www.adventmoravianchurch.com

**Central Church**
73 West Church Street
Bethlehem PA 18018
O: 610.866.5661 or 610.866.0607
F: 610.866.7256
email:
office@centralmoravianchurch.org
www.centralmoravianchurch.org

**College Hill Church**
72 West Laurel Street
Bethlehem PA 18018
O: 610.867.8291
F: 610.865.3067
email:
church@collegehillmoravian.org
www.collegehillmoravian.org

**East Hills Church**
1830 Butztown Road
Bethlehem PA 18017
O: 610.868.6481
F: 610.868.6219
email: office@easthillsmc.org
www.easthillsmc.org

**Edgeboro Church**
645 Hamilton Avenue
Bethlehem PA 18017
O: 610.866.8793
F: 610.866.8583
email:
churchoffice@edgeboromoravian.org
www.edgeboromoravian.org

**West Side Church**
402 Third Avenue
Bethlehem PA 18018
O: 610.865.0256
email: mail@westsidemoravian.org
www.westsidemoravian.org

**CANADENSIS -
Canadensis Church**
Route 447
Canadensis PA 18325
*Mail:* PO Box 209
Canadensis PA 18325-0209
O: 570.595.7114

**COOPERSBURG -
MorningStar Church**
234 South Main Street
Coopersburg PA 18036
O/F: 610.282.1908
email: coopmoravian@aol.com

**EASTON -
First Church**
225 North 10th Street
Easton PA 18042
O: 610.258.6317
email: eastonmoravian@rcn.com
www.firstmoravianeaston.org

**Palmer Township Church**
2901 John Street
Easton PA 18045-2544
O: 610.253.2510
F: 610.253.7401
email: pmc@palmermoravian.org
www.palmermoravian.org

**EMMAUS -
Emmaus Church**
146 Main Street
Emmaus PA 18049
O: 610.965.6067
F: 610.966.5420
email: pastor@emmausmoravian.org
www.emmausmoravian.org

**HELLERTOWN -
Mountainview Church**
331 Constitution Avenue
Hellertown PA 18055
O: 610.838.9344
F: 610.838.2807
email:
mountainviewmoravian@verizon.net
www.mountainviewmoravianchurch.com

**LANCASTER -
Lancaster Church**
1460 Eden Road
Lancaster PA 17601
O: 717.397.9722
F: 717.431.3809
email: office@lancastermoravian.org
www.lancastermoravian.org

**LEBANON -**
**Lebanon Church**
1115 Birch Road
Lebanon PA 17042-9123
O: 717.273.5864
F: 717.273.0255
email: lebmoravian@nbn.net
www.freewebs.com/lebanonmoravian

**LITITZ -**
**Lititz Church**
8 Church Square
Lititz PA 17543
O: 717.626.8515
F: 717.626.8258
email: office@lititzmoravian.org
www.lititzmoravian.org

**NAZARETH -**
**Nazareth Church**
4 South Main Street
Center Square
Nazareth PA 18064
*Mail:* PO Box 315
Nazareth PA 18064-0315
O: 610.759.3163
F: 610.759.3175
email: nazmoroffice@rcn.com
www.nazarethmoravian.org

**Schoeneck Church**
316 North Broad Street Extension
Nazareth PA 18064
O: 610.759.0376
F: 610.759.9762
email:
schoeneck@schoeneckmoravian.org
www.schoeneckmoravian.org

**NEWFOUNDLAND -**
**Newfoundland Church**
Route 191
Newfoundland PA 18445
*Mail:* PO Box 221
Newfoundland PA 18445-0221
O: 570.676.8201

**PHILADELPHIA -**
**Redeemer Church**
2950 South 70th Street
Philadelphia PA 19142
O: 215.365.6448
www.redeemermoravianphiladelphia.org

**READING -**
**Reading Church**
1116 Perry Street
Reading PA 19604-2005
O: 610.374.0886
email: readingmoravian@1USA.com
www.readingmoravian.org

**YORK -**
**Covenant Church**
901 Cape Horn Road
York PA 17402
O: 717.755.3269
email: covenantpastor@comcast.net
www.covenantmoravianyork.org

**First Church**
39 North Duke Street
York PA 17401
O: 717.843.2239
email: yorkfirstmoravian@verizon.net
www.firstmoravianchurch.worthyofpraise.org

**VIRGINIA (SP):**
**ARARAT -**
**Willow Hill Church**
577 Willow Hill Road
Ararat VA 24053
email: info@willowhillmoravian.org
www.willowhillmoravian.org

**CANA -**
**Crooked Oak Church**
1641 Bear Trail Road
Cana VA 24317
email: ijeaster@ccpsd.k12.va.us

**Mt. Bethel Church**
127 Mt. Bethel Church Road
Cana VA 24317
O: 276.755.4690
www.mountbethelmoravianchurch.com

**WISCONSIN (NP, WD):**

**APPLETON -**
**Freedom Church**
W3457 Center Valley Road
Appleton WI 54913-8937
O: 920.734.1278
F: 920.734.9932
email: freedommoravian@gmail.com
www.freedommoravian.com

**CAMBRIDGE -**
**London Church**
W9682 Main St.
Cambridge WI 53523
O: 608.764.1482
email:
pastor@londonmoravianchurch.org
www.londonmoravianchurch.org

**DEFOREST -**
**Christian Faith Church**
805 East Holum Street
DeForest WI 53532
O: 608.846.5876
email: cfmcoffice@gmail.com
www.cfmoravianchurch.org

**EPHRAIM -**
**Ephraim Church**
9970 Moravia Street
Ephraim WI 54211
*Mail:* PO Box 73
Ephraim WI 54211-0073
O: 920.854.2804
email: worship@ephraimmoravian.org
www.ephraimmoravian.org

**GREEN BAY -**
**West Side Church**
1707 South Oneida Street
Green Bay WI 54304
O: 920.499.4433
F: 920.499.9966
email: office@wsmoraviangb.org
www.wsmoraviangb.org

**LAKE MILLS -**
**Lake Mills Church**
301 College Street
Lake Mills WI 53551
O: 920.648.5412
F: 920.648.3669
email: lmmc3@frontier.com
www.lakemillsmoravianchurch.org

**MADISON -**
**Glenwood Church**
725 Gilmore Street
Madison WI 53711
O: 608.233.8709
F: 608.233.2595
email: glenwoodmoravian@tds.net
www.glenwoodmoravian.org

**Lakeview Church**
3565 Tulane Avenue
Madison WI 53714
O: 608.249.1973
email: lakeviewrev@sbcglobal.net
www.lakeviewmoravianchurch.org

**PITTSVILE -**
**Veedum Church**
County Road E
Pittsville WI 54466
*Mail:* PO Box 244
Pittsville WI 54466-0244
O: 715.884.6911

**Rudolph -**
**Rudolph Church**
1490 Main Street
Rudolph WI 54475
*Mail:* PO Box 144
Rudolph WI 54475-0144
O: 715.435.3333
email: rmchurch@solarus.net

**Sister Bay -**
**Sister Bay Church**
10924 Old Stage Road
Sister Bay WI 54234
O: 920.854.4080
www.sisterbaymoravianchurch.org

**Sturgeon Bay -**
**Sturgeon Bay Church**
323 South 5th Avenue
Sturgeon Bay WI 54235
O: 920.743.6218
F: 920.743.0440
email: sbmc@sbmoravian.org
www.sbmoravian.org

**Watertown -**
**Ebenezer Church**
N8071 High Road
Watertown WI 53094
O: 920.206.0222
email: emc1853@aol.com
www.ebenezermoravianchurch.org

**Watertown Church**
510 Cole Street
Watertown WI 53094
O: 920.261.7494
F: 920.206.9030
email:
watertownmoravianchurch@yahoo.com
www.watertownmoravianchurch.org

**Wisconsin Rapids -**
**Kellner Church**
Junction of County Hwys U and W
Wisconsin Rapids WI 54494
*Mail:* 8016 County Road FF
Wisconsin Rapids WI 54494
O: 715.423.2688

**Saratoga Church**
11131 52nd Street S
Wisconsin Rapids WI 54494
O: 715.325.3081
email: smoravch@wctc.net

**Wisconsin Rapids Church**
310 First Avenue South
Wisconsin Rapids WI 54495-4155
O: 715.423.0180
email: moravian@wctc.net
www.wrmoravian.org

## NEW & EMERGING CHURCHES

**INDIANA:**
**Indianapolis**
Zaccheus' Tree Moravian Church
The Rev. Rebecca Craver
*Church Planter*
7001 S Arlington Avenue
Indianapolis IN 46237
O: 317.881.6204
www.newhopeindy.org

**MINNESOTA:**
**St. Michael**
New Horizons Community Church
The Rev. David Glasser
*Church Planter*
405 5th Street NW
St. Michael MN 55376
O: 763.497.9024
email: newhorizonstma@aol.com
www.newhorizons-stma.org

**PENNSYLVANIA:**
**Lehigh Valley**
Esperanza for Bethlehem
The Rev. Tracy Robinson
*Church Planter*
617 East 4th Street
Bethlehem PA 18015
O: 484.895.5581
email: pastortracy@
esperanzaforbethlehem.org

**Macungie**
SONrise Community Church
Kate Dekker
*Lay Church Planter*
2923 Lifford Lane
Macungie PA 18062
O: 610.965.1879
email:
moravianchurchlady@verizon.net

**ALBERTA, CANADA:**
**Sherwood Park**
The Connection
The Rev. Ian Edwards &
The Rev. Dr. Eileen Edwards
*Church Planters*
15 Davy Crescent
Sherwood Park AB T8H 1P3
Canada

## MORAVIAN FELLOWSHIPS

**CALIFORNIA:**
### Guiding Star Fellowship
Ethel Brown
324 Los Encinos Drive
San Jose CA 95134

Meiling Hentz
1831 Washu Way
Stockton CA 95206

Meeting Location:
957 Colorado Avenue
Palo Alto CA 94303

### Hope Fellowship
Gina Antonio
1147 Hollyburn Avenue
Menlo Park CA 94025

Maicie Cunningham
27789 Mandarin Avenue
Hayward CA 94544

Meeting Location:
1199 East Bay Shore Road
East Palo Alto CA 94303

**FLORIDA:**
### Margate Fellowship
The Rev. Joe Nicholas
1880 NW 183rd Street
Miami FL 33056
O: 305.628.2061, F: 305.625.5365

Meeting Location:
4700 N State Road 7, Suite 108
Lauderhill FL 33319-5803

### New Covenant Fellowship
The Rev. Ofreciano Julias
1621 Quail Drive Bldg 203
West Palm Beach FL 33409
H: 561.313.3651

Meeting Location:
West Palm Beach Moravian Church

### Nueva Esperanza Fellowship
Illovis Gonzalez, *Provincial Acolyte*
c/o 6001 SW 127 Avenue
Miami FL 33183

Meeting location:
New Hope Moravian Church

### Suriname Moravian Fellowship
Armand Sabar, *Coordinator*
245 NE 191 Street Unit #3009
Miami FL 33179
O: 305.401.5479

Meeting Location:
Prince of Peace Moravian Church

### Rayaka Ingnika Fellowship
Jose Willis, *Coordinator*
2125 Constitution Boulevard
Sarasota FL 34243
O: 941.922.6413
email: willis1011@verizon.net

Meeting location:
Primera Iglesia Bautista
4445 South Lockwood Ridge Road
Sarasota FL 34231

### Tampa Fellowship
Federico Velasquez, *Coordinator*
6602 North 24th Street
Tampa FL 33610-1310
O: 813.476.7969

Meeting Location:
St. Paul Lutheran Church
5103 North Central Avenue
Tampa FL 33610

## MORAVIAN FELLOWSHIPS CONTINUED

### NORTH CAROLINA:
**Morning Star Fellowship**
Cliff Dodson, *Coordinator*
34 Baton Lane
Asheville NC 28803
O: 828.778.2411
O: 828.253.0043 (Morning Star)
*Mail:* PO Box 8608
Asheville NC 28814

Meeting Location:
St. Mark's Lutheran Church
10 North Liberty Street
Asheville NC 28801

### Community Fellowship
Jack Nance, *Coordinator*
3733 Konnoak Drive
Winston-Salem NC 27127
H: 336.784.5252

Welcome-Arcadia Road
Welcome NC 27374
*Mail:* PO Box 397
Welcome NC 27374-0397
O: 336.731.8265

### Mountain Laurel Fellowship
George Bloodworth, *Coordinator*
239 Laurel Lane
Jefferson NC 28640
H: 336.846.7038
email: ghb43@skybest.com

Meeting Location:
Transou UMC
2nd and 4th Sundays at 11:00am
Laurel Springs NC 28644

### ONTARIO, CANADA:
**The Journey Fellowship**
Winston Josiah, *Administrator*
1508 - 3605 Kariya Drive
Mississauga ON L5B 3J4
Canada
O: 905.897.1212

Meeting Location:
6945 Meadowvale Town Center Circle
Mississauga ON L5N 2W7

### SOUTH CAROLINA:
**Palmetto Fellowship**
Martha Stocks, *Coordinator*
105 Pine Tree Circle
Spartanburg SC 29307
O: 864.582.1442
email: palmettomoravian@aol.com
www.palmettomoravianfellowship.org

Meeting location:
Central United Methodist Church
233 North Church Street
Spartanburg SC 29307
O: 864.597.0200

### WASHINGTON:
**Seattle Fellowship**
Richard and Joan Thomas
20904 3rd Avenue South
Des Moines WA 98198
O: 206.824.6411
email: jmpthomas@comcast.net

### WISCONSIN:
**Mamre Fellowship**
Don Wegner, *Coordinator*
W5884 Church Road
Johnson Creek WI 53038-9736
H: 920.699.3272

Meeting Location:
N9015 County Highway Q
Watertown WI 53094

# MORAVIAN CHURCH IN NORTH AMERICA
# PROVINCIAL & DISTRICT OFFICES

### *The Provincial Elders' Conference -*
### *Northern Province*

The Rev. Dr. Elizabeth D. Miller, President
Office: 1021 Center St., PO  Box 1245, Bethlehem, PA 18016-1245
O: 610.867.7566, 800.732.0591, Ext. 19
email: betsy@mcnp.org
www.mcnp.org

### *Northern Province - District Executive Boards*

### **Eastern District**

The Rev. David E. Bennett, President
1021 Center St., PO Box 1245, Bethlehem, PA 18016-1245
O: 610.865.0302, 800.732.0591, F: 610.866.9223
email: edeb@mcnp.org
www.mcnp.org/easterndistrict

### **Western District**

The Rev. James T. Hicks, President
PO Box 12677, Green Bay, WI 54307-2677
O: 920.883.2212
email: jamesthicks@aol.com
www.moravianwest.org

### **Canadian District**

The Rev. Stephen A. Gohdes, President
600 Acadia Dr. SE, Calgary, Alberta T2J 0B8, Canada
O: 403.271.2700
email: sgohdes@shaw.ca
www.moravian.ca

### *The Provincial Elders' Conference -*
### *Southern Province*

The Rev. David B. Guthrie
459 S. Church St., Winston-Salem, NC 27101
O: 336.725.5811, 888.725.5811, F: 336.723.1029
email: dguthrie@mcsp.org
www.mcsp.org

## PRAYER DAYS AND SPECIAL EMPHASES

The following prayer days or special emphases have been authorized by the Northern Provincial Synod or by the Provincial Elders' Conferences of the Northern and Southern Provinces of the Moravian Church in North America:

Ecumenical Sunday: The last Sunday in January.

For Retired Ministers (optional): The last Sunday in January.

For Moravian Unity Work: The first Sunday in March.

For Board of Evangelism and Home Missions (Southern Province):
The last Sunday in April.

Moravian Music Sunday: Fifth Sunday of Easter (fourth Sunday after Easter).

For Moravian Retirement Community (Southern Province):
The second Sunday in May.

For Outdoor Ministries (Northern Province): The Sunday after Trinity.

For Camps & Conferences (Southern Province): The Sunday after Trinity.

For World Peace and Nuclear Disarmament (Northern Province):
The first Sunday in August.

For Public Education and Moravian Educational Institutions
(Southern Province): The last Sunday in August.

For Public Education (Northern Province): The last Sunday in August.

For Christian Education: The second Sunday in September.

For Church Development (Northern Province): The third Sunday in September.

For the Church's Ministry to Older Adults (Northern Province):
The fourth Sunday in September.

For Older Adults (Southern Province): The fourth Sunday in September.

For Children: A Sunday in October.

For World Mission: The second Sunday in October.

For Peace with Justice and Freedom (Northern Province):
The third Sunday in October.

Moravian Women's Sunday (Northern Province):
The first Sunday in November (date optional).

For the Bible Society: The Sunday before Thanksgiving.

For Moravian College and Theological Seminary (Northern Province):
The Sunday on or immediately after November 20.

World AIDS Day: December 1.

## CHURCH CAUSES
### Northern Province

Members and friends of the Moravian Church can show continuing interest in its work by making the Church a beneficiary in their will or by making an outright monetary gift. For the address of any corporation listed below, please see pages immediately preceding. The programs of the Northern Province are administered by the following incorporated boards:

Moravian Church, Northern Province

The Society for Promoting the Gospel

Trustees of the Moravian Larger Life Foundation

The Provincial Women's Board

The Moravian Archives

The Executive Board of the Eastern District of the Moravian Church in America, Northern Province

The Executive Board of the Eastern District of the Moravian Church in America, Northern Province for the Foster Fund

The Executive Board of the Western District of the Moravian Church in America, Northern Province

Hope Conference and Renewal Center

Moravian Hall Square Historic District, Inc.

Moravian Hall Square Retirement Community, Inc.

Moravian Manors, Inc.

Moravian Open Door, Inc.

Sperling-Zimmerman Memorial Home

Marquardt Memorial Manor, Inc.

Moravian Care Ministries, Inc.

Mt. Morris Camp and Conference Center

The Board of Elders of the Canadian District of the Moravian Church in America, Northern Province

Canadian Moravian Foundation

Van-Es Camp and Conference Centre

Board of World Mission of the Moravian Church

Moravian Music Foundation, Inc.

Linden Hall School for Girls at Lititz, Pennsylvania

Moravian Academy

Moravian College

Moravian Theological Seminary

Interprovincial Board of Communication

## Southern Province

The programs of the Southern Province are administered by the following boards and agencies:

The Provincial Elders' Conference
The Board of Evangelism and Homeland Missions*
Mission Society of the Moravian Church, South, Inc.
Board of World Mission of the Moravian Church
Salem Academy and College
The Board of Christian Education*
Laurel Ridge, Moravian Camp, Conference, & Retreat Center*
The Archives*
Salemtowne
The Pension Fund*
Moravian Music Foundation, Inc.
Provincial Women's Board*
Moravian Theological Seminary
Sunnyside Ministry*
Interprovincial Board of Communication

*Not incorporated. Bequests to these boards and agencies should be made for their use to the Moravian Church in America, Southern Province.*

### REMITTANCES
Contributions for provincial or general church causes should be sent to the provincial treasurer:

**NORTHERN PROVINCE:** Christina Giesler, Controller
1021 Center Street, PO Box 1245, Bethlehem, Pennsylvania 18018-1245

**SOUTHERN PROVINCE:** Ted Leinbach, Treasurer
459 South Church Street, Winston-Salem, North Carolina 27101

**PLANNED GIFTS AND BEQUESTS:** For information about estate plans or information about charitable trusts, annuities, and other forms of planned gifts to support one or more of the above ministries or your church, contact Paul McLaughlin, President of Moravian Ministries Foundation at:
455 South Church Street, Winston-Salem, North Carolina 27101
Phone: 1.888.722.7923

## THE UNITAS FRATRUM
*(International Moravian Church)*
for the year ending December 31, 2010
*Provided by the Chair of the Unity Board*

| Province | C | O | M | COM | T |
|---|---|---|---|---|---|
| Alaska | 23 | 1 | 11 | 1,904 | 1,904 |
| America, North | 93 | 10 | 106 | 17,298 | 21,633 |
| America, South | 56 | 9 | 65 | 13,096 | 15,737 |
| Burundi*** | 18 | 44 | --- | 26,648 | 26,648 |
| Congo** | 65 | 13 | 20 | 11,050 | 15,360 |
| Costa Rica | 6 | 1 | 6 | 400 | 1,803 |
| Cuba*** | 5 | --- | 3 | --- | 700 |
| Czech Republic* | 23 | 5 | 28 | 800 | 4,800 |
| Czech Unity Undertaking | 8 | --- | 7 | --- | 600 |
| EasternWest Indies* | 50 | 3 | 45 | 12,040 | 17,121 |
| European Continental* | 25 | 35 | 47 | 11,475 | 16,361 |
| Garifuna*** | 14 | --- | 9 | --- | 500 |
| Great Britain* | 30 | 2 | 18 | 1,448 | 1,787 |
| Guyana** | 8 | --- | 4 | 681 | 940 |
| Honduras* | 104 | 11 | 30 | 45,000 | 45,000 |
| Honduras Unity Undertaking | 68 | --- | 24 | --- | 14,000 |
| Jamaica | 65 | 5 | 35 | 5,180 | 8,549 |
| Kenya*** | 16 | --- | 2 | --- | 731 |
| Labrador**/* | 4 | 2 | 2 | 519 | 1,981 |
| Malawi** | 9 | 4 | 30 | 3,282 | 4,000 |
| Nicaragua | 215 | --- | 96 | 25,995 | 88,262 |
| Rwanda*** | 5 | --- | --- | --- | 1,861 |
| South Africa* | 84 | 140 | 64 | 30,569 | 42,740 |
| Suriname | 80 | 7 | 17 | 23,000 | 45,000 |
| Tanzania, East/Zanzibar** | 40 | 10 | 30 | 16,000 | 20,000 |
| Tanzania, Kigoma** | 22 | 121 | 20 | 23,150 | 26,512 |
| Tanzania, Northern** | 22 | 3 | 24 | --- | 3,350 |
| Tanzania, Rukwa | 47 | 396 | 88 | --- | 60,129 |
| Tanzania, Southern* | 128 | 10 | 150 | 167,062 | 172,776 |
| Tanzania, South West* | 240 | 410 | --- | --- | 215,000 |
| Tanzania, Western | 45 | 261 | 60 | --- | 102,250 |
| Uganda*** | --- | 10 | --- | --- | 160 |
| Zambia** | 15 | 39 | 12 | 4,000 | 4,012 |
| **Total, Dec, 31, 2010** | **1,633** | **1,552** | **1,053** | **440,617** | **984,665** |

C = Congregations
O = Outstations
M = Ordained Ministers
COM = Communicants
T = Total Membership

\* no membership statistics received for 2010
\** Mission Province
\*** Mission Area

## OFFICIAL HEADS OF FULL UNITY PROVINCES
## COMPRISING THE MORAVIAN UNITY

(Phone numbers do not include international access code numbers. The international direct dial access code from U.S. phones is 011 except for calls to Labrador, Eastern West Indies, Jamaica.)

### President of the Unity Board
The Rev. Dr. Paul Gardner
*President, Jamaica Province*
The Moravian Church Office
PO Box 8369
3 Hector Street
Kingston CSO
Jamaica West Indies
O: 876.928.1861
F: 876.928.8336
email:
moravianchurch@cwjamaica.com
or moravianchurchja@yahoo.com
www.unitasfratrum.org

### Unity Business Administrator
The Rev. Dr. Jørgen Bøytler
Lindegade 26
DK-6070 Christiansfeld
Denmark
O: 45.7456.1420
C: 45.4036.1420
email: boytler@ebu.de

### Alaska
The Rev. Peter Green
PO Box 545
371 Third Avenue
Bethel AK 99559-0545
O: 907.543.2478
F: 907.543.3942
email: peterg11@alaskamoravian.org
www.alaskamoravian.org

### America (North)
The Rev. Dr. Elizabeth D. Miller
1021 Center Street
PO Box 1245
Bethlehem PA 18016-1245
O: 610.865.3137
F: 610.866.9223
email: betsy@mcnp.org
www.mcnp.org

### America (South)
The Rev. David Guthrie
459 South Church Street
Winston-Salem NC 27101
O: 336.725.5811
F: 336.723.1029
email: dguthrie@mcsp.org
www.mcsp.org

### Congo
The Rev. Moise M. Tshimanga
Eglise Morave au Congo
PO Box 126
Muene-Ditu Congo
O: 24.381.603.0558
email: tshimangamoise@yahoo.fr

### Costa Rica
Dr. Leopold Pixley
Iglesia Morava en Costa Rica
Apartado Postal 2140-1002
Paseo de los Estudiantes
San José Costa Rica
Central America
H: 506.250.0311
F: 506.227.1542
email: lpixley@costarricense.cr

**Czech Republic**
The Rev. Evald Rucky
Bozeny Nemcove 54/9
CZ 460 05 Liberec V
Czech Republic
O: 420.484.847916
email: rucky@jbcr.info
www.jbcr.info

**Eastern West Indies**
The Rev. Dr. Cortroy Jarvis
Cashew Hill
PO Box 504
St. John's Antigua West Indies
O: 268.560.0185
F: 268.462.0643
email: cjarvis.ewip@gmail.com
www.moravians.net

**European Continental**
The Rev. Frieder Vollprecht
Badwasen 6
D-73087 Bad Boll Germany
O: 49.7164.942130
F: 49.7164.942199
email: frieder.vollprecht@bb.ebu.de
www.ebu.de

**Great Britain and Ireland**
The Rev. Robert Hopcroft
Moravian Church House
5-7 Muswell Hill
London N10 3TJ United Kingdom
O: 44.208.883.3409
F: 44.208.365.3371
email:
Robert.Hopcroft@moravian.org.uk
or office@moravian.org.uk
www.moravian.org.uk

**Honduras**
The Rev. Isai Granwell
Iglesia Morava, Puerto Lempira
Depto. de Gracias a Dios
Honduras Central America
O: 504.433.6595
F: 504.441.0627
email: henriquez1960@yahoo.com

**Jamaica & the Cayman Islands**
The Rev. Dr. Paul Gardner
The Moravian Church Office
PO Box 8369
3 Hector Street
Kingston CSO
Jamaica West Indies
O: 876.928.1861
F: 876.928.8336
email:
moravianchurch@cwjamaica.com
www.jamaicamoravian.com

**Nicaragua**
The Rev. Gonzalo Piaz
Iglesia Morava en Nicaragua
Puerto Cabezas RAAN Nicaragua
Central America
O/F: 505.792.2222
M: 505.835547
email: gonzalomoravo@gmail.com

**South Africa**
The Rev. Lennox Mcubusi
PO Box 24111
Lansdowne
7780 Republic of South Africa
O: 27.21.761.4030
F: 27.21.761.4046
email: mcsa@iafrica.com

**Suriname**
The Rev. Renard Pansa
Evangelische Broeder Gemeente
PO Box 1811 Maagdenstraat 50
Paramaribo Suriname
South America
O: 597.473073
F: 597.475794
email: ebgs@sr.net or
renoldpansa@yahoo.com
www.moravianchurch.sr

**Tanzania (Rukwa)**
The Rev. Nebort Kipeta Sikazwe
PO Box 378
Sumbawanga Rukwa
Tanzania East Central Africa
O: 255.25.280.2714
F: 255.25.280.2079
email: sikazwenebort@yahoo.com

**Tanzania (Southern)**
The Rev. Clement Mwaitebele
Moravian Church in Tanzania
PO Box 32
Rungwe Tukuyu
Tanzania East Central Africa
O: 255.25.255.2030
F: 255.25.255.2298
email: ctebele@yahoo.co.uk

**Tanzania (Southwest)**
The Rev. Nonsigwe Buyo
PO Box 377
2643 Mbeya
Tanzania East Central Africa
O: 255.25.250.2643
email: mctswp@hotmail.com

**Tanzania (Western)**
The Rev. John Italazyo
PO Box 29
Tabora Tanzania
East Central Africa
O/F: 255.26.260.4822
email: jitalazyo@yahoo.com

## MISSION AREAS
*(Parenthesis indicate the supervising province -*
*correspondence should be directed to the supervising province)*

**Moravian Church in Belize**
(Honduras)

**Moravian Church in Burundi**
(Tanzania - Western)

**Moravian Church in Cuba**
(Jamaica)

**Moravian Church in Fr. Guiana**
(Suriname)

**Moravian Church in Garifuna**
(Honduras)

**Moravian Church in Kenya**
(Tanzania - Western)

**Moravian Church in Peru**
(Board of World Mission - USA)

**Ruvuma and Njombe, Tanzania**
(Tanzania - Southern)

**Moravian Church in Rwanda**
(Tanzania - Western)

**Moravian Church in Sierra Leone**
(Board of World Mission - USA)

**Moravian Church in South Asia**
(Great Britain)

**Moravian Church in Uganda**
(Tanzania - Western)

**Moravian Church in Zanzibar**
(Tanzania - Eastern)

## MISSION PROVINCES

### Guyana
The Rev. Brinmore Phaul
The Moravian Church in Guyana
53 New Garden Street
Queenstown Georgetown
Guyana South America
O: 592.226.2524
F: 592.227.4590
email: brinmorep@yahoo.com

### Labrador
Linda Saunders Mc-Lean
PO Box 220 Station B
Happy Valley-Goose Bay
Labrador A0P 1E0 Canada
O: 709.923.2262
email: thebigland@aol.com or
moravianhv@hotmail.com
www.labradormoravian.blogspot.com

### Malawi
The Rev. Henry Mwakibinga
Moravian Church in Malawi
PO Box 119
Karonga Malawi
email: moravian_cmm@yahoo.com

### Tanzania, East/Zanzibar
The Rev. Clement D. Fumbo
Eastern Tanzania & Zanzibar
PO Box 16416
Dar Es Salaam Tanzania
email: cfumbo@gmail.com or
moravian07@gmail.com

### Tanzania, Kigoma
The Rev. Ernest Vuzuka
Moravian Church in Kigoma
PO Box 1267
Kigoma Tanzania
email: evuzuka@yahoo.com

### Tanzania, Northern
The Rev. Peter Malema
Moravian Church, Northern
Tanzania
PO Box 12320
Arusha Tanzania
O/F: 255.27.250.7901
email: mcnt2007@yahoo.com

### Zambia
The Rev. Joseph Silaywe
Moravian Church in Zambia
PO Box 38508
Lusaka Zambia
O: 260.262.1215
email: edsilaywe@yahoo.co.uk or
moravianchurch2003@yahoo.com

## UNITY UNDERTAKINGS
*(Parenthesis indicate the supervising province)*

**Czech Unity Undertaking**
(European Continental Province)
The Rev. Jiri Polma, *Chairman*
Komenskeho 603
CZ - 46822 Zelezny Brod
Czech Republic
O: 420.483.38923
email: jiri.polma@seznam.cz

**Honduras Unity Undertaking**
Rev. Salomon Ordonez
Ahuas Gracias A Dios
Honduras
email:
ordonezsalomon@yahoo.com.mx

**Star Mountain
Rehabilitation Center**
(European Continental Province)
Ms. Ghada Naser, *Director*
PO Box 199
Ramallah Palestine
O: 972.2.296.2705
F: 972.2.296.2715
email: starmountaincenter@gmail.com
www.starmountain.org

**Unity Archives of the
Moravian Church**
Dr. Rüdiger Kröger, *Director*
PO Box 21
Zittauerstrasse 24
D-02745 Herrnhut
Germany
O: 49.358.734.8731
F: 49.358.734.8766
email: unitaetsarchiv@ebu.de

## RELATED TO THE AMERICAN PROVINCES

### Unity of the Brethren in Texas
The Rev. Claren Kotrla, President
1501 Echo Bluff Cove
Austin TX 78754
512.491.7802

# HISTORICAL NOTES

Organization dates of congregations in the United States and
Canada and dates of the worldwide Moravian Church:

## JANUARY

1- 1815 Sharon, Tuscarawas, Ohio

1858 Chaska, Minnesota

1915 Waconia, Minnesota

1968 United, New York, New York, merger of New York III and IV

3- 1856 Ordination of John Andrew Buckley, the first Moravian
minister of African descent, Antigua, West Indies

1932 First service of confirmation of Moravians in Honduras

5- 1992 New Hope, Miami, Florida

12- 1757 The first Moravian convert baptized on Antigua, West Indies

19- 1964 Rio Terrace, Edmonton, Alberta, Canada

20- 1889 Wisconsin Rapids, Wisconsin

21- 1951 Konnoak Hills, Winston-Salem, North Carolina

28- 1996 Palm Beach, West Palm Beach, Florida

30- 1864 Sturgeon Bay, Wisconsin

31- 1971 St. Paul's, Upper Marlboro, Maryland

## FEBRUARY

2- 1891 Bethel, Leonard, North Dakota

1964 Trinity, New Carrollton, Maryland

3- 1957 Official organization of Morongo Moravian Church,
Banning, California; result of Indian mission work begun in
1889

9- 1749 Warwick, now Lititz, Lititz, Pennsylvania

12- 1978 Covenant, Wilmington, North Carolina

1989 Good Shepherd, Kernersville, North Carolina

13- 1870 Unionville, Michigan

1983 New Hope, Newton, North Carolina

## MARCH

| | | |
|---|---|---|
| 1- | 1457 | Date observed in commemoration of the founding in Bohemia of the Unitas Fratrum, now known as the Moravian Church |
| 5- | 1939 | Calvary, Allentown, Pennsylvania |
| 14- | 1849 | Arrival of first Moravian missionaries in Bluefields, Nicaragua |
| | 1886 | Great Kills, Staten Island, New York |
| | 1951 | Mountainview, Hellertown, Pennsylvania |
| 15- | 1925 | Grace, Mount Airy, North Carolina |
| 21- | 1993 | King of Kings, Miami, Florida |
| 23- | 1975 | First, Stone Mountain, Georgia |
| 24- | 1799 | The first Moravian converts baptized on Tobago, West Indies |
| 25- | 1752 | First, York, Pennsylvania |
| | 1995 | Morning Star, Asheville, North Carolina |
| 27- | 1966 | John Hus, Brooklyn, New York |
| 28- | 1954 | Lakeview, Madison, Wisconsin |

## APRIL

| | | |
|---|---|---|
| 1- | 1756 | Arrival on Antigua, West Indies, of Samuel Isles, the first Moravian missionary on that island |
| | 1888 | First, Easton, Pennsylvania |
| 3- | 1896 | Sister Bay, Wisconsin |
| 4- | 1773 | Friedberg, Winston-Salem, North Carolina |
| 6- | 1851 | Olivet, Winston-Salem, North Carolina |
| 7- | 1929 | Glenwood, Madison, Wisconsin |
| 9- | 1917 | Veedum, Pittsville, Wisconsin |
| 10- | 1949 | Palmer Township, Easton, Pennsylvania |
| | 1988 | Good News, Sherwood Park, Alberta, Canada |
| 11- | 1898 | Enterprise, Arcadia, North Carolina |
| 13- | 1732 | The first Easter sunrise service of the Moravians conducted in the Hutberg cemetery at Herrnhut, Germany |
| | 1760 | Bethania, North Carolina |
| | 1859 | Egg Harbor City, New Jersey |
| | 1885 | Windsor, now Christian Faith, DeForest, Wisconsin |
| 21- | 1929 | Leaksville, Eden, North Carolina |
| | 1976 | Our Savior's, Altura, Minnesota, merger of Bethany and Hebron |

| | | |
|---|---|---|
| 25- | 1890 | Arrival on Trinidad, West Indies, of Samuel Thaeler and John Holmes to organize Moravian work on that island |
| 27- | 1790 | Arrival on Tobago, West Indies, of John and Mary Montgomery (parents of hymnwriter James Montgomery) to begin Moravian work on that island |
| | 1852 | New York II, now Tremont Terrace, Bronx, New York |
| | 1969 | Christ, Calgary, Alberta, Canada |

## MAY

| | | |
|---|---|---|
| 3- | 1728 | Beginning of Losungen (Daily Texts) in Herrnhut, Germany |
| | 1931 | Rural Hall, North Carolina |
| 5- | 1822 | St. Philip's, Winston-Salem, North Carolina |
| | 1895 | Fairview, Winston-Salem, North Carolina |
| 6- | 1860 | West Side, Bethlehem, Pennsylvania |
| | 1895 | Bruderheim, Alberta, Canada |
| 9- | 1760 | Count Zinzendorf dies. (b. May 26,1700) |
| 12- | 1727 | Unanimous adoption of the first statutes, or Brotherly Agreement, by the settlers at Herrnhut, Germany, the first definite step toward reorganization of the Unitas Fratrum |
| 17- | 1863 | Palmyra, Cinnaminson, New Jersey |
| 18- | 1902 | Calgary, now Good Shepherd, Calgary, Alberta, Canada |
| 19- | 2002 | New Beginnings, Huntersville, North Carolina |
| 22- | 1966 | Redeemer, Philadelphia, Pennsylvania |
| | 1983 | Christ's Community Church, Maple Grove, Minnesota |
| 24- | 1856 | Macedonia, Advance, North Carolina |
| | 1878 | Goshen, Durbin, North Dakota |
| 25- | 1844 | West Salem, Illinois |
| | 1986 | Faith Church of the Nation's Capital, Washington, D.C. |
| 26- | 1853 | Ephraim, Wisconsin |
| | 1963 | Acceptance of Saratoga Union, Wisconsin Rapids, Wisconsin, as a Moravian congregation |

## JUNE

| | | |
|---|---|---|
| 1- | 1895 | Rudolph, Wisconsin |
| 5- | 1898 | Willow Hill, Ararat, Virginia |
| 6- | 1954 | Downey, California |
| 9- | 1957 | East Hills, Bethlehem, Pennsylvania |
| 11- | 1857 | Fry's Valley, New Philadelphia, Ohio |
| 12- | 1905 | Edmonton, Alberta, Canada |
| | 1943 | Fargo, now Shepherd of the Prairie, Fargo, North Dakota |
| | 1955 | Battle Hill, Union, New Jersey, continuing the Elizabeth, New Jersey, congregation begun in 1866 |
| 14- | 1777 | Arrival of the first Moravian missionaries on St. Kitts, West Indies |
| 17- | 1722 | Beginning of the building of Herrnhut, Germany, by the emigrants from Moravia |
| | 1830 | Hope, Indiana |
| | 1853 | Ebenezer, Watertown, Wisconsin |
| 18- | 1932 | Hopewell, Winston-Salem, North Carolina |
| 20- | 1884 | Arrival of first Moravian missionaries in Bethel, Alaska |
| 21- | 1621 | The Day of Blood, so called because on that day 27 patriots, most of them members of the Brethren's Church, were executed at Prague, Bohemia |
| | 1924 | Advent, Winston-Salem, North Carolina |
| | 1958 | Grace, Westland, Michigan |
| 25- | 1742 | Central, Bethlehem, Pennsylvania |
| | 1747 | Nazareth, Pennsylvania |
| | 1876 | Fries Memorial, Winston-Salem, North Carolina |
| 26- | 1988 | Fellowship, Brooklyn, New York |
| 27- | 1895 | Bruderfeld, now Millwoods, Edmonton, Alberta, Canada |
| 29- | 1924 | Ardmore, Winston-Salem, North Carolina |

## JULY

| | | |
|---|---|---|
| 6- | 1415 | Burning at the stake of John Hus, Bohemian martyr and forebear of the Unitas Fratrum |
| | 1763 | New Dorp, Staten Island, New York |
| | 1800 | Gnadenhutten, Ohio |
| 14- | 1912 | Trinity, Winston-Salem, North Carolina |

17- 1955   Grace, Center Valley, Pennsylvania
      1927   Crooked Oak, Cana, Virginia
26- 1846   New Philadelphia, Winston-Salem, North Carolina
      1896   Heimtal, South Edmonton, Alberta, Canada
30- 1747   Emmaus, Pennsylvania
31- 1752   Arrival of first Moravian missionaries in Labrador

## AUGUST

13- 1727   Manifestation of the unity of the Spirit, at the Holy
              Communion service held in the Berthelsdorf, Germany,
              church; regarded as the spiritual birthday of the Renewed
              Moravian Church
      1837   Newfoundland, Pennsylvania
      1900   Clemmons, North Carolina
21- 1732   Departure of the first Moravian missionaries from
              Herrnhut for St. Thomas in the West Indies; the beginning
              of Moravian missions and of the modern missionary
              movement of the Protestant church
26- 1780   Hope, Winston-Salem, North Carolina
      2001   The Promise, Lewis Center, Ohio
27- 1727   Beginning of the Hourly Intercession
      1872   Formation of the Moravian Prayer Union
31- 1873   Castleton Hill, Staten Island, New York

## SEPTEMBER

3-  1780   Friedland, Winston-Salem, North Carolina
5-  1869   Northfield, Minnesota
10- 1911   Daggett, Michigan
11- 1854   Watertown, Wisconsin
13- 1893   Union Cross, Winston-Salem, North Carolina
      1896   Mizpah, Rural Hall, North Carolina
15- 2003   Holly Springs, North Carolina
16- 1741   Recognition and acceptance of Christ as the Chief Elder of
              the Moravian Church
      1858   Canadensis, Pennsylvania

## SEPTEMBER (continued)

|       |      |                                                                                          |
|-------|------|------------------------------------------------------------------------------------------|
|       | 1984 | New Dawn, Toronto, Ontario, Canada                                                       |
| 18-   | 1768 | Baptism of the first Moravian convert on Barbados, West Indies                           |
| 25-   | 1887 | Oak Grove, Winston-Salem, North Carolina                                                 |
| 26-   | 1765 | Arrival of John Wood and Andrew Rittsmansberger on Barbados, West Indies, from Herrnhut to begin Moravian work |

## OCTOBER

|       |      |                                                                                          |
|-------|------|------------------------------------------------------------------------------------------|
| 2-    | 1807 | Beginning of the Moravian Theological Seminary at Nazareth, Pennsylvania, in 1858 transferred to Bethlehem |
| 3-    | 1762 | Schoeneck, Nazareth, Pennsylvania                                                        |
|       | 1896 | Moravia, Summerfield, North Carolina                                                     |
| 4-    | 1953 | Raleigh, North Carolina                                                                  |
| 5-    | 1908 | First, Greensboro, North Carolina                                                        |
|       | 1924 | King, North Carolina                                                                     |
| 6-    | 1889 | London, Cambridge, Wisconsin                                                             |
| 7-    | 2002 | Immanuel-New Eden, merger of Immanuel (1912) and New Eden (1923)                         |
| 8-    | 1758 | Graceham, Thurmont, Maryland                                                             |
|       | 1967 | Rolling Hills, Longwood, Florida                                                         |
| 10-   | 1885 | Moving into the first house in Bethel, Alaska, by missionaries John Kilbuck and William Weinland |
| 12-   | 1851 | East Side, Green Bay, Wisconsin                                                          |
| 17-   | 2004 | Cordero de Dios, Winston-Salem, North Carolina                                           |
| 18-   | 1889 | Stapleton, now Vanderbilt Avenue, Staten Island, New York                               |
| 20-   | 1985 | Church of the Redeemer, Dublin, Ohio                                                     |
| 22-   | 1899 | Bethesda, Winston-Salem, North Carolina                                                  |
| 23-   | 1881 | Canaan, Davenport, North Dakota                                                          |
| 24-   | 1874 | First, Uhrichsville, Ohio                                                                |
| 25-   | 1896 | Christ, Winston-Salem, North Carolina                                                    |
|       | 1914 | Edgeboro, Bethlehem, Pennsylvania                                                        |
| 31-   | 1858 | Lake Auburn, Victoria, Minnesota                                                         |

## NOVEMBER

| | | |
|---|---|---|
| 7- | 1920 | The Little Church on the Lane, Charlotte, North Carolina |
| 9- | 1980 | Grace, Queens, New York |
| 10- | 1867 | Kernersville, North Carolina |
| 11- | 1893 | Fulp, Walnut Cove, North Carolina |
| 12- | 1909 | Kellner, Wisconsin Rapids, Wisconsin |
| 13- | 1741 | Formal announcement to the congregations of the Moravian Church of the immediate Headship of the Lord Jesus Christ in his church on earth |
| | 1771 | Home, Winston-Salem, North Carolina |
| | 1893 | Calvary, Winston-Salem, North Carolina |
| | 1965 | Covenant, York, Pennsylvania, merger of Bethany and Olivet |
| 14- | 1779 | Baptism of the first Moravian convert on St. Kitts, West Indies |
| 16- | 1924 | Pine Chapel, Winston-Salem, North Carolina |
| | 1980 | Unity, Lewisville, North Carolina |
| 17- | 1753 | Arrival of the first Moravians from Bethlehem, Pennsylvania, on the Wachovia Tract in North Carolina to establish a settlement; observed as the anniversary of Bethabara, the first congregation of the Southern Province |
| | 1850 | Fort Howard, now West Side, Green Bay, Wisconsin |
| 18- | 1930 | Beginning of Moravian work in Honduras by George Heath in Cauquira |
| | 1951 | Messiah, Winston-Salem, North Carolina |
| 21- | 1880 | Providence, Winston-Salem, North Carolina |
| 24- | 1963 | Park Road, Charlotte, North Carolina, name Peace adopted in 1999 |
| | 1991 | Christ the King, Durham, North Carolina |
| 25- | 1852 | Mt. Bethel, Cana, Virginia |
| 29- | 1896 | Mayodan, North Carolina |
| 30- | 1746 | Lancaster, Pennsylvania |
| | 1986 | Prince of Peace, Miami, Florida |

## DECEMBER

| | | |
|---|---|---|
| 4- | 1874 | Berea, St. Charles, Minnesota |
| 7- | 1754 | Missionaries arrived in Kingston, Jamaica. |
| 9- | 1883 | Coopersburg, Pennsylvania |
| 11- | 1887 | College Hill, Bethlehem, Pennsylvania |
| 13- | 1732 | Arrival of Leonard Dober and David Nitschmann, the first foreign missionaries of the Moravian Church, on St. Thomas, West Indies |
| 16- | 1877 | Fries Memorial, Winston-Salem, North Carolina |
| 17- | 1914 | Reading, Pennsylvania |
| 19- | 1747 | Lebanon, Pennsylvania |
| 21- | 1856 | Lake Mills, Wisconsin |
| 22- | 1866 | Freedom, Appleton, Wisconsin |
| 25- | 1862 | First, South Bethlehem, Pennsylvania, now Advent, Bethlehem, Pennsylvania |
| 27- | 1748 | First, New York, New York |
| | 1842 | First, Dover, Ohio |
| 31- | 1865 | First, Riverside, New Jersey |
| | 1947 | Schoenbrunn, New Philadelphia, Ohio |

**To Order *Moravian Daily Texts 2013* Contact:**
Interprovincial Board Of Communication
Moravian Church In North America
Po Box 1245 • 1021 Center Street
Bethlehem, Pa 18016-1245
610.867.0593 Or 610.867.7566, Ext. 38

**Or Order Online At:**
www.moravian.org

# 2012

## JANUARY
| S | M | T | W | T | F | S |
|---|---|---|---|---|---|---|
| 1 | 2 | 3 | 4 | 5 | 6 | 7 |
| 8 | 9 | 10 | 11 | 12 | 13 | 14 |
| 15 | 16 | 17 | 18 | 19 | 20 | 21 |
| 22 | 23 | 24 | 25 | 26 | 27 | 28 |
| 29 | 30 | 31 | ... | ... | ... | ... |
| ... | ... | ... | ... | ... | ... | ... |

## FEBRUARY
| S | M | T | W | T | F | S |
|---|---|---|---|---|---|---|
| ... | ... | ... | 1 | 2 | 3 | 4 |
| 5 | 6 | 7 | 8 | 9 | 10 | 11 |
| 12 | 13 | 14 | 15 | 16 | 17 | 18 |
| 19 | 20 | 21 | 22 | 23 | 24 | 25 |
| 26 | 27 | 28 | 29 | ... | ... | ... |
| ... | ... | ... | ... | ... | ... | ... |

## MARCH
| S | M | T | W | T | F | S |
|---|---|---|---|---|---|---|
| ... | ... | ... | ... | 1 | 2 | 3 |
| 4 | 5 | 6 | 7 | 8 | 9 | 10 |
| 11 | 12 | 13 | 14 | 15 | 16 | 17 |
| 18 | 19 | 20 | 21 | 22 | 23 | 24 |
| 25 | 26 | 27 | 28 | 29 | 30 | 31 |
| ... | ... | ... | ... | ... | ... | ... |

## APRIL
| S | M | T | W | T | F | S |
|---|---|---|---|---|---|---|
| 1 | 2 | 3 | 4 | 5 | 6 | 7 |
| 8 | 9 | 10 | 11 | 12 | 13 | 14 |
| 15 | 16 | 17 | 18 | 19 | 20 | 21 |
| 22 | 23 | 24 | 25 | 26 | 27 | 28 |
| 29 | 30 | ... | ... | ... | ... | ... |
| ... | ... | ... | ... | ... | ... | ... |

## MAY
| S | M | T | W | T | F | S |
|---|---|---|---|---|---|---|
| ... | ... | 1 | 2 | 3 | 4 | 5 |
| 6 | 7 | 8 | 9 | 10 | 11 | 12 |
| 13 | 14 | 15 | 16 | 17 | 18 | 19 |
| 20 | 21 | 22 | 23 | 24 | 25 | 26 |
| 27 | 28 | 29 | 30 | 31 | ... | ... |
| ... | ... | ... | ... | ... | ... | ... |

## JUNE
| S | M | T | W | T | F | S |
|---|---|---|---|---|---|---|
| ... | ... | ... | ... | ... | 1 | 2 |
| 3 | 4 | 5 | 6 | 7 | 8 | 9 |
| 10 | 11 | 12 | 13 | 14 | 15 | 16 |
| 17 | 18 | 19 | 20 | 21 | 22 | 23 |
| 24 | 25 | 26 | 27 | 28 | 29 | 30 |
| ... | ... | ... | ... | ... | ... | ... |

## JULY
| S | M | T | W | T | F | S |
|---|---|---|---|---|---|---|
| 1 | 2 | 3 | 4 | 5 | 6 | 7 |
| 8 | 9 | 10 | 11 | 12 | 13 | 14 |
| 15 | 16 | 17 | 18 | 19 | 20 | 21 |
| 22 | 23 | 24 | 25 | 26 | 27 | 28 |
| 29 | 30 | 31 | ... | ... | ... | ... |
| ... | ... | ... | ... | ... | ... | ... |

## AUGUST
| S | M | T | W | T | F | S |
|---|---|---|---|---|---|---|
| ... | ... | ... | 1 | 2 | 3 | 4 |
| 5 | 6 | 7 | 8 | 9 | 10 | 11 |
| 12 | 13 | 14 | 15 | 16 | 17 | 18 |
| 19 | 20 | 21 | 22 | 23 | 24 | 25 |
| 26 | 27 | 28 | 29 | 30 | 31 | ... |
| ... | ... | ... | ... | ... | ... | ... |

## SEPTEMBER
| S | M | T | W | T | F | S |
|---|---|---|---|---|---|---|
| ... | ... | ... | ... | ... | ... | 1 |
| 2 | 3 | 4 | 5 | 6 | 7 | 8 |
| 9 | 10 | 11 | 12 | 13 | 14 | 15 |
| 16 | 17 | 18 | 19 | 20 | 21 | 22 |
| 23 | 24 | 25 | 26 | 27 | 28 | 29 |
| 30 | ... | ... | ... | ... | ... | ... |

## OCTOBER
| S | M | T | W | T | F | S |
|---|---|---|---|---|---|---|
| ... | 1 | 2 | 3 | 4 | 5 | 6 |
| 7 | 8 | 9 | 10 | 11 | 12 | 13 |
| 14 | 15 | 16 | 17 | 18 | 19 | 20 |
| 21 | 22 | 23 | 24 | 25 | 26 | 27 |
| 28 | 29 | 30 | 31 | ... | ... | ... |
| ... | ... | ... | ... | ... | ... | ... |

## NOVEMBER
| S | M | T | W | T | F | S |
|---|---|---|---|---|---|---|
| ... | ... | ... | ... | 1 | 2 | 3 |
| 4 | 5 | 6 | 7 | 8 | 9 | 10 |
| 11 | 12 | 13 | 14 | 15 | 16 | 17 |
| 18 | 19 | 20 | 21 | 22 | 23 | 24 |
| 25 | 26 | 27 | 28 | 29 | 30 | ... |
| ... | ... | ... | ... | ... | ... | ... |

## DECEMBER
| S | M | T | W | T | F | S |
|---|---|---|---|---|---|---|
| ... | ... | ... | ... | ... | ... | 1 |
| 2 | 3 | 4 | 5 | 6 | 7 | 8 |
| 9 | 10 | 11 | 12 | 13 | 14 | 15 |
| 16 | 17 | 18 | 19 | 20 | 21 | 22 |
| 23 | 24 | 25 | 26 | 27 | 28 | 29 |
| 30 | 31 | ... | ... | ... | ... | ... |

# 2013

## JANUARY
| S | M | T | W | T | F | S |
|---|---|---|---|---|---|---|
| ... | ... | 1 | 2 | 3 | 4 | 5 |
| 6 | 7 | 8 | 9 | 10 | 11 | 12 |
| 13 | 14 | 15 | 16 | 17 | 18 | 19 |
| 20 | 21 | 22 | 23 | 24 | 25 | 26 |
| 27 | 28 | 29 | 30 | 31 | ... | ... |
| ... | ... | ... | ... | ... | ... | ... |

## FEBRUARY
| S | M | T | W | T | F | S |
|---|---|---|---|---|---|---|
| ... | ... | ... | ... | ... | 1 | 2 |
| 3 | 4 | 5 | 6 | 7 | 8 | 9 |
| 10 | 11 | 12 | 13 | 14 | 15 | 16 |
| 17 | 18 | 19 | 20 | 21 | 22 | 23 |
| 24 | 25 | 26 | 27 | 28 | ... | ... |
| ... | ... | ... | ... | ... | ... | ... |

## MARCH
| S | M | T | W | T | F | S |
|---|---|---|---|---|---|---|
| ... | ... | ... | ... | ... | 1 | 2 |
| 3 | 4 | 5 | 6 | 7 | 8 | 9 |
| 10 | 11 | 12 | 13 | 14 | 15 | 16 |
| 17 | 18 | 19 | 20 | 21 | 22 | 23 |
| 24 | 25 | 26 | 27 | 28 | 29 | 30 |
| 31 | ... | ... | ... | ... | ... | ... |

## APRIL
| S | M | T | W | T | F | S |
|---|---|---|---|---|---|---|
| ... | 1 | 2 | 3 | 4 | 5 | 6 |
| 7 | 8 | 9 | 10 | 11 | 12 | 13 |
| 14 | 15 | 16 | 17 | 18 | 19 | 20 |
| 21 | 22 | 23 | 24 | 25 | 26 | 27 |
| 28 | 29 | 30 | ... | ... | ... | ... |
| ... | ... | ... | ... | ... | ... | ... |

## MAY
| S | M | T | W | T | F | S |
|---|---|---|---|---|---|---|
| ... | ... | ... | 1 | 2 | 3 | 4 |
| 5 | 6 | 7 | 8 | 9 | 10 | 11 |
| 12 | 13 | 14 | 15 | 16 | 17 | 18 |
| 19 | 20 | 21 | 22 | 23 | 24 | 25 |
| 26 | 27 | 28 | 29 | 30 | 31 | ... |
| ... | ... | ... | ... | ... | ... | ... |

## JUNE
| S | M | T | W | T | F | S |
|---|---|---|---|---|---|---|
| ... | ... | ... | ... | ... | ... | 1 |
| 2 | 3 | 4 | 5 | 6 | 7 | 8 |
| 9 | 10 | 11 | 12 | 13 | 14 | 15 |
| 16 | 17 | 18 | 19 | 20 | 21 | 22 |
| 23 | 24 | 25 | 26 | 27 | 28 | 29 |
| 30 | ... | ... | ... | ... | ... | ... |

## JULY
| S | M | T | W | T | F | S |
|---|---|---|---|---|---|---|
| ... | 1 | 2 | 3 | 4 | 5 | 6 |
| 7 | 8 | 9 | 10 | 11 | 12 | 13 |
| 14 | 15 | 16 | 17 | 18 | 19 | 20 |
| 21 | 22 | 23 | 24 | 25 | 26 | 2 |
| 28 | 29 | 30 | 31 | ... | ... | ... |
| ... | ... | ... | ... | ... | ... | ... |

## AUGUST
| S | M | T | W | T | F | S |
|---|---|---|---|---|---|---|
| ... | ... | ... | ... | 1 | 2 | 3 |
| 4 | 5 | 6 | 7 | 8 | 9 | 10 |
| 11 | 12 | 13 | 14 | 15 | 16 | 17 |
| 18 | 19 | 20 | 21 | 22 | 23 | 24 |
| 25 | 26 | 27 | 28 | 29 | 30 | 31 |
| ... | ... | ... | ... | ... | ... | ... |

## SEPTEMBER
| S | M | T | W | T | F | S |
|---|---|---|---|---|---|---|
| 1 | 2 | 3 | 4 | 5 | 6 | 7 |
| 8 | 9 | 10 | 11 | 12 | 13 | 14 |
| 15 | 16 | 17 | 18 | 19 | 20 | 21 |
| 22 | 23 | 24 | 25 | 26 | 27 | 28 |
| 29 | 30 | ... | ... | ... | ... | ... |
| ... | ... | ... | ... | ... | ... | ... |

## OCTOBER
| S | M | T | W | T | F | S |
|---|---|---|---|---|---|---|
| ... | ... | 1 | 2 | 3 | 4 | 5 |
| 6 | 7 | 8 | 9 | 10 | 11 | 12 |
| 13 | 14 | 15 | 16 | 17 | 18 | 19 |
| 20 | 21 | 22 | 23 | 24 | 25 | 26 |
| 27 | 28 | 29 | 30 | 31 | ... | ... |
| ... | ... | ... | ... | ... | ... | ... |

## NOVEMBER
| S | M | T | W | T | F | S |
|---|---|---|---|---|---|---|
| ... | ... | ... | ... | ... | 1 | 2 |
| 3 | 4 | 5 | 6 | 7 | 8 | 9 |
| 10 | 11 | 12 | 13 | 14 | 15 | 16 |
| 17 | 18 | 19 | 20 | 21 | 22 | 23 |
| 24 | 25 | 26 | 27 | 28 | 29 | 30 |
| ... | ... | ... | ... | ... | ... | ... |

## DECEMBER
| S | M | T | W | T | F | S |
|---|---|---|---|---|---|---|
| 1 | 2 | 3 | 4 | 5 | 6 | 7 |
| 8 | 9 | 10 | 11 | 12 | 13 | 14 |
| 15 | 16 | 17 | 18 | 19 | 20 | 21 |
| 22 | 23 | 24 | 25 | 26 | 27 | 28 |
| 29 | 30 | 31 | ... | ... | ... | ... |
| ... | ... | ... | ... | ... | ... | ... |